Dear Reader,

As a full-time buyer and bookseller at an independent bookstore (Loganberry Books in Cleveland, OH), I'm not a typical writer of editorial letters. But the story behind this book isn't a typical story, either.

Once upon a time, Rebecca Schiller and I were Instagram friends who connected over shared passions for gardening, duck husbandry, and books. When she offered me an early read of her forthcoming memoir, I eagerly accepted.

While the first few pages of taut plotting—such a rarity in memoir!—drew me in for their own sake, it was the solution to Rebecca's medical mystery that shot to the heart of my own life. Both my wife and mother were, like Rebecca, diagnosed with ADHD in adulthood: my mother, in her fifties, and my wife, in her early thirties—mere weeks before Rebecca's memoir first landed in my inbox. I've lived my life witnessing (albeit from the outside) the suffering that a neuro-normative world inflicts on neurodivergent women, and I've read so much about ADHD—little of which offers a fraction of the compassion and complexity that Rebecca's memoir holds on any single page.

I excitedly wrote to Matthew Lore with a slightly more polished version of "if you publish this book, I will sell the **** out of it." Matthew founded The Experiment, and gave me my first publishing job more than twelve years ago. To my surprise, he replied not only as the friend he's become but also with an invitation—to pursue acquiring the book, and to help Rebecca edit the UK's *Earthed* into the revised edition that The Experiment will publish as *A Thousand Ways to Pay Attention*: this ARC now in your hands.

So, yes, I write to you as an editor—but also as a bookseller, jumping up to show you a book I love, longing for you to take it home and be transformed by it, as I have been. "Do you like books about trees?" I'd exclaim. "Wait til you meet the three-hundred-year-old oak tree in this one!" Or, "Seeking histories overlooked and erased by dominant narratives? You must meet the outsider women whose histories Rebecca uncovers here." I'd push the book into your hands, saying, "This is about wrestling with that part of yourself you most fear and refusing to let it go until you can know it and name it and—against all odds—even begin to love it."

And, just as I tell every customer I convince to take a chance on a book I love, I'd tell you, "I can't wait to hear what you think."

Gratefully yours,

Elisabeth Plumlee-Watson
Bookseller, Loganberry Books, and Editor-at-Large, The Experiment

A THOUSAND WAYS
TO PAY
ATTENTION

https://bit.ly/TheExperimentIN
May Nominations due February 28, 2022

https://bit.ly/TheExperimentLR
May nominations due March 1, 2022

Edelweiss   https://bit.ly/EdelweissAThousandWays

A THOUSAND WAYS TO PAY ATTENTION

A Memoir of Coming Home to My Neurodivergent Mind

REBECCA SCHILLER

THE EXPERIMENT

NEW YORK

The Experiment, LLC
220 East 23rd Street, Suite 600
New York, NY 10010-4658
theexperimentpublishing.com

THE EXPERIMENT and its colophon are registered trademarks of
The Experiment, LLC. Many of the designations used by manufacturers and
sellers to distinguish their products are claimed as trademarks. Where those
designations appear in this book and The Experiment was aware of a trademark
claim, the designations have been capitalized.

The Experiment's books are available at special discounts when purchased in bulk
for premiums and sales promotions as well as for fund-raising or educational use.
For details, contact us at info@theexperimentpublishing.com.

Library of Congress Cataloging-in-Publication Data TK

ISBN 978-1-61519-880-1
Ebook ISBN 978-1-61519-881-8

Cover and text design by Beth Bugler
Cover illustration by Sarah Moore
Author photograph by TK

Manufactured in the United States of America

First printing April 2022
10 9 8 7 6 5 4 3 2 1

January

I FALL

t is dark on this moonless night, the ground is uneven, and the half bottle of wine makes me forget to place each foot deliberately as I have trained myself to do. I am laughing one moment and the next, side lit by the pub window, I am falling through three places at once: upright and moving forward, tilting and tumbling down, stationary and horizontal. I land eventually, my knees and palms pressed into the wet pavement. I try not to cry.

Down here I spot mud and grass smeared on the side of my good shoes—a gift from my field, no doubt. My hands are skinned and there's a pain somewhere else too, but I pay more attention to the two men in front of me turning their heads in interest and amusement.

"I'm fine. So like me. What a klutz," I say to the friend I'm out with for the night, rolling my eyes faux-affectionately at myself and performing my best version of a capable, calm, and unhurt woman with an unfortunate but cute habit of tipping herself onto the floor. It's a routine I do well. "I'm okay, really, don't worry. Let's go on somewhere, have another drink," I say to her, smiling, as I jack-in-the-box up. My friend has had a tough time of late and I know she needs me for an uncomplicated night out. As I walk through the narrow streets of the old town with her, I let myself feel the pain in my knee for a moment, and I can tell that I'm probably not so OK after all.

This fall is a thing to be carefully managed by my internal PR agency. I play a tactical game of deflection, telling my friend lightly about the four-year-old me who went to school and was swiftly given the "girl with two left feet" tag. I paint a funny picture of my scruffy little self emerging from the classroom dragging a grungy teddy behind me; sweetly stuccoed with bandages, ripped clothes, and undone braids. I compress the story into three minutes, ending with four weeks ago when, attempting to show my children that I could leap, gazelle-like, from one wooden stepping stone to the other, I fell, idiot-like, in the adventure playground and bruised both knees so badly that I couldn't drive for a week. I draw a line under all this with minimizing laughter and then return to celebrating my friend's brave new life, which, with as much of my heart as I can muster, is what I am here for.

In the background, as I pay attention to her, I also think of my clumsiness. The part of me that's still constantly tripping over, bruising my hips and shins on the edges of furniture, ripping waistbands off jeans, and destroying my overalls by catching the straps on door handles. This me is still a four-year-old, unsure where the edges of her body are, where the floor and walls begin, but not having any idea why.

I can't bear that I fell in front of strangers, and an image of the men swiveling in amusement keeps popping up in my thoughts as we walk. A little vignette of embarrassment and self-loathing that will stay on a loop for much longer than it should, taking turns with the playback of my stepping-stone fall. That time no one noticed me hit the ground. Not the children, racing joyfully away from me, the backs of their sweaters covered in leaf mold, or my husband sitting on the nearby bench looking at his muddy boots. I stayed down there for a while, my nose against the bark chippings for long enough to spot a wood louse creeping between two logs and to realize how like a tiny armadillo it looked. As it worried its way into the woody darkness, my shock and embarrassment coalesced into anger, but, as ever, I wasn't clear who it was I was angry with.

Later tonight, in a wine-bar bathroom, I sit on the cold toilet seat and try to pull down my tights. They are stuck fast to my skin: glued with blood from the four-inch gash that runs from the bottom of my knee on a diagonal that splits my shin. I instantly hate this cut and the little limp it is making me do.

So I cover it up. I go back out into the bar, glad of my long skirt; I refuse to limp and am extra witty, extra clever, and extra outgoing. Later, lying on my friend's spare bed with the ceiling spinning gently above me, I will think that while most people are made of 60 percent water, I am largely composed of smoke and mirrors held together with shame.

The next morning I scrape the ice from my car before driving back across the flat, reclaimed land that lies between my rare night away and our home: a patch of frozen mud, a two-acre plot of land that Jared, our two children, and I moved to in 2017 in hopes of living a simpler, more self-sufficient life.

The light is low and clouds hang heavily over the reeds that border the water along the roadside. It's stark and beautiful with occasional glimpses of swans and a liberal sprinkling of Romney sheep. In summer we'll all walk lazily along the reclaimed salt marsh that this sheep breed is named for, enjoying the gentle power of English sunshine, spotting wildflowers, butterflies, and bees and arguing about whether 10:00 AM is too early for our picnic lunch.

Today, as I return to our plot, I notice the mess first, as always: the weeds and grass that encroach on the gravel driveway, piles of leaves we have found time to rake but not collect, a heap of broken bricks we plan to use as hardcore when we finally get around to filling in the flood-waiting-to-happen car-inspection pit dug by the previous owners. The paddock gate reveals a motley collection of field shelters, sheds, and henhouses that contain an even motlier crew of geese, goats, chickens, and ducks. Their comforting cacophony starts as I exit the car—desperate to let me know that they haven't yet been fed.

Even though I'm in my good clothes and nice shoes I walk straight through my garden toward the animal sheds. My borders offer the first glimpse of primroses telling winter to move along now. Hellebores and the spidery leaves of *Anemone coronaria* give welcome respite from the endless brown, and my boots inadvertently trample a host of particularly keen daffodil shoots that ring the fruit trees in our little orchard. The season's early adopters are out in force this morning, but it still takes the faith I've been cultivating to believe in spring's coming in the sharp cold of this January day.

I pass the almost empty vegetable garden and tuck behind our beech hedge to let the animals into the field. The gang cheer me as they always do: a chuckle at the way the ducks chase our cats—beaks down, sheer gumption making them the unlikely winners in every encounter; the goats' distinct preferences for being stroked and scratched (Amber on her ear, Belle on the sides of her golden face) and their daily attempts to escape and nibble my rose cuttings—the hairy little fools. The white hen who streaks straight to the end of the field every morning to get into the hollow tree where she insists on laying her eggs.

Limping a little, I crouch down by the chicken shed to check if anyone remembered to collect the eggs last night, and as my knee bends, the new scab breaks, letting blood through. It barely hurts but I wince anyway with the thought of the night before. Out in today's morning quiet, I put my ungloved hands on the ground and try to be *here now* instead of *there then*. The earth feels cold: grass crispy with a light coating of frost, a present-moment shimmer camouflaging something more permanent below.

I brush a few of the frost crystals aside with my fingers and put more pressure on the field's surface. Today the frozen crust gives way easily, revealing only the wet clagginess beneath. My ground. My mud. It is why I am here: this clay, this land. To return to it, get back to it, to raise my children in it, to try naively to live the good life, the simple life, a life where this ground supports us.

Today, and every day this week, our plot of land is hard with the cold. The pond is a solid brown lump of ice, much to the surprise of the ducks, who waddle over to it every hour or so on a *Groundhog Day* loop of bewilderment. I find myself humming "In the Bleak Midwinter" as I do my morning rounds with the animals and discover that the hose, rain barrel, and all the buckets and drinkers have turned to solid ice. I replace the frozen drinkers with makeshift troughs and bowls (which will themselves freeze over in an hour) and take the others inside to start a constant cycle of thawing that leaves chicken-poo-infused puddles on the living room floor.

As I finish my morning jobs I spot a blackbird with a distinctive necklace of featherless skin around his throat. There is something about the framing of this view, and the very same blackbird in it, that makes today fade into the background and a matching day, two years ago, appear in front of it. The air is the same: a kind of deep cold that refuses to let the sun bring its usual warmth and tastes sharp. I breathe it in, it freezes my lungs, and I cough my way into the memory.

We were stuffed into the car: two adults, two children, and two cats. Sparks of stress and excitement pinged off the sunroof, the windows, and the box in the trunk containing a kettle, cups, and a corkscrew. We'd done this house-moving thing before and knew there would be an urgent need for hot caffeine on arrival, followed later by wine.

The stench hit us about ten minutes into the journey. I'd day-dreamed about this trip from our former home in a seaside town to the new house, just over an hour away on the edge of the Weald of Kent. I'd imagined the salty seaside air slowly mingling with country-side smells before disappearing entirely, every inhalation filling our noses with the iron tang of earth or perhaps an unseasonal breath of new-mown hay. An olfactory metaphor for the big adventure ahead. But before we'd even made it to the highway, the smell in the car made me want to be sick.

We stopped at the side of the road, sniffed three-year-old Ar-thur warily and then opened the boot. The horror was definitely in there somewhere. We found him—the culprit—in his blue carrier, meowing desperately. Perhaps we'd scooped him up and stuffed him into the car on his way to the litter tray. Maybe the stress of moving day had worked a kind of unholy magic on his feline bowels, but, for whatever reason, Bruce had smeared himself and the carrier with pungent cat shit. It was all we could do not to leave him by the side of the road. Instead we cracked the windows, turned the heat up, and I carried on driving, feeling a little chastened.

Then we were here, turning the car into the driveway. Jared got out before any of us, then the children, and finally me. "I can't be-lieve that we live here, that this is all ours!" I said, though the words, once out in the freezing air, didn't sound quite right. But I moved on quickly, taking it all in: the plot, the work, the plans, the ideas already piling up and spreading out in my head—each one connect-ing to the other and spawning its own cascade of electric darts of thought. Little fizzy hits of I-spot-something-new, adding more and more dimensions to the plan for our life in this place.

We walked along the path, past the stacked firewood, under the wooden arch that would soon fall down, and took out unfamiliar keys to open the porch for the first time. The stress of mortgages, of lawyers, of packing, and the journey dulled instantly. There's nothing like watching your children run in circles, shrieking with excitement and arguing about who gets which bedroom, to make you forget that ten minutes ago you were shouting and that your near future involves washing an angry cat. As we walked through the door now, this place that we had spent only minutes in before became our shelter and, though the kitchen was falling apart and the central heating didn't exist, every corner was transformed by the hopes we were piling in them. We were home.

A little later, despite chattering teeth, the children and I did our tenth excited loop around the plot, trying and failing to stay out of the way of Jared and the movers. We'd already clocked potential sites for dens and chicken coops by the time I spotted a row of leeks waiting to be harvested in the neat, otherwise bare, vegetable patch that sat (and still sits, somewhat less neatly) directly behind the south-facing house. A few hours later, our possessions stacked in each room and the moving van finally gone, I knew exactly what I wanted to do to mark the beginning of our lives in this squat bungalow with its wraparound garden and tree-lined field—and it involved leeks.

I strolled over to the vegetable patch, my first real encounter with its soil squares, and felt consumed by the romance of harvesting produce sown nearly a year ago by the garden's previous caretaker. She had lived here for over thirty years and raised her family in this place where I would now raise mine. Our first meal in our new life would be a ritual dinner, a gift from the past. So I took hold of a leek by its peeling casing and pulled gently, savoring the poignant moment.

Nothing happened.

I tried again. This time I snapped off an inch or so of the inedible top but was no closer to actually harvesting a leek. Undeterred, I tried a new technique: grabbing it at the bottom where its thick white stem met the soil. I yanked really hard this time, but it didn't budge a millimeter. Was it a trick leek? I was flailing about by now, using every ounce of strength to get the damn thing out of the ground and feeling increasingly ridiculous. It would not yield to me. Fuck that fucking leek.

Twenty minutes later, having figured out where the movers had left the gardening tools, finding only three impossibly heavy spades—and something pointy and unfathomable—I improvised with a teaspoon and set about digging. The soil was much harder than I'd expected, so I was chipping away at it like just-out-of-the-freezer ice cream. Every now and then I gave the damn thing an experimental wiggle and shouted to my increasingly impatient family that *everything was great! I wouldn't be long!!*

What felt like hours later, I could finally see its gnarly base and the first signs of white wormlike roots clinging fast to the clods of clay. This was it; I would conquer this leek. Ha!

Red in the face and sweating profusely despite the January cold, I grabbed it once again and it seemed to give a little. I wiggled it and—yes—it yielded some more. I took the reluctant vegetable in both hands and, grunting with effort, pulled upward from the depths of my being, from my soul. Finally, I felt the exquisite freedom of release as it gave up and came to me.

And then: *snap.* I was thrown backward onto the hard ground. Only the tasteless green part was clutched in my red-raw hands and the white prize of its leeky, savory goodness was still firmly one with the clay. Double fuck that fucking leek and the realization that this was all going to be much harder than I'd thought.

At lunchtime today I am wearing my third-best overalls over leggings, thick gloves, and a ridiculous bobble hat. The cold is a slap in the face as I go outside, but it distracts from the pain in my leg as I start digging close to where this year's leeks wait for a more successful harvest. That's for another week though, as right now there's a huge pile of wood chips that need loading onto wheelbarrows, dumping on my paths, and spreading evenly with a rake. My spade cuts through the chippings easily enough with a whooshing sound of man-made meeting nature, and then a satisfying *shhhunk* as I lift the mulch and tip it into the barrow bed. One spade, two spade, three spade, four. It takes about twenty spadefuls to fill it and then, reckless, I usually gamble on another couple on the top. Back and forth, back and forth, I pass bare branches and juicy, duplicitous holly berries as I take out the crappy week I'm having on this mound of bark.

My body craves this movement but even now, as I throw every muscle fiber into it—arching forward, back, and to the side—it isn't quite enough to calm me. At the moment I seem to need this physical release of accumulated energy more regularly and more intensely than ever. The quivering restlessness inside me has to be discharged into anything I can find, otherwise it builds inside me: sunbeams on a magnifying glass, creating warmth, then heat, then fire.

I give the task my all, and more besides, but fight against the urge to break into a jog. Motion is good but I have learned it has its traps for me too. I'm juggling the instructions of several of my mental sticky notes to avoid the pitfalls of the past. I must remember to shake things off with energetic movement and practice the stillness that eludes me. I must also find a sweet spot between the two. The elusive equilibrium that must live between these seemingly opposite states and will help me to discover a less hysterical pace.

An overwhelming urge to keep moving so as to travel almost instantly from job to job, radically limiting any gaps in productivity, has been with me for as long as I can remember. No task is ever so big that perspective, determination, and speed can't see it realized. I didn't learn to walk as a baby; I learned to sprint—so swift that there was never time to find my point of balance. But I am learning that while moving at a pace of "pretend I am being chased by a rabid dog and then go a bit faster" gets things done for a while, there are consequences. If I keep it up for too long I risk an abrupt and jarring stop.

Even though my every instinct is to slide from moving to rushing, I grit my teeth and try to take my time. Moderating myself seems to take as much energy and effort as the job of refreshing the paths itself. But finally I finish covering the area with its fresh layer of chippings and I do feel better. Daily pressures and nagging voices have receded. This task—the smoothing over and hiding of imperfections—appeals to me. The quick payoff, the miniature *Grand Designs*–reality-TV reveal, suits my natural impatience. I feel bad, I come outside, I see the sky, I dig a hole, I stroke a hen, I make over a path, and I feel calmer. Every single time. This was a good idea.

Then I look to my right and see days-I-don't-haves'-worth of paths that also need weeding and chipping. They actually look worse now that they have a tidy neighbor. And then there's the literal ton of compost I need to cover my veg and flower beds with. Not to mention the leaves smothering the crocuses and the grass growing in between every paving stone. I think about the trays I need to fill with soil to allow seedlings to push their way to the surface. Seeds still to buy. Poultry coops to disinfect. Worlds yet to conquer. My children, Jared, the house, my work, the political mess, the world's slide toward climate disaster, and everything else start jumping up and down and waving at me from inside my head. They are equally loud, equally important, and are all speeding away from me at an equally fast pace.

My hips, thighs, and knees start to move. My breathing quickens.

I am running out of time.

I am running out.

I am running.

In the shortchanged light of the January afternoon the birds are going about their end-of-the-day business. A dunnock (I think) on the hawthorn, blue tits having relay races from gutter to rose branch, a collared dove getting a head start on nest building, and my unimaginative favorite, the robin, hopping across the grass. I know this chap from all the others. He's charmingly potbellied with a tilt of his head that makes me think of a 1920s dancer with a top hat and cane: "Robbo the Robin."

"He's so fat, Mummy!" says Sofya, who's come outside to hunt me down. Good old Robbo defuses my irritation at the feeling she's pursuing me and the swift guilt that follows. I don't want to be this person who reacts to my daughter as if she were an intruder in a rare five minutes of rest. I kiss the top of her dark, tangled head and take a moment to breathe her in. Over the past couple of years my capacity for almost everything in life has shrunk dramatically. The generous, patient, and unboundaried energy required to meet my children in the loud, needy, giving-of-myself places they often ask me to be is just not there anymore.

I cheat by taking them in like this: smelling them and letting that basic prompt connect us via the deep-buried hillock of my limbic system—the mammalian part of my brain. Its companion, the newer humanity of the neocortex, squats over this center of my motherhood—at times obscuring it with complication analysis and then melting away selectively at others to allow adrenaline's ancient signals to block me in another way.

I get round these barricades by spending time stroking my children's cheeks, kissing their foreheads, and saying loving things to them as they sleep, knowing that here in the dark they won't argue, talk incessantly, or drop a fork on the floor—the clatter plucking every one of my nerves. I find a Canadian soap opera about a horse whisperer for us to watch together in almost silence, snuggled close, and I make it into an exclusive mother-child club. I find the truth of our bond tangentially, give them what I can, and hope it makes up for how little I have left.

Sofya and I also find a way to be together in our roles as Director and Deputy Director of Animal Husbandry. And we look at the dimness that has abruptly claimed the afternoon and scramble to our end-of-day chores done before the light fails completely. She mucks out the goats' pen using a red dustpan and brush. I refill their hayrack and put hard feed in buckets, sprinkling it with a supplement and listening to my daughter spill the contents of her mind into the little animal shelter we inherited. Always wanting to want to hear more of her sideways take on the world, always longing for a stretch of settled quiet.

As we walk back to the house I am already deep in the week ahead, but Sofya's voice breaks through: "Look, Mummy!" I turn and find her behind me, absorbed by the sky. I was rushing again, running while walking, and nearly missed this January sunset laid out above the trees. But my eight-year-old moves at another pace; eyes open, ready to receive gifts like this and this feels like a small victory. I walk back toward her smiling and put my arm around her shoulders.

We stare at the red on the horizon and see it fade up to orange and then yellow. There's a band of green above, spreading like watercolor into the blue. Higher up, the clouds are shocking pink and—behind witchy, black branches—the dusk is crushed berries. We say nothing—there is nothing that needs to be said as the animals' jaws work at their dinners, the birds sing their good-nights, and our quiet breathing slowly synchronizes.

The cold got to me eventually and I've retreated inside to the bath where the warm water soothes my muscles and gives my cut leg an overdue rinse. The tub has magic powers. A soapy shield protecting me from being drained by demands that usually come from both inside and out. With my body stilled by the water, my mind often takes its chance to roam and clear. Now, as I move soapy hands up and down my arms, I traipse over one of my favorite topics, taking a more leisurely circuitous route than I would on dry land.

Since our move here I have been unsystematically researching smallholdings and other smaller ways of living on and from the land. *Smallholding*: a very British and very vague term for a small plot of land that isn't a commercial farm but is more than a house with a garden. At first my motivation was pure instruction: I wanted to find others who were living and working similar-sized acreages, with similar intent, so that I could learn what to do—and what not to do—by following their lead.

It has been a struggle to find them. The more I read, the more confused I became. It was hard to find people whose plans and plots matched mine when no one seems to agree what defines a smallholder and differentiates the land they work from a small farm or a large garden. "Smallholding" sits outside officialdom. For many of those who are drawn to it, this outsider status is an attraction in and of itself. But with no official qualification, size bracket, or shared purpose to unite us, finding my kind of people in this tangled new world has been a challenge.

Some believe a smallholding is defined by its size: a figure of twenty acres or less quoted most often. Many smallholders talk about their growing of crops, raising animals, and working on the land as being less commercial than the work farmers do. Yet one report I read considered a four-hundred-acre wildflower seed business under the smallholding umbrella. Ethos and priority vary wildly: from a rigid dedication to backbreaking self-sufficiency to Martha Stewart coffee-table-book-worthy lifestyle setup in which the gingham bunting is the most important part.

The more I researched, the more grey areas and gaps I discovered, and when I couldn't find myself or my land reflected back at me, the need I was trying to meet changed. Smallholding had seemed like an answer but had become many questions instead. I felt less sure about what I was doing and why. I started to look at how a life on land can work in other countries, looked for those with values that might remind me of mine in different setups and began to trace the history of how we got to all this from where we were in times past.

I am immersed. The sounds of the outside world are distorted by the water that my ears are now under. This plot of land distorts in the presence of other things too. It expands and contracts in response to how I feel in it. When I'm overwhelmed, it is a universe whose edges I can never hope to touch—let alone weed—and when I am fired up by a new idea that just won't fit, it becomes an insignificant speck, and I become a privileged preschooler playing in the shadow of "real" rural life.

The smallholding also changes size and significance according to who is looking at it with me. Vast when reflected in the eyes of our city friends; yet, when our farmer neighbor Victor brings over bales of hay in a barrow, it shrinks again to fit neatly in his pocket. With him I don't even use the word *smallholding*. I remember that he makes a real living from his land and so far, ours has cost far more than it has repaid and I am embarrassed to have called the place where we live and work anything but a garden with a few pets.

I work conditioner through my hair while rummaging through the internal filing cabinet where I keep my favorite discoveries. They are never far from the front of my thoughts and neither is the plot itself: the jobs, the plans, the difficulties, the point of it all, exert such a force on me. And as I press the elderly showerhead into service, I see that the tub has worked its magic again and something new and clearer has floated up while I've been in the water.

Perhaps my determination to grasp my land's size and importance and the repeated failure to do both sit within that force. Though it is a tiny acreage, the power it has over me—and the power that a small patch of earth to call your own exerts on many others—is enormous, and I cannot leave a paradox like this alone. These things agitate and compel me; wrinkles that can't be smoothed promising something important I know is there, hidden under the surface that I must work away at in order to find. Under this wrinkle there must be the powerful thing or things that keep pulling me and have kept pulling humans back to the land again and again. That is what I am searching for, and, if I can find it, I feel sure I will find my people and that my own land will settle into its proper place

I step out onto the cold bathroom floor and, removed from the bath's watery safety, my thoughts take a familiar dive along an opposing track. This tiny place means nothing outside my overactive imagination. It and I are too small to count. Everything is still distorted and I don't know which track is the right one. But underneath my uncertainty I can't ever shake the feeling that many of us have been kidding ourselves with our reverence for largeness. Conned by the idea of expansion—of bigger, slicker, and more streamlined being better. I think it's the small things, sometimes (often); the tiniest things—their presence, their absence—that can have an earth-smashing, big-bang-ing, universal impact. *Boom!*

Smallholding. Small holding. I want to get the measure of it, not in feet and inches but on a scale of importance and meaning. I need to know what it is made of, what it means, what it has meant. As I dry my hands, I think of another route toward discovering meaning and reach for my phone to call up an etymological dictionary, asking it to reveal what's hidden "smallholding"—this thing I have that is not much, yet all too much for me:

> "Small": a pale-yellow flower of a word on the stalk of the Old
> English *smæl*, which had a thin meaning: "slender," "fine."
> Deeper under the soil is its tangled root ball: the proto-Germanic
> *smal*, the Gothic *smalista*, old Norse *smali*, church Slavonic *malu*.
> The original meaning of "narrow" almost lost to us unless we
> apply it to our waists or (worse) intestines.

Sm—all: there are only five letters, two sounds—all in, in "small." These thirteenth-century diagraphs pushed out of an embryonic base to become not big, not large, but "compact."

As the decades passed, this little word became diminished: a small person of small means and small import. Small change, small talk, small fry, small potatoes—though when I dig them up, they are surprisingly heavy in my hand.

"Holding": from the Middle English *holden, back* to the Old English *halden.* The word's meanings peel away like layers of the onions: sharper than you'd think with a side effect of tears.

"To hold": containing something that would otherwise escape: water, petrol, grain. A "firm hold" a "handhold," a "strangle hold." "Hold your breath!" "Hold your ground!" "Hold on!" "Hold me!"

Last of all—"a hold": the void in a ship's belly where cargo is stored. Empty and echoing or stuffed full of flowers, treasures, breaths.

It's a small thing—not much. It's holding everything together.

A small holding: "beholden," "held."

It is the last day of the month and I walk across the garden's snowy ground as night gives into morning. I let the hens and goats out and then stand on the yard looking over the gate at what, in summer, will be a grassy hollow in the paddock but in these winter months is an accidental pond. Today, the dip is hidden by snow and Honk the goose's orange feet are slapping down comedically on a newly hard surface that has appeared overnight as water below snow became ice. I feel tired and flimsy, without the energy to fling my agitation away physically but sensing it in every pore nonetheless. The bite in the air isn't enough to enliven my outside or calm what's within. I need something more—a real connection to something (a goose will do)—

JANUARY

to help me shake off the creeping feeling that something inside me has started to come loose. A cobblestone, agitated by generations of foot traffic, working its way up to become a trip hazard.

There is nothing uneven about Honk, though, as she stretches; long and balanced, opening her wings in parallel to the ground, standing straight on her left foot and stretching her right out behind her: a perfect arabesque. I force myself to leave my head for a moment, eased down into my body by the view of her elegant form. It is tight in the chest, a little dehydrated, achy in the lower back and there's the sticky constriction of a wound dressing on my leg.

I ended up at the doctor's office within a week of my pavement dive outside the pub. As he peered professionally at the gross pus-y mess of my shin, I was embarrassed by what, under his professional gaze, looked like lack of self-care: black hairs poking out of the weeping yellow and—how had I missed it?—a line of mud along my ankle bone.

There is not much I can do about the mud—a little of this earth is always on me now: a smear of boot edge catching the skin over my fibula, a grain of brown down the side of my nail that no amount of brushing can reach. I take the land with me on the train to smart London meetings, on the school run, to my desk. There's dirt on my knees at the end of the day and it's there when I turn to Jared in the morning wanting to be touched.

And there is more of it, no doubt, making its way onto me now as I look back at Honk and hear a crack as she lumbers to the center of the ice. Liquid appears from below the thin surface as her weight and the heat from her feet fracture the hardness below. I flinch, but she doesn't plummet; sinking slowly, gracefully instead—as if she knows what matters in this moment and even an abrupt change in the state of the matter that holds her up can't distract her from it. She raises her head on a pipe-cleaner neck and plunges it into the newly revealed pool; grooming herself with a twist of her beak; splashing her back and in between her feathers in the way, I have learned, geese love to do.

I envy Honk's knowledge of who she is and what she needs and how that surety doesn't make her any less able to roll with the changes too. I stay here a little longer trying to harvest something from the sight of my white goose under the lightening sky. Though I'm trying to ignore and fight it in turns, part of me knows that—unlike her—I am plunging. This could go one way or the other.

It is present in every moment: concentration, pressure—from within—to stop falling, hold steady as the sun tracks east to west like this beautiful bird with her ridiculous name, and stretch out and up despite the fear. Solve the mystery. Work it out. Find stillness. Find movement. Find the mythical place of rest where they meet. These instructions run through my head as the minutes pull a little further from the dark. I am apprehensive; prepping for what feels like might be coming. But I want it too: the energy, the force, the powerful thing that pulls me to the land. Its distant vibrations already shake me, half-threaten to break me, yet I long for the moment of arrival and the strength that might be released when everything cracks and then melts.

BEGINNINGS

Breakfast time and I am readying the children for school, when Arthur throws up his cereal into my instinctively cupped hands. I drip his vomit on the floor as I rush to the bin, the sink, find a bowl, paper towels, and a glass of water; all the while watching to see if there is more to come. His little face registers a mixture of confusion and upset as I cuddle him and notice that the tender feeling of wanting to help is fusing with rising panic as the reality of a missed eight hours at my desk hits.

I keep up the comforting patter, but thoughts begin sliding out from the sides of my brain. Slowly at first and then faster and faster, a mechanized spitting of competing ideas that manage to gang up on me and go to war with each other. Worry, love, and care are all there, but there's annoyance, too, and the guilt at feeling it. Then plans, tasks, and to-do lists start to intrude, with each thought spawning at least two more—a family tree whose descendants multiply at speed. If I don't send this email, plant this seed, finish this work, order this part, then I won't be able to do something else tomorrow; the impact of today traveling down a chain that stretches far into the future.

I am becoming familiarly lost in this interior pile-on. The tendency to think in many directions at once has been there in one form or another for as long as I can remember, but the intensity and frequency have upped of late. With the smallest of triggers now, my mind is both clogged and stretched. I'm quickly out of control and afraid yet can't pin down what's frightening me or remember how it all began.

Arthur is sitting on a towel, bowl on lap and tissues close by. As I turn to wash my hands again—the smell has stuck to my skin—I try to reel in my mind like a life belt. It's an effort that's made just about possible by his little wobbly lip and the mother I want to be for him. I am trying so hard to ensure our journey through Tuesday morning doesn't get stuck in this tangled place, though the pressure of wanting to succeed threatens to get me stuck all the faster. I clench my jaw and tell myself not to be held fast by the fear, the confusion, or the rising anger. I remind myself in mutters that I have time to take a day off, that everything can wait, and that Arthur is the most important thing, which, of course, he is. As I stroke his hair and notice that his ears are dirty, I whisper to myself that I've changed my life over the past two years and work isn't quite the pressurized vessel it once was. This is not a disaster; I've just programmed myself to think it is.

The trouble is that, despite the tangible scaling back I've done within my career, the stock feeling of running red-faced behind my life—reaching out to grab it as it keeps sprinting away—has not disappeared. This year is the year I am supposed to be back to my old capable self after the long, bad patch I've been in since we moved here. I have done the work, made the sacrifices, and I should be feeling better. *Yet maybe*—I think it as I scrabble in the drawer for a clean hand towel—*maybe, almost definitely, what I am feeling this year is worse.*

Forty minutes later and the color is coming back to Arthur's cheeks, he's eaten, has a normal temperature, and seems absolutely fine. It was a one-off but school rules say we must keep out of the classroom for twenty-four hours anyway. I am still working hard to keep myself in check, so I throw myself into finding something to occupy us both. First I read him our favorite nonsense rhyme, "The Jumblies," who despite everything their friends could say went to sea in a sieve and proceeded to sail to a land all covered with trees, went on a very odd shopping spree and bought an owl, a useful cart, a pound of rice, a cranberry tart, no less than a whole hive of silvery bees, a pig, some green jackdaws, a lovely monkey with lollipop paws, forty bottles of Ring-Bo-Ree (which I always rather like the sound of) and, most important, no end of Stilton cheese.

Once the Jumblies have returned from their twenty-year voyage, Arthur's enthusiasm for poetry abruptly ends, and the day stretches out endlessly in front of us. I can't face the cartoon he wants to watch, nor can my allergic-to-numbers brain bear to dive into the math puzzles that he loves. We compromise on a story now and a math TV show later, and I pull him on to my knee to think of a tale that will absorb us both.

He leans in, ready to listen, his back pressing against bulges in my clothes—I push him away quickly before he crushes the eggs I'd forgotten about. Like a mad, ripped-overall-wearing magician, I pull a duck egg, two hens' eggs, and, the pièce de résistance, a bright white goose egg out of my pockets.

At more than three times the size of a chicken's egg, the goose egg completely fills my palm with its smooth, ceramic-like surface and pleasing pointedness. We are not goose experts by any stretch. I'm not even certain how many males and females we have and, as this is our first year with laying geese, every egg is a thrill. Arthur and I gaze at it for a while and I think that finding a goose egg in my pocket on a difficult morning is exactly the kind of fairy-tale thing I want my life to be made from.

I nearly start the fable of the goose who laid the golden egg but stop after "Once upon a time." I'd like to keep believing that one day I might actually find a golden egg glinting at me from the straw-sided, feather-lined nest that the geese have built in the wonky field shelter we bought off eBay. I won't make it a myth just yet.

We are silent as I search for inspiration, waving to Jared as he passes the window leaving for work. When he's gone my eyes remain focused on the land, scanning the vegetable patch, the fruit cage, and then our field. I am looking for a story out there, trying hard to keep level by noticing every blade of grass and wind-cracked twig and breaking the quiet to point out a shimmer of catkins on the hazel copse.

I am holding Arthur close, for my comfort as much as his, when a local farm cat appears, being chased—yet again—by our ducks and goats. We watch the scene together, laughing as they noisily round up the cat, who flees over the fence in a shriek of black fur, into Victor's field, where he spooks the ponies. I can't really hear the drum of their hooves galloping off into the distance from here, but my brain knows the sound well enough to color it in. I heard it almost every day as a teenager coming from the fields behind the yard as we pitched in to keep our fees down at the dilapidated stables by the highway bridge. I heard it again when I rode through the nearby valley, flanked by housing projects and busy roads, but still retaining a calming air of the quiet, old place. And so I can hear it now even with the windows shut: an urgence of percussion fading to nothing as the horses disappear down the hill.

Our plot sits at the top of this gentle slope that then tips down southward for a mile toward the village school. When I first stood here I clapped my hands and grinned: a classic English countryside scene with fields, hedges, small patches of woodland, and the occasional faraway cottage. This, I thought, is what I need to see every day. Lately though, when I look into that distance, I think I see other things too: indistinct but intriguing. I look out beyond the paddock fence now, relaxing and then sharpening my gaze, and soon glimmers begin to appear across this February morning, as if a film were being projected on a too-bright day. An unknown scene is being offered to me gently at a time when most things feel as though they are flung at my head. I take it—this shadowy mystery—and try to bring it toward the light and find the story of the start of this plot.

Once upon a time, I say again in a lower voice, a really long time ago, everything we can see out of this window would have been different. Let's go there, Arthur: back to when all this—I pause as one of the shimmers becomes more distinct—was the middle of a huge forest that covered everything for hundreds of miles and there were no humans here at all. We are inside it now—and it feels as though it has been here forever: a density of trees growing undisturbed for hundreds of thousands of years. Thick trunks stretch way up, further than we can see, and little ones are dotted in between, sprung up when others, tired of holding their branches, blew over.

My senses adjust and everything becomes clearer still: It is dark in here, isn't it, Arthur? A nice darkness, like a soft blanket. It's not exactly quiet—quite noisy in fact—but the sounds are dampened. The trees—so many—take some of the rustles, shrieks and the noise of the wind into their bark. Can you hear it? I turn to him—his gaze matching mine, holding my hand—and he nods solemnly.

This world grows out of the clay and somewhere inside me. We scan the scene for animals, birds, and insects and it takes a little time because they are shy, though they don't yet know to be afraid of humans. What animals do you think live here? I ask. Rabbits, he guesses. Worms? Yes, I say, lots of worms, and hares and foxes too. Red squirrels, dormice, earwigs, voles, and owls—can you see any? We try, looking up toward where the sky should be and our eyes are so sharp when turned on this forest that we see them all.

There's a nightjar sitting on her ground nest of two mottled eggs and we watch her blending in with the moss and leaves of a clearing to the east, giving herself away only by tiny movements of her folded breast. A louder sound next: over there. A wild boar rooting for acorns and—a sharp inhalation as I see them—wolves, beyond the marshy part where willows are growing. Arthur's eyes widen—he can see it as clearly as I can: a grey wolf, less translucent with every minute. We watch the pack, a couple of cubs playing in the dust, and then I spot something large and feline: black-tipped ears and a spotted back. Arthur, it's a lynx, a big cat. *Shhhh.*

I think he's hunting—I tell Arthur—there must be roe deer nearby, and my son looks upset at the thought of jaws and claws meeting a fawn's spotted coat. I nod, understanding and feeling the same but, I say, the lynx's mate has kittens now. I point to where the lynx queen is occupied with washing them, her rough tongue pressing against their fur. The new family is sheltered by huge roots and the curved trunk of what can only be the greatest and most ancient of trees. A mother tree, I tell him—in charge of protecting the whole forest. A few weeks ago—I know it somehow—the mother cat lay down here to give birth, choosing this spot to raise her family because it felt like a place of protection to her too.

We look on as the babies start to feed. Arthur, I remind him gently, she needs to eat to make the milk. He thinks for a few seconds: "The daddy will have to kill the deer, then." I put my arms around him a little tighter as the tom lynx passes right in front of us on his murderous but life-saving quest. We stare at the canopy above and this world that has become so real that it almost obscures the sight of our tabby cat slinking through the open field on her way to hunt mice.

Late morning and the sun is high enough to shine directly outside the kitchen. We drag cushions outside to bask in the heat, remembering how nice it is when the air is warm, not biting. The sky is spookily blue for February; not the usual determined cerulean of late winter but a soft summerlike periwinkle. It's odd to see bare branches against a shade of sky that is usually paired with leaves, and even the crocuses seem shocked as they open and spin like satellites to stalk the sun.

This is all Arthur really remembers. He is tuned into the outdoor world we have foisted on him; noticing the moon's daily changes and knowing how to hold a hen so her wings don't flap. I wonder if he will choose something similar for himself or if, later, he'll resent us for taking him away from the big city where his sister was born. Whether deciding between city and countryside life will even be something his generation gets to do. But I try not to project into the future today, to avoid stepping any closer to the internal agitation that would otherwise catch light.

We eat lunch early and then I open three envelopes that came in the post, happy to hear a promising rattle from within. Money is tight this year, but seeds are a cheap dopamine fix and I have a burgeoning addiction. A pound or two brings me an assurance of summer and buys my freedom from the sensory assault of the vegetable aisle. I love them and they are useful too—the perfect thing to keep my son occupied and me distracted without it all feeling like a waste of precious time.

I take out the packets excitedly and my enthusiasm spills over to Arthur, who squeals and shakes them, doing a funny little dance that I join in with. I tear the paper, pour seeds carefully out onto our palms and we consider them reverently: the pepper's pale curve; the darker, chunkier teardrop of the squash. These are the essential ingredients for a magic spell I am about to cast, and I resist the instinct to rush on. I roll them between thumb and finger for a moment instead, hoping that their ugly duckling promise of eventual swan will rub off.

We sow them together sitting on the grass, getting seed compost everywhere. After we've done all the vegetables we can, Arthur agitates for more and, as I can't face a tantrum today, I fetch the jumbled box of flower seeds, taking out the ones I am most excited about: Cosmos Rose Bon Bon. They sound like something a wacky celebrity would name a child, and as we push these brown new moons into the compost, I am pressed closer to the pink, double-petaled flowers of July. Arthur must feel this forward motion too, chatting happily about what else we will grow for him to eat this summer. Raspberries, corn, peas, strawberries, carrots, beans, sugar snaps, lettuce (but not arugula—too spicy), cucumbers, potatoes, mint, beets (but only if I cut them into ribbons) and, finally, even more raspberries.

I'd better get to work.

The next morning, both children are at school and I am typing quickly. Thrown off by yesterday's unplanned holiday I'm skittering from task to task as if each is an emergency and yet entirely meaningless. I feel frantic but then catch myself staring gormlessly out the window. When I get up to do something, I've forgotten what it is by the time I reach the next room. Finally, I settle to scrolling through the headlines, clicking through to a story on how yesterday was the hottest in a British February since record keeping began.

It's confusing to look at the still-seductive blue sky and know there's something sinister about it. Everything feels easier when the air is balmy, the light streams in, and no one needs a coat. Being reminded that this heat is a symptom of a climate lurching out of balance makes these simple joys feel like betrayals. I should be outside now working the plot to make our lives less reliant on things that make the temperature climb. But—the follow-up thought comes quickly—surely it's absurd to even try to meet a problem of this scale by growing a few beans?

I read on and discover that yesterday's temperature record was logged somewhere not usually famed for its good weather—the place where the idea for our smallholding life first germinated. While Arthur and I sowed our seeds, the thermometer in the Trawsgoed Estate in Ceredigion, West Wales, crept up to 70 degrees Fahrenheit. Less than three years previously, on working holiday we'd passed that very spot and it was near there, with the children in the background running happily toward a stream, that Jared and I first talked about making a shift to a more outdoor life.

I remember that summer as one continuous picnic in the August grass—the memory already heat hazed. Days passed and we turned browner and our hair sun bleached. The world of trains, laptops, cafés, and shops drifted away down the River Teifi and out into the sea. After nearly ten years of marriage, Jared and I smiled more easily again, laughed often, played with the children in the day, and talked and loved at night as if we'd discovered a secret compartment in one another with something new within every morning. I recognized a difference in myself too—not completely novel, but a return to something I'd lost and then forgotten.

Soothed by the sounds of crickets, we found the space for thoughts usually pushed aside by work, vacuuming, and getting to childcare on time. Late-night fireside chats evolved into a plan that felt like the only logical response to where we and everything around us seemed to be headed. I don't know who said it first—the wish to capture some of the freedom and energy we felt then and bring it to our everyday lives. But there was a shared certainty, I know there was, a realization that we didn't miss much of the life we were away from and that there was a lot to gain in beginning again a little closer to the earth. Both our heads swiveled in a new way when we passed solar panels, vegetable patches, and farm For Sale signs. And, as the fire turned to embers and we turned our feelings into a vision, we found that we were also talking about our biggest fears. That this plan we had somehow segued into making contained the worries we had about our family, our town, our country, and our world.

The memory of our idealistic hopes gives me an idea and I jump up and, using scraps of paper, start arranging nuggets of information in chronological order on the floor. We aren't the first people to put things together and turn the land into the answer. I use the notes I've been making to create a rough timeline of the many attempts to protect a living-from-the-land way of life across English history. A bill of Parliament in the time of Elizabeth I, legal fences, government-sponsored schemes and privately funded projects—all saying in their different ways that a small life on a small piece of land was something to hold to.

A little land offered by rulers as a token to keep the peasant classes from starving and rioting and hold them in their place. Offered again to their descendants, nineteenth-century workers, but this time to empower them to realize their rights and rise up against the class system. Innovative urban projects of recent times defying the way things have always been done yet coming back to the old idea of putting our hands in the soil.

I see some of what connects these things beyond the floor I've put them on but what interests me most is their shared contrariness. These many attempts to dig into the land haven't worked. Land was taken, fences enclosed communal grazing sites, farms swallowed other farms and became bigger, and rural folk moved for a city life and wages. Yet the land has continued to call and we hear it most clearly when times are hardest: enthusiasm for a good, simple life following hot on the heels of recession, war, and political crisis.

The stubborn insistence on marching in one direction while everything points to another is so familiar. If I can get at it, pull it apart, and see why it matters on this macro scale, then maybe my own micro version will make more sense and feel less contentious. And it does feel contentious; a good thing wrapped in bad things and struggle.

I was thirty-four the summer before our move when we started to sketch the life we wanted. I feel a hundred and thirty-four, only three years on. It was 2016, the summer that Jared and I stood up from the fireside, scooped up the sleeping children, and set off without a backward glance. The summer of the Brexit vote and the Trump presidential campaign. When, belatedly, climate change and the wrecking of the natural world transitioned for us from abstract worries to active threats. The summer when I started to tense against a feeling that there was a point of confluence ahead for which we needed to be ready.

I was thirty-four that summer; the summer of striding out toward a life of open fields and sacks of corn. And I brought my kids, Jared, two cats, three jobs, and a confused black hole of something pernicious but not yet acknowledged along for the ride.

This afternoon I am trying to focus on the progress I have made and not let myself think about the rest of it: everything else still to be completed, and how I feel when it piles up. This is why I am looking for materials to sow yet another batch of seeds. The tangle of energy, certainty, ambition, thoughtfulness, panic, self-loathing, anger, confusion—and all the other things not found or named—is pulling me in too many directions. Over these impossible feelings I choose the anticipation of a speck of green against black every time. I want to watch each one become a seedling, noticing its cotyledons, the temporary first leaves, open as if trying aboveground existence on for size before making a commitment. It feels as if identifying the precise moment that photosynthesis takes over could make the expanse of my thoughts manageable.

Despite these efforts this wide internal space opens up now. I see Jared and me sharing a mouse-infested shithole of an East London flat with five others. Just-out-of-university friends, thrown together as we tried to persuade the others to move farther out for more space and light. We fell in love in my messy bedroom looking out over the twenty-four-hour Beigel Bake on Bethnal Green Road. Six months later we decamped to a tiny flat overlooking a courtyard, then another with a sliver of outdoor space in which we immediately, unnecessarily, installed two rabbits. The dense undergrowth of our current life is seeded in these beginnings. Getting married the week after my twenty-fifth birthday, a curly-haired baby at twenty-seven; always wanting to tangle ourselves up with where we lived. Jared keener to stay still for a while and me always restless and ready for the next thing.

There's a lurching strangeness making itself obvious within me now but it doesn't feel new. It has been growing for a long time. It's the same out there in the world—the leaves of this month's record-breaking heat forming their first tiny buds one hundred, five hundred, perhaps a thousand years ago.

Once I start, it is hard for me to stop going along this trail to the uncertainties of the future, the demand for a response and solution following quickly behind. I'm too jittery for it today so I force my focus away from pursuing the truth, leave the shed, and concentrate on tugging out some weeds. My thoughts drop unwilling, but then with relief, and make their way through the place these roots have been growing.

Since the forest of our home's past told itself to me and Arthur as a fairy story, I have added a new branch to my research interest, under the broad heading of making sense of *now* by understanding *then*. It's no longer just land in general that I am examining. My own land's very specific past has now captured my attention too, and I have started by looking for its beginning and found 130 million years ago, when the clay was laid down, to be a contender. The sun has risen and fallen over it 46 billion times since, and though land became sea and became land once more, its earth remained solid underneath. Next, it was topped by a warm, wet jungle that was stopped by sudden extinction and followed by a winter almost without end.

I can smell spring as I inhale: it always comes eventually—even out of that ancient eternity of cold—small thickets sprouted and massed, becoming the prehistoric, prehuman forest of the Weald. A green wave of leaves, a density of trunks, and a wholeness of many sounds that I have already found, thanks to a horizon haze, a little boy, and a story that I am proving is real and true.

The weeding takes only a sliver of my thoughts, the rest directing a whistle-stop tour across hundreds of thousands of years. Bacteria, plants, birds, insects, reptiles, and mammals emerged from the great woodland, altered, and gradually disappeared. Slowly, slowly creatures whose descendants would eventually stand up as humans moved across its leaf-mold floor. And when the Holocene came to this patch of land, sucking soils and dense woodland acted as a barrier, shielding the forest and lightening the touch of people for longer than elsewhere.

By and by—a little over a thousand years ago—this land finally felt the force of permanent human inhabitation. Small clearings for pigs and tents multiplied and expanded; a tsunami of change had started. Axes met saplings and large trunks alike. Within three centuries, the forest's 500 square miles had shrunk to 150, and sunlight hit grass more often than leaf. In time even the Mother Tree—the oldest in the forest, charged with protecting this woodland (with a sideline in sheltering generations of lynx)—became ship's hull, fence, and mantelpiece.

Coit Andred. Andredesleage. Andredes weald. I am collecting these old names for the forest that grew where my house now stands. The sound of a crow overhead makes me look up and away from the pile I've made of fast-shriveling roots. At first I see only sky and bird. Then a clearing: grazing and a place to grow food. Now—only a fleeting glimpse in the window—an unblemished expanse of trees;

so beautiful that I mourn it despite knowing that if it were still here, this smallholding and I could not be.

The past doesn't seem keen to stay in textbooks anymore. As I look and listen, it comes more clearly into view, refusing to step out of the present's way as time travels like a river through today. Holes in the canopy, paths through the darkness, the smell of woodsmoke, and human voices getting louder, life getting better. Land that had just existed, just was—a place to walk across, scurry on, climb up or fly over—becoming somewhere that was owned. A safer world of hospitals, welfare state, and lifesaving vaccines, yet one where trees became the exception and fields—dotted with houses, bordered by roads—the rule.

By the time our family began our new life here, there were only 23 square miles of ancient forest left—half damaged and a quarter overgrazed. There are still so many clues to what it was both below and above the surface: holiday cottages named for the earliest settlers; villages, roads, and shops inheriting the titles of the first clearings made. As I made a start on smallholding, turning this soil with my fork, I had no idea that this wasn't only gardening; it was a kind of archaeology too.

January and February have taken too long to get over themselves and I'm done. These first two months are always so full of important dates and not enough light hours to stuff the remembering of them into. New Year's, both our mothers' birthdays, then Jared's, Sofya's, and my father's; by the time Valentines comes all I want as a gift is not to have to celebrate at all.

As I check on the now-germinated cosmos seedlings, I take note of the welcome extra light. The days have lengthened by a full two hours since the start of the month and once again today the last of the sunshine lands a few minutes later and a ray or two farther on the daffodils. Winter is over and I can see the summer garden emerging from pots in the propagator and on windowsills. Sweet peas are snaking up canes and the garden peas that overwintered in a plastic pop-up tent are already beginning to reach the tops of their short stakes. The extra light is helping me check off some long-overdue chores and I finally feel a little satisfied as I take stock of the garden and my plans for its year to come.

Most of the seeds Arthur and I sowed have germinated and I'm thinning them out; pulling the weakest from the soil to give the healthiest the best start. Too sentimental to be cutthroat about it, I know I've left more than I should to battle it out. This garden knowledge has grown in me quickly over the past few years. Until I was thirty-four, and those warm weeks of summer in Wales did their work on me, I'd never picked up a trowel and was convinced that I couldn't successfully cultivate so much as a layer of mold on jam— let alone grow a whole plant from a seed.

Our last home—a tall, narrow townhouse—had a garden that pleased and terrified me in equal amounts. I wanted our family to be out in it and for it to be lovely, but I had no idea where to start. I worried that I would kill the plants and break the rules, not realizing that they were my plants and my rules to make. Stopping the house from falling down, working, looking after a toddler, being pregnant again, and having a new baby were more than enough to help avoid looking outside too much and ignore the guilty, neglectful feeling I got when I did.

When the mess became too much to block out, a gardener friend planted a low-maintenance flower bed and I panic-turfed the rest. Slowly the little collection plants worked on me. I watered them sometimes, began noticing the buds form and turn to flowers, and knew I'd played a small part in that transformation. It was quiet out there, by myself, with only the hose and a ladybug for company.

One late-spring day I felt ready to take the next step and create something of my own. I remembered the impulse-purchase strawberry plants I'd picked up the previous year, found them looking half-dead at the bottom of the garden, and planted them up in pride of place near the house. I nurtured those strawberries tenderly for two months; snipping off brown leaves and evicting weeds in my first real taste of gardening. By the time we set off for our summer in Wales my pet plants had quadrupled in size and my gardener buddy, who was watering in our absence, promised to pay them special attention.

When we returned five weeks later, ready to ditch town life for the call of the countryside, the strawberry plants had fruited. There's an addictive sense of achievement and self-reliance that comes when the work of tending to a plant turns it into food and it flooded through me, validating the decisions we'd made while we were away.

It was a week later that I realized I'd been scammed. I couldn't shake the realization that my plants, which hadn't even had buds on them when we'd left, had become covered in ripe fruits in a suspiciously short time. I texted my friend and she confessed. The plants I'd bought twelve months previously had no doubt died within a matter of weeks of their purchase, because if you leave a plant, any plant, even a cactus, in a tiny plastic pot for a hot summer with no water, it will shrivel to nothing. Then, when the spring rains watered wind-scattered seeds, a new crop had appeared. A crop of weeds that I'd cared for like children for months. My kind friend had worked it out in seconds, dug my mistakes up and swapped them for the garden center's best strawberries.

Somehow, even though my cheeks were as red as those berries when I realized what had happened, her ploy worked. Though the fruits hadn't been mine, I had an inkling of what it might take and a hunch as to how it might feel if they were. Six months later I was planting real strawberries in the old fruit cage of our new smallholding. Putting my hands into the earth and growing something akin to survival in it was my new obsession, the good old story of going back to the land in defiance of a world that seemed to be walking away from it.

After washing the worst of the garden off my hands, I take the hour before a work call to add to my growing dossier. Over the past week I've spread out from English history and gone global, looking for meaning in my Australian cousin's arid acres, idealistic 1960s Tennessee communes, the lives of Scottish crofters of today, and even Russian dachas—tiny parcels of rural land providing food and respite to city dwellers. But I am not a crofter, a hippie, or a dachinki—not quite.

I have started reading about contemporary American homesteaders and some of it feels a little closer. I'd barely uttered the word *homestead* until a few days ago. It's not a word heard often on this side of the Atlantic, and though most homesteads appear to be a lot bigger than two acres, the word seems to have some similar associations with size, self-sufficiency, idealism, and outsider spirit as smallholding does.

The thought of the work call is ever present, and the time to stop reading gets annoyingly close. I want to find something, anything, that I can consider a success before I'm interrupted. I click quickly through the Homesteaders of America, look up "neo-homesteaders," and spend a little while in the bunker with "preppers," whose homesteading is bound up in a belief that they need to be ready for disaster to come.

I am not a prepper; these are not my people either; yet I do think we need to be prepared. I always have an eye on the horizon—scanning—and my alarm bells have been going off for quite some time. In 2016 I knew something was wrong. Many things were wrong.

And I needed to be ready when they arrived— in here and out there.

As my reminder app lets me know I've only ten minutes left, I feel a little panic and then a bigger shot of something negative directed sharply at myself for being so ridiculous. I'm panicking because I can't find something. I have no idea what the something is, or if and why it matters. It isn't work, it isn't for the children, and it isn't even making me feel good. And yet I can't tear myself away.

I snooze the reminder for five minutes and read one last thing. The end of a master's thesis on contemporary homesteading, which I started blurrily in a 4:00 AM insomnia session. One paragraph enlarges and phrases embolden as I read. "Homesteaders transvalue their possessions, homes, work, and identities . . . in order to reinscribe them with new meanings . . . Their vocational labor . . . means what they *want it to mean*, not what history says it ought to."

There's another wrinkle here, another clue but no time to unravel it now. The freedom to define my own life excites me. I want to live outside a norm if the norm is bad. But if you make a life on your own terms no one shows you what to do, and it's all too easy for everything to spin, alter, and become something else entirely. All too easy to find yourself wanting it to mean one thing so much that you refuse to see what's really there.

Whether they are around the corner or thousands of miles away in Peredelkino, Russia, or Minnesota, others are working their small patches of earth as I work mine. In the absence of anything more certain I try to take comfort in this simple thought. However, what I am really comforted by is the fifty-page thesis. There's so much that chimes for me within its intelligent, earnest inquiry, but it is the fact of its mere existence that has lightened me. Though it has taken a couple of years, finally I've found her and I love her: This someone from another land who has overthought the whole thing even more than me.

March

FRAG MENT ATION

Over breakfast something small finally tips me off that ledge—the one I have been balancing on for quite some time. I hold the glass jar of coffee beans in both hands over my head and bring it toward the floor, via the top of my skull, with force. Under the instant landslide of adrenalin, I realize I've been waiting for this moment: secretly hoping it will come, rigid with the effort of preventing it. It's almost a relief to give into the flood.

I'm hoping for blood: a gash and then a warm trickle that fills the creases of my forehead and drips rhythmically onto the kitchen's grainy tiles. I am sick of trying to explain this with words that I can't get right and that everyone seems to ignore or forget. So today, in a split-second reaction, I try to leave enough of a mark so that even when I wipe my eyes and pull myself together later, neither Jared nor I will be in any doubt that there is something very wrong.

Shelf, hand, forehead: the jar hits the floor, rolls and barely even chips. Jared looks shocked, angry even, but not full of realization. I put my fingers to my forehead and they come away clean. There is only a dull ache and a stupid little egg on my hairline and it doesn't meet the need for self-destruction or match the strength of the charge within.

So then something else: better, louder, more painful. Four delicate pottery cups, handmade to look and feel like wood and just the right size in my hand. A decade-old gift from my mother that I had wrapped and unwrapped each time we moved, relieved that they hadn't accidentally cracked along the way. Today I throw them all at my favorite piece of furniture, an antique dresser that displays our family treasures. Photographs of the children, our wedding; 1940s Martini glasses collected for Jared's birthday; a card hand printed by a friend, reading only "Peace."

The dresser door smashes as the first cup hits. The second takes out the objects within. I barely register the third and the fourth meeting my palm and leaving again a split second later. But they do. Last of all, perhaps for completeness, I pick up the matching jug. The final piece of a set that had been chosen with care and given with love. I lob it like a grenade.

There is rubble when the protective shell of a person explodes. Glass everywhere mixed with shards of ochre, duck-egg blue, deep black, and wintergreen. A tasteful rainbow of destruction underscored by little breathy sounds of shock and a rooster crowing outside.

I am blank. I hear static noise, the ends of my fingers tingle but the whirling anger and panic has finally gone. Something of me is all in pieces on the floor and that's fine. I sure as hell don't want to stick her back together again. I stand there, numbly, waiting for the fallout, the reaction, the judgment to be handed down. For Jared's strong arm to land on mine and march me out and, in a shout-whisper, tell me that I can't behave like this ever again. Or maybe to be scooped up and put to bed with an ice pack and instruction to sleep. Perhaps he'll insist I cancel my day of meetings and get some help right now. I don't know what it is that I want from him, apart from his acknowledgment, apart from a response.

There is only silence. Jared is rooted to the spot, and the children, who have just appeared, are looking on with huge eyes and pale faces. Centuries pass while I wait for him to see me as I am, without my armor, here in this awful place—a corner with no way out, where everything is dangerous and broken, and I am not even trying to hide it anymore. The spring air cools my damp skin quickly as the nothingness stretches out and out.

I stand as firm as I can and wait, letting my eyelids fall shut for a moment. Underneath them I'm naked and shivering. Freshly emerged from an old tin bath under the trees where my skin has been scrubbed red with the effort of removing a long winter's dirt. The fire isn't lit and I am waiting for him to do it. To come out of the log house with a blanket and see me without my coverings, pathetic as I am, and know me and love me.

But he doesn't come. I just stand there in the quiet, feeling a cold wind hitting my back and knowing I am turning from red to blue. It is just me. I am alone in the forest, in the clearing, just as I feared I was all along. And the all-aloneness is more obvious and more dangerous because I've broken through the casing I have been hiding it within. Still nothing and no one and it is unbearable. I am moments from hypothermia. I jump back in that bath and I skim the scum off the water's top and slather myself with it. The filthy clothes I'd thought not fit for purpose warm me as I put them back on. I climb back into the safety of what I know, protecting myself again as suddenly as I dared to make myself so vulnerable.

I open my eyes. I pour myself a cup of coffee, open the cutlery drawer and use a knife to spread peanut butter onto bread. I collect my bag and keys—an odd calm bolted over the adrenalin rush—and pick through the room hearing fragments hit the walls as my feet send them skittering. As I leave to catch my train, turning back with a shout of "Have a nice day," there is no reply. All three of them look at me as though I've lost my mind.

Which of course I have.

My day of work goes well despite the preface. I'm good at this stuff, whatever the run-up. I put the morning away somewhere I can't reach—pushing it further as the train takes me to the city—and creating distance between me and the "her" who did the bad thing. When I'm working and meeting people, I don't have time or space in my head for anything else. As well as actively reminding myself to listen to what's being said, I am also instinctively taking in the bigger picture and decoding the dynamics of the room.

My antennae are tuned to the unspoken things that matter: a shadow under someone's eyes; a micro-glance at the water bottle as they balance thirst with not wanting to interrupt; the way they hold themselves taut at the mention of someone else's pregnancy. I am at capacity with the effort of putting all this together, making a formula, and turning myself into its answer, so it's only when I'm walking through the streetlamp-lit station parking lot that this morning becomes real again and I start to feel a bit sick.

At home there's the kind of quiet that tells me the children are in bed; a hush that highlights how nervous I am about facing the intervention to come. The house is spotless—tidier than when I left. All traces of what happened earlier have been removed, and if you didn't know the things that were here before I destroyed them, you wouldn't miss their presence.

"Hi," I say with studied casualness as I walk toward Jared in the kitchen. "Hello," he replies, a little wary perhaps, but not hostile. He asks about my day and so I tell him: the meetings, the promise of something exciting, the annoying email. He offers things up from his day and, though we are stilted, a light remark and half laugh seem to go over OK.

It takes me half an hour of this to realize that the conversation I have been expecting is not in the cards. If I don't bring up what took place over breakfast, it might never be mentioned again. I know I should do it: be brave, apologize, try to explain why it happened and how I am going to make sure it doesn't happen again. Make a plan to fix this, fix us, fix me; but I have been doing versions of this for a while now, and I don't have anything left. It's too tempting, the knowledge that if I pretend it didn't happen I can convince myself it never was.

So I say nothing and, after eating and watching something I can't remember, lie on the precipitous edge of our bed and think about that summer day three years ago when we started to talk about the future and ended up, five months later, on this plot. Excitement, shared purpose, and a plan—I tell myself that these things propelled us, but I wonder if there's another story that's also true. In this story it's all my fault. I'm the impulsive one who pushes harder and has it all scoped out with the answers to every possible question prepared in advance. A story in which I have good ideas and a need to bring them to life so Jared plays along. And somehow our new life becomes my solo project—though I'd never have set out to do it alone. I am unchecked and leading the charge and so the stakes rise and my effort rises in turn. I take the responsibility, the credit, and the blame as we move apart instead of together and I meet a challenge that no amount of trying seems to overcome. Maybe that's the real story. Maybe not.

I want to understand what went wrong, but the narrative has split and I don't know which version is the original. I don't know whether it's normal that we are not talking about the way I shattered into sharp pieces this morning. I can't tell if something big and bad happened today or if everything is fine.

There are so many possible scenarios and I have tried to make a plan for each, just in case. But these responses, every one given an equal weighting, don't resolve anything and instead become staccato fragments arguing in my head. Sleep will shush them for a bit though, and so I try to get to it by focusing on the only thing that feels certain: the ceiling, the air, and, above it all, the expanding infinity of space, which is tiny compared to the distance between my husband and me on the mattress tonight.

The next morning we carried on ignoring everything that matters. Still, I took the last bit of bravery I must have stored in my little toe for such emergencies and began the one piece of repair work I knew I had to do: apologizing to the children. I pulled them close to show them that my knee was still a safe place. I told them that I understood how they might feel because when I was a little girl it frightened and upset me when people would volcano their feelings seemingly out of nowhere. I said that I was so sorry and that I would do better. They appeared to be fine, taking it all as read, relaxing into my arms, and, now they are at school, I try to reassure myself that it's the apology that counts, that all I have to be is good enough as often as I can. But this was not good enough and I know it.

I have already written off today's work. I'm drained and wired and at my desk reading the news. "Apocalyptic," says a BBC story about the burning of Saddleworth Moor, one of the largest-ever moorland fires that sparked up a week ago as my little son and I sowed seeds. The story is a big one. We are not used to wildfires here, not often, not in the cool north of England, not in winter. Yet, fanned by one of the driest and warmest Februarys on record, six-foot-high flames moved swiftly across the early-spring land as if it were the end of a long Californian summer. As if it were the end of the world as we know it.

I read eyewitness reports and follow the hashtags that fly out from the story taking hold online like sparks on dry bilberry and cross-leaved heath. We have spent the past two hundred years sucking the life out of the moors and now they are dying. But as our future is tangled up with these great carbon sinks, people are trying to save them. Last year volunteers were down on their knees planting a million sphagnum moss plants to help restore this land to a featherbed bog of moss and cotton grasses.

Much of their effort has just burned away to nothing—the peat giving up its treasure and pumping carbon into the atmosphere at a rate of thousands of tons per hectare. "Apocalyptic," says the story, but I wonder at what point "apocalyptic" becomes "apocalypse" and whether it's possible to catch the moment before the adjective becomes that definitive, deafening noun.

I close my eyes against the weight of these facts and thoughts, but since they are inside my skull this only intensifies the smash of jagged edges as they collide. I needed a calming morning, but instead I am keyed up, and my thoughts are flinging themselves against a heavy tiredness made of yesterday and *its* yesterdays. I should be doing more, be out on the moor on my knees planting sphagnum moss until the trowel handle bursts the blisters on my hands and begins to make new ones beneath.

My heart is full of more and moor, but I can't calibrate whether I am twiddling my thumbs and being lazy or if I am already at capacity. The space in my head is a wild moorland filling with a snarl of leaves, stems, and roots that make an ecosystem of thoughts and plans. Golden plover, dunlin, and short-eared owls take turns to run and fly and dive across it in random bursts until I lose my place and everything starts to spin.

Zooming out and seeing many things at once, piecing them together to spot patterns and construct self-supporting plans that capture everything from the micro to the macro—this used to be my biggest strength. But my brain has turned against itself and me, so this hasn't been true for a while. Perhaps I was denser, heavier, and at less risk of wafting up and out of control in the past. Maybe I weighed myself down previously: used pegs and a rope or wore a protective suit made of something like sphagnum moss, a soft, acidic layer to stop anything evaporating or decaying. Yet I've lost sight of whatever it was that I used to keep safe and anchored, and, until I discover what to lash myself tightly to, I can't go farther into the moorland, not after yesterday. Feeling guilty, I close the browser and go outside to look for something more solid than peat bog on which to rest.

I walk toward and along the boundary, tracing its route from roadside to field. The trunks are what I notice at first; different widths and barks, all lined up either side of the fence like security guards and it's then that the extraordinary span of the largest oak's canopy registers. I look at the underside of its umbrella for a while, relaxing in my insignificance. The shade I cast wouldn't shelter more than a handful of bluebells but this tree could shadow a planet. I know to be reassured by its size somehow and maybe, yes—another idea—its age. I should try to work out how old it is.

A quick google sends me looking for the dressmaker's tape measure inherited with my grandmother's sewing box. I approach the fattest oak trunk and put my palms on it, focusing on the way the bark feels under my nervy hands. It is quiet and still under the canopy, with decades of leaves that make it slippery underfoot. As I try to get the tape measure around the trunk I lose my balance and brace for another fall, but the catch I've been hoping for comes this time. Spinning to see who held out their arms, I find only a laurel branch.

I measure in sections and make slapdash calculations on my phone until an answer appears: 335. The numbers settle slowly on me: dandelion seeds following the breeze's path until they finally land. This tree I have been ignoring is 335 years old. It has been growing here since 1684.

I take it, this direct link that feels like a way out, and travel from the sharp pieces of now to when everything came together then.

Piecing together those perfect moments that followed the acorn's fall.

The year 1684 has become a gap that I need to fill. Inside and on the internet, I click, skim, highlight, and soon have twenty tabs open. This feels like a safe place to get lost. Nothing in 1684 can be my fault and no one from 335 years ago is expecting my call. I feel free to spread out across the year and, as I do, I find scraps that might fit together if I find enough of them.

The acorn's taproot began to tunnel under the earth as England struggled through the coldest winter in living memory and a "little ice age" gripped the land. South from here, in Romney Marsh, the *Anopheles* mosquitoes' malarial bites were stopped for a short while by the chill, and the sea froze for two miles toward France. In Paris, poet and philosopher Anne de la Vigne took one last breath before dying, supposedly of sheer devotion to studying a world she had challenged with her words, thoughts, and gender. And eastward from her deathbed, Pope Innocent XI gathered a Holy League of nations and ushered in the Ottoman Empire's defeat.

In England, north of where this oak nut's stem broke the soil's surface, Charles II lived out his final year. As the seedling's lateral roots worked outward, the King threw his rule wider too; to Massachusetts, where he demonstrated power by punishing the puritan leanings of his New England subjects, despite the Atlantic between them.

In Lithuania, punishment for faith was also a recent reality and a baby girl—Marta Skowronska—was born to peasant parents who would never know their orphan would grow to be Catherine I, Empress of all Russia.

As she fed, New England reeled, and old England's freeze set in harder, Isaac Newton kept warm by his Cambridgeshire fire and scratched away with a goose-feather quill to prove and explain much of what had seemed mystical until then: tides, comets, equinoxes, eclipses, and the relationship between the way objects moved here on Earth and in the big skies above. "My" acorn hit the clay below, as every acorn has ever done, because of these laws of gravity. But perhaps it was the first to fall in a time when we knew what force was holding us, and it, to the earth's surface.

More changed across that year than our understanding of the invisible. The thirty-eight babies baptized in our village church who survived infancy would grow up with a chance to go to the school that had just opened. The community had gained a blacksmith: John Illenden, who felt the heat of the new forge's fire on his face every day as our oak grew to a sapling. Snow, ague, empire, war; celestial bodies, water splashing on thirty-eight foreheads, and a horseshoe glowing white in the heat—single random stitches, faces becoming distinct in the crowd, only the start of a tapestry, but fabric in the making nonetheless.

I would like to continue to travel in time, finding it less urgent and more solid than my present day research but when I look at the clock I see the day has all but gone. As I drive to school, anonymous houses, trees, hedges, and fields seem to have become individual question marks. Histories that want to bump up against mine. But right now I have to leave all this in the glove box, open my arms to the children, and hope they will find me a little steadier this afternoon because I've lashed myself to the ground with gravity and acorns.

March has nearly passed and the daffodil show is at its peak. Thick ribbons of lemon white and yolk orange enclose the trees in the orchard. Even on difficult days, it is impossible to ignore them in this volume. As if the plot has been building to this all winter and is releasing the stored energy in a six-week-long circular breath.

I am picking them now—daffodils for the kitchen table and others to give to a friend who needs cheering. With each diagonal snip of a stem I have the feeling of settling into a pre-made mold. My fingers on the scissors, my boots pressing into the squelchy grass, and the sap leaving viscous smears on my gloves. Another woman planted the bulbs that became these flowers. Every spring she would cut them as I am and bring them in to die vibrantly in the warm air of the house.

As I take my bunch inside, I see birds overhead, returning from winter travels. Their size, the delicate point of their beaks, and contrasting scope of their wings: all instant clues that these are geese. I hear their echoing bugle sound now and know it well. It feels a worthwhile thing to have learned here alongside the discovery that there are many more than four seasons. I used to think that spring arrived overnight with blossom and summer showed up just as suddenly on the first hot day. I would know autumn only when I couldn't see the pavement for leaves and winter would wait until, pulling on my hat, I realized the branches were bare. Now that I am lucky to be so close to its daily signals I see the idea of seasons as something humans constructed rather than one of nature's truth. The year's cycle turns continuously, every day a little advance, every year a little different.

After lunch I remember to go to the shed to check for more plant labels. There are a few on the shelf but not enough, so I rummage around on the floor, lifting the boxes where the remaining dahlias wait to be potted up. There aren't many so I tackle them now, inspecting each tuber for rot, using a utility knife to divide the largest into three smaller sections and enjoying the thriftiness of making three plants from one. I plant each piece into a good-size pot for growing on, sheltered until the frost has definitely passed and the slugs have lost their first ravenous interest.

As I move the final dahlia box, the shed fills with the noise of broken china. Inside the lid, instead of the earthy potential of tubers, shards of pottery and glass confront me. Final. Broken. Undeniable.

My arms and legs throb with desire to dump this box in the bin and run away from the crash it makes with my fingers in my ears. I want to deny its existence and have been very busy doing so all month. But the mementos within—made into weapons by my hands, in my kitchen, less than thirty days ago—seduce their way around my amnesia.

Sharp things call to me like Sirens these days and these fragments pull me in. I sit on the floor running my fingertips over their jaggedness and wondering if it is possible to change your fingerprints forever if you have something sharp enough. I imagine their journey to this garden shed as I press into their points. While I was journeying to London, having lifted myself out of my body and most of my mind—othering myself—Jared must have been tidying up. Standing in the rubble, sweeping the floor and holding the dustpan. Looking at this box and so wanting it to not to exist. Finding this dark corner of my garden domain, shoving it away out of sight and not mentioning it since.

I can't blame him. Rubbing things out of the story has been a joint project. I've been doing it too. Pretending that I and everything around me are fine, whole, fixed. There have been plenty of what looked and felt like good days this month to corroborate the censored version. We are desperate to believe in it and in the steady springtime version of me: smiling, efficient, and calm. I have tried to convince myself that she is real and that the woman who exploded was a blip. Except she wasn't. The angry and desperate feeling of that morning is still there and though I haven't lobbed any more heirlooms at the furniture, neither have I worked out why I did it or found a way to be sure I won't do it or something worse again.

At the beginning of this month I stood in my kitchen and smashed things that I loved in an attempt to break out of a shelter that was turning into a prison. I stopped ignoring the hairline cracks and surface chips made by my own hands and let them become fractures revealing the inescapably raw and wet me that had been incubating underneath.

It was too hard though, wasn't it? I chickened out and did what I always seem to do—plastered it all back on and hoped for the best. I am doing it now: taking the dahlia pots outside, leaving the box of brokenness with the recycling, and cutting some more daffodils to cheer up the darker corners of the house. Before I take them inside, I go to the oldest oak tree, look up at the branches' spread, and feel called out. The me who stands under this tree doesn't buy my own bullshit and refuses to corroborate the all-singing, all-dancing lie that I am fine.

BLACK HOLES

'**ve** been waiting for the reminder that has just appeared on my phone screen instructing me to CANDLE THE EGGS. Not that I needed it—I've been excited to check on their progress since I set sixteen eggs to hatch a week ago. I turn the incubator off and load the warm shapes into boxes as quickly and carefully as I can, imagining the gory scene if one drops to the floor. In a darkened room I hold each up to the bright light of a special lamp bought in our first summer here. Several hatches on and I know more or less what I'm looking for. I no longer need to watch fifty-seven YouTube videos to be sure that these red veins spidering out from a little blob are good news.

There are, as always, some duds and disappointments. Two glow clear apart from the circle of yolk, suggesting they were never fertilized. There are a few where life must have started and then stopped, its brief flicker captured by a telltale ring—a blood line—and little pieces of tissue floating in the albumen catching the light of the torch like dust in sunshine. I discard these to protect the developing eggs from bacteria, but as I've learned to set more than I need, I'm feeling good about my chances of a clutch of chicks in two weeks' time.

I put the promising eggs back into the warmth, rotating them as a mother hen would, top up the water, and check that the temperature is beginning to rise to 99.5 degrees Fahrenheit. There are plenty of flashy incubators that would do all this for me and make a better job of it, no doubt. Yet even if I could afford one, I like being tied tightly to our smallholding for the three weeks this process takes. The continual focus on these precise and regular tasks is helping to contain me—soft little walls on which to lean periodically throughout the day. The expansions and contractions of last month need to be dealt with, but I am still putting it off in blossom-scented, downy-soft ways. Each laborious turn of an egg is really a distraction and an act of faith: There will be a chick in my pocket, new breeds for the flock, and rainbow colors in my egg boxes again.

Several days have passed and Arthur and I are watching a news report before bed. The reporter speaks calmly but the scientists' excitement is betrayed by their high, fast voices and my space-loving boy is excited too. The screen shows the world's observatories working together, each dish swiveling in time; a synchronized, global dance that turns them into one giant "event horizon telescope."

The picture cuts to the main event: the screen black apart from a glowing circle of orange and red with a dark disk at its center. Arthur and I look at it, the first ever image of a black hole captured. It is mesmerizing, pulling us both in. In my parents' lifetime black holes have gone from science fiction to million-ton science fact. At first humans couldn't see them so we didn't know they were there. Then, as we still couldn't see them, most of us didn't believe those who said black holes were there. But now we can see them: here they are, here one is—a real life black hole. Exactly where those who didn't need their eyes to confirm what they knew had said it would be.

When the program ends I put Arthur to bed and instead of a story we look up the new words and ideas it has given us. We learn about different kinds and sizes of black holes, the smallest made when the universe began. We read that some are made during the death throes of stars but that we do not have to worry about our sun becoming a black hole because it is far too small.

I read aloud to him about the sheer gravitational pull of these places, so strong that it can bend space and light around it. Together we learn that when light and the information it holds are pulled across the event horizon they are rendered invisible. "Event horizon": a boundary beyond which events cannot affect an observer. At a certain point of proximity, unless you are going in yourself, you can't see or be part of what happens in a black hole. Even if you could watch an object approaching you would only witness it slowing to a permanent stop at the event horizon. Gravity, distance, and the speed of light work together in ways I can't grasp to make it impossible for anyone to witness the moment of crossing over. We have to trust that the black hole has pulled the object in and that from there it travels toward the singularity, a one-dimensional point at its center of impossibly huge mass. Inside, density and gravity will become infinite and the laws of physics give up on themselves.

We talk, I type, and he looks at pictures until his yawn reveals it is far too late for this kind of thing. I'm usually going through the motions with Arthur's space obsession, finding it dull myself, but tonight since watching telescopes dance and turn fiction into fact, the backdrop of outer space seems a lot more interesting.

I leave Arthur looking at the pictures in a large space encyclopedia and see my own shelf of dull-but-not-dull reference books, bought as the air started to warm in our initial February here, and I began to take wobbly, introductory steps as a smallholder. The secondhand books promised to teach me about vegetable gardening, companion planting, how to grow without any backbreaking, microcosm-disturbing digging, about living self-sufficiently on an acre, keeping poultry, and more. I borrowed Sofya's colored pencils to sketch elaborate vegetable-planting plans: orange for carrots, green for cabbage, yellow for the onions planted around the edges to keep the root fly off the scent.

I sowed my first-ever seeds in trays (badly) and covered the beds with sheets of blue plastic found in the shed, on a hunch that it was the right thing to do. By March I'd decided it was time for animals and brought home three ducklings who panicked every time they saw us and I panicked right back at them when they refused to go under the heat lamp. It would be twenty weeks before we could poach duck eggs for breakfast, but as that first spring warmed to summer we started to eat other produce. I cut asparagus with a sharp knife and, though I didn't yet know what to do with the flower beds or how to keep on top of the weeding or the pruning, the garden rewarded me anyway with roses, clematis, and irises.

We were hardly ever indoors: a family delighting in our surroundings and how they changed us. Sending Sofya out to gather kindling and marveling at her strength when she came back dragging a twelve-foot branch. Watching Arthur strolling easily in the field pointing at our neighbor's sheep and lambs, the sun sliding sideways casting a halo around his head. Always out doing, digging, and making plans. Idyllic.

Two years on, as I look at this time, I see another, less idyllic, side to all that doing: the beginning of many things becoming wound up far too tightly. In the blur that those twelve months have become, it is hard to tease out the moment I went wrong.

Perhaps it was a few weeks in when, even though I was always working at something—ten things—I was falling behind. I didn't know what was needed or how to do it. I hadn't got any shortcuts or handed-down secrets and neither Jared nor I could easily knock up a frame for beans to climb up or fix a broken shed door. Just doing some of it badly with lots of googling, and swearing was a full-time job. Yet the harder it felt, the more vigorously I attacked the project. I am good in a crisis and this unexpectedly was starting to feel like just that. Every part of me was locked on to the work and the ideas behind it and it was hard to think of anything else. Pausing was not an option because it had become everything and I couldn't even stop to listen to myself or the sound of the marsh frogs in the distance.

Maybe it went wrong a couple of months later, when I had to face up to a big pile of work projects that stretched me in all directions. On top of this I needed to get the builders in: we didn't have heating, the hot-water system was about to give out. I didn't think it could wait. Or perhaps it was not a single moment but the creeping, not-really-realized feeling that Jared, while happy to help when I asked, wasn't diving in too. I worried that I had taken over and elbowed him out, or that he was regretting the move. It became a small sore spot that I tried to heal by showing him that the dream we'd planned together was coming true. I attempted to do everything, all at once, and tried to do it bigger and better in the hopes he would join back in. "We" became "I": I, I, I, I, I. And soon I, I, I, I, I started to feel quite different from ever before.

I was in emergency mode and not listening to the danger signs: tight in the chest, irritable, unable to sit still, to speak slowly, or make decisions. I did not go gently into my garden and potter but instead planned and executed a full-scale vegetable assault. I wanted to expand the growing space of our already-large plot with the addition of three more raised beds. This felt very urgent because when someone mentioned a vegetable or herb I wasn't growing I felt a very real sick-making stab of anxiety that I couldn't rationalize. If I grew everything, though, and grew it well, this would not be a problem. If I had enough growing space I might get rid of the sensation of running up an escalator moving rapidly in the opposite direction—knees, arms, and heart pumping away furiously only to find that I remained static or had slipped back.

I had tied bits of myself, of us, to this project, and so I couldn't stop, I couldn't fail. Instead of resting when I felt shredded, I hammered the nails into the wooden frames for the new beds myself in the early morning. *Bang. Bang. Bang.* The sound of someone increasingly out of control but doing a very good impression of having the time of her life. The beat of Jared's feet stepping back from what we had started together.

The work dial turned up then in tandem with the summer's extra watering. Everything was enormous and urgent and I would start each day almost high with it, a feeling that increased as the hours passed: adrenalin bursts accompanying every pulse. I wrote very long lists, thwacking the side of my skull with my hand regularly to try to keep my brain on the task in hand, even as it ran off like spilt toadflax seeds across the kitchen counter.

By midsummer I was faster, clumsier, and planning out my day from 6:00 AM to 10:00 PM in thirty-minute increments. At night I would hit a physical wall of exhaustion and thick sleep would come almost instantly. In the cracks of time between my day job running a small but busy charity, writing a book, speaking at events, sowing, growing, digging, feeding, mucking out, fixing, and reading about ground-source heat pumps, I tried to be a friend, a good mother, and a wife but found only impatience and an urge to be left alone.

So, I took up running, tried to fit in hobbies I had enjoyed in the past—as if what I needed was more not less. I was spinning through space; except space was my desk, the plot, and the inside of my head. I was both stuck in it and I *was* it. Gravity—that constant—seemed to have given up on me. To anyone outside, to Jared most of the time, and often to myself, all that was visible was the excited smile of an ambitious woman. I didn't know which of these stories was true: the idyll, the person wrestling with a full but rewarding life, or the feeling of complete disintegration.

I kept going though. I hid it really well: how I was feeling, the loneliness, the fear, and the truth that this land no longer felt like a sanctuary but a battleground. By the end of that first summer I had finished my book, grown zucchini, and the raised beds were full of ripening peppers—our first chicks pecking in the dirt beside them.

I had achieved something else too, though I didn't know it then. I had exposed a short-circuit in my brain and, to this April day two years on, I haven't been able to work out exactly where it is or how to stop the sparks from burning me.

Eighteen days after I put the eggs in the incubator I candled them a final time. The children watched as I held each up to the lamp. There was less to see now—the chicks filling almost all of the space apart from the slowly expanding air cell. It's now three days on, late at night, and the blue egg chick has already broken through the membrane into this place of transition. The egg wobbles as it bashes a pointed egg tooth—a tiny temporary axe on the end of its beak— against the calcium carbonate wall.

Sometimes the chicks don't break through before the oxygen runs out. As advised, I try not to intervene for fear of killing a healthy chick, but it is hard to wait. I have peeled away the shell too late before and seen the little creature a millimeter or two from life, all wet and tucked up—a kernel of not-to-be. I try not to hold my breath as I watch and hope.

Then it pips—breaks through into the air and after a rest it starts unzipping—as if worked at by some internal can opener. The top of the shell is almost off and, as I watch it alone with the heavy duvet of midnight around me, hours of slow progress are over in a moment and confinement becomes liberty. The shell is empty and broken, instantly meaningless as it wobbles from side to side on the floor of the incubator. There's not a trace of yolk or white inside to tell of the journey that has just ended. The chick isn't the fluffy handful of greetings cards—but a smear of a creature, its down oiled with the contents of the egg and its new body pushed to breaking point by the effort of escape. I wonder if it has already forgotten becoming something from nothing and then smashing its way out. I let it rest while the other chicks, still in the invisible prelude to being, try to emerge from a fracture line into the night.

I've been trying to work since 9:00 AM but am distracted. When the children rushed in at seven this morning to tell us two chicks had hatched and two more were giving it a good go, I pretended I hadn't been up since five and seen it all already. Now I want to check on progress once more but have promised myself I will wait until lunchtime, and so I start on a new piece of research that my daughter suggested to me.

"Why is it called egg 'candling,' Mummy?" she asked after we'd finished checking the eggs that last time. The answer seemed obvious at first so I gave it unthinkingly. "People used an actual candle to do it before they had electricity." I told her confidently. She was satisfied with this and moved on instantly but I have not. The question has been tapping on the inside of my skull for the past three days. I don't know anything about it and I find I want to. My fingers type out the odd-sounding word and I'm soon looking at instructional videos, overpriced hatching tools, and reading the occasional mention of a lit wick and a steady hand.

I find no indication of when a person first picked up an egg, held it to a flame and thought, *This could be a handy way to count my chickens before they've hatched.* Yet there must be a history to this process. Some confluence of curiosity, economic necessity, and ingenuity that compelled someone to try and see what was inside. The knowledge was surely passed along too—that's how it works, isn't it? Information, tips, and facts passed horizontally and vertically across place and time. So why can't I find any trace of the path this knowledge took?

I have my teeth around this, so I keep going, looking through the elderly but new-to-me books about small farms and Kent piled on my desk—the results of late-night eBay sessions. There are three surveys of the county, written by a series of men who seem to have jumped up every hundred years or so with an urge to walk across southeast England for no other reason than that they could. The books made from their journeys are full of interesting snippets but they make me uncomfortable and cross.

It is not reasonable to be this irked by long-dead Williams and Henrys, but I am. Their words read like an attempt to capture the land and tip it onto the page in a way that would hold up their interests and enshrine their views as all there was and ever would be. It's all too robust and monolithic and they walked too fast—and at times too slow—not seeming to look sideways, underneath, or around corners and wonder.

Of them all, Edward Hasted, who trampled over this countryside at the end of the eighteenth century, is the one I resent least. He names our road in his book and there's a thrill in knowing for certain that this particular person, with his name and date of birth, walked where I live. Hasted has given something else too, words for the very first clearings the settlers made in the Wealden forest: *dens*, *denberies*, *wealdberies*. I keep finding myself rolling them around in my head and muttering them under my breath like a mantra.

I want more than bald facts inked into existence as if there were no room for interpretation and no stories to be found. To know if, where, and when in a denberie someone noticed that an eggshell was no longer opaque if held up to a bright-enough light. So I hurry Hasted along his way out of my thoughts and he travels north along our road to hand the writing baton on. William Henry Ireland, like the two fellows before him, has not written a syllable on the poultry farmers who must have been here. Not a sentence about candling.

There is a history to be found, though. Everything in the equation points to its existence even if it doesn't appear to be visible to the naked eye.

When I wake it is dark and I know without checking that it is still so early in the morning that it is also night. Sleep falls lightly over me when a hatch is underway—the poultry part of me remaining switched on and excited. Pulling on a dressing gown I move carefully through the unlit house and depress the creaky door handle as quietly as I can. Another chick is out and it shouldn't be long before the fourth joins its sort-of siblings.

There's no point in going back to bed now. Instead I watch the new bird's feathers fluff up while other little beaks work at the inside of their shells which rock from side to side. The invisible void of egg candling is bothering me more than it should. I know it's there but how do you find something that seems to eat both light and information?

My desk is next to the incubator, which I placed in here so it was less likely to be knocked over and because I like to be distracted by it. I give my timeline and the document where I keep the latest chunks I've cut and pasted from websites a cursory skim—not reading the words as such; more trying to climb into the partially painted picture that together they make. Taking the tangent that this suggests, I start a new expedition. Coming closer to home again and looking for UK equivalents of the American homesteaders of today who write about meaning and work in a way that understands and excites me.

The Landworkers' Alliance: I find the group, who describe themselves as a UK union of farmers, growers, foresters, and land-based workers, quickly. Their website speaks of food sovereignty, agroecology, and a hoped-for future in which dignity; local, healthy, and affordable food, fuel and fiber; social and environmental justice; and farming in a deep and respectful dialogue with nature are shared priorities.

Outside the wind lobs another bucket of rain at the window but the stormy weather does nothing to dent how joyful I feel reading their report on small farms. Here they really do mean "small." One featured case study is just over an acre, yet it manages to provide part-time jobs to four people. This fits well—at last. A world where non-commercial holdings like our plot count and the people who work them are supported and matter. Where wealth is much broader than money, its definition including what the natural world could gain when we work the land in the right way.

Following a link, I move on to La Via Campesina, an international association of peasants. Here landworkers from Ethiopia, Andalusia, South India, Colombia, people who are too often bullied and criminalized, braid their experiences together to make a heavy rope that ties much together for me. Within minutes I've learned what my chromosomes could have told me if I'd asked. That despite often being ignored, marginalized, and rendered invisible, women produce 70 percent of the world's food.

I have been looking for a community and this early morning research has shown me a new direction to point my torch toward as I search. I shouldn't need a report with the Alliance's logo to confirm my smallholding plans have value and exist in dialogue with the work of others. But I do, and it helps. In times of uncertainty definitions are deliciously solid and, according to the United Nations definition I have just read, I am a peasant. One of the most privileged peasants there is, no doubt, but a peasant nonetheless. And I am a woman too, working the land, and this adds more layers of specificity and more places and people to connect to and search amongst.

A small sound turns me from screen to incubator, where the newest chick has woken up and is running in circles bashing into the others. I check the eggs haven't been too disturbed and decide it's worth risking the humidity dip of opening the lid to rescue one whose egg has rolled over on to its air hole, cutting off the oxygen supply. It is warm in my hand, fragile now the shell's integrity has been damaged, a gift to know how a hatching egg feels against my skin. The sensation lingers after I have put it back, my fingers tingle and so does my brain.

Women. Peasants. Eggs: There, but not there. The books bend around them, turning presence into absence and leaving a darkness that is so easy to ignore until you see the empty space and wonder what should be there. I want to drop out of the William/Edward/ Henry narrative and into that of the wives they left behind to survey my county. But how, if the women of today still struggle to get their voices heard? There's a gap, a chasm in history, where their lives should be. I knew it intellectually already but today it's a personal loss that aches out of my solar plexus.

Teachers whose lessons I need and want to have been taught, hidden by a skewed system and its rules. The room is darkened as I sense more lightless places where the missing should be, and I need to start filling them in before it becomes any more oppressive. A red paperback detailing the social history of our village catches the light that's left. I've only half read it, but I think there's something in there that will help. The pages move between my thumb and forefinger as I look and . . . yes, here it is. Here she is: one of the missing.

Joane Newman: a seventeenth-century "thrice-married farmer's wife." I really like the sound of her as I read the single-page biography, pieced together from church records and archives by a local woman—her great-granddaughter eight times removed.

Born in 1635, Joane lived through the execution of Charles I, Cromwell's brief Commonwealth that followed, and her life spanned the reigns of a further six kings and queens, from before our oak was an acorn to its becoming a strong young tree.

By nineteen she had a son by a married man and, according to court proceedings, a physical fight with his wife. She lived like the times she was in: tumultuously, outrageously even, with the key players changing again and again. One farmer husband, two farmer husbands (they kept on dying), four sons and a daughter later, and at forty-eight she married for a third time. As Newton published the *Principia*, leaving clues pointing to the existence of unseen dense dark stars, fifty-one-year-old Joane left her own clues behind. Other than her death, the last mark she left on paper was ownership of a large piece of land on our road—near, or perhaps even on, this very spot.

This smattering of information isn't much—not five hundred pages of walking and musing—but unlike those it invites me in. The words are made of her, and it's her I want. If I squint I can almost catch fragments of the real woman who was here in this very place and who, after all that living, would have known so much. I close my eyes and try to imagine her. There's nothing on this page about her hair or whether she walked with a limp, but she finally settles as a person behind my eyes: seventy or so, done with husbands, ruling her own roost.

Joane would have kept hens on her land: small-time poultry keeping to feed her family and put a little extra in her purse. She learned what was needed from her mother, sister, grandmother who all knew how a warm shell hatching felt in their hands. This is one of the reasons for the gap and it's why I can't find anything about the development of egg candling in books and on websites. This is knowledge of another kind and it doesn't exist in those places. Like the herbs of birth and death and all the struggles and joys they existed in and around, this is one of the quiet backstories that no man bothered to write down and few women ever needed to or even could. Egg candling was passed from lips to lips until the conversation ended and the memory of it faded out.

Joane has moved from *was* to *is* with these realizations—evidence of her stretching her hand up and out of the past to gift me all this and more. There is a route opening up. A different sort of research project made of these gifts; finding them, seeing them in the dark and working out how to open them. If I want to know what it was like to hold an egg to a candle, what clusters of hurt, love, and hunger led to that moment, then I'm going to have to stretch my hand out to meet this woman who has already forced herself a little way through the gap and back into the world.

I open my window, take the rainy air into my lungs, and let it out into Joane's flat outline made of dusty records. Nothing. It's a big ask: recomposing yourself centuries later from a smattering of snippets; another big ask to believe it is possible. She can't do it alone; too much of her is missing and I am going to have to help fill it in.

My breath comes again and now I look consciously for the empty places where pieces of her once were: dead pixels on a screen. In their place I insert what I know to be true because I have felt, suspected, witnessed, or intuited it. She begins to swell into three dimensions: fleshy, palpable, and buoyant. This work is not the same as reading a hard-edged document and making bullet-point notes; it is better. Joane is now a record of the past whose chest expands and contracts. Whether I am falling into her life, or she into mine, is not clear but we are meeting on earth that knows both our weights. It—she—has a smell, a taste, of salt, bacteria, and linen.

I look on, watching her and waiting. At first I can't see where she is or hear what she says. Joane is pottering about slowly, muttering to herself as she walks into her pasture from the woodland beyond. She looks over her shoulder at me, making eye contact, and giving a little nod: permission to watch and listen.

I follow as she bends a little stiffly, reaching toward a broody hen on a nest and speaking softly to the creature as she does. "Here biddy, biddy, biddy, don't you peck me, broody as you are. Here. It's only my hand, the one that gives you the corn." She slides her fingers under the chicken gingerly, pausing at a low growling squawk and, once she's sure she won't get viciously pecked, Joane begins removing eggs from the bed of hay and feather.

I know how those eggs feel, smooth and warm as the fireside. I smell the mix of ammonia and sweetness momentarily released as the nest is disturbed: I know that too. After putting half a dozen eggs in a basket she stands and stretches; speaking low to herself and—I think—to me. "That will do—my back no longer likes to bend the way it did. I'm three-husbands-buried-older now and there is a gain and a loss in all of that."

By the flicker of a lantern she begins to pick her way through early evening to the house, chatting more freely as if getting into her stride. "I only ever really mourned the one husband: Robert. I think of him still and feel his hand on me." She pauses, remembering the surprise of his electric touch on her skin. "He was not my first"—a knowing smile. "But he was the first to walk me into the church, the only one who looked me in the eyes and kept on looking. Oh, I'm sure the gossips' tongues wagged aplenty about the two of us making the best of it; me with the baby and no man, him with the baby and no woman. It was more than that soon though—he let me find my own way across the bed to him. Which didn't take long once he'd shown me his smile with just one of his brows raised."

The corner of her mouth moves up at the thought of the smile, the brow, and the bed, and her lust is so infectious that I can barely meet her eye. She catches herself and me and pulls us from our moment of indulgence. "That's enough evening reverie about the dead. We are needed by the living for a while longer."

Joane has slid from "I" to "we" as we enter the house and I like everything about that shift. At the table she whispers to herself as she takes out the first egg and holds it up to a candle flame. "Don't be too hot and hasty, Joane—you have broken many a shell that way." Then a nod, that I find I am copying, as she sees something lit up within, the start of life. "Girl!" a sharp shout to someone out of the room. "Hurry up, moppet! I have a need of your sharp eyes. Mine are tired after gathering the wood betony and you must be good at something and it isn't sweeping, that's for certain." She pours a little scorn on the hapless maid-of-all-work, who seems quite terrified as she holds the egg to impatient cries of "careful" and "don't tremble so."

But the girl nods in confirmation that this egg is developing and then all three of us smile. Joane gives her an affectionate squeeze, thanks God, the biddy, and herself. Together they check the rest of the eggs in turn—all but one passing the test and I feel myself receding a little. By the time Joane hurries outside to give the hen back her nestful, it is dark and the scene is at the end of a tunnel. I haven't quite left her, yet I already miss the woman sliding eggs under the hen and chatting as she does. "Not much is certain, chick, but the signs are there. You are a good biddy, a fine girl. I am sure of that." Her words just reach me as I move from past to the present, unsure if it is the bird or me she is speaking to.

The computer screen has gone to sleep and I see myself in it now: happily drained by the late night, the hatch, this quest, and now, by something else—an infusion of shared imagination and memories that aren't mine. Underneath, there is still a fast heartbeat and something that could be the moment before panic, but it is spring and I have chicks and I want everything to be fine. I want to be fine. I want to be more than guided by Joane—I want to *be* her: wise, stubborn, brave, tough. I want to be a good biddy, a fine girl—I want that to be true. Perhaps that's why I find myself pressing the keyboard one more time—not quite sure whether to believe in her and myself.

Then, and I'm not aware of the series of queries and mouse movements that make it appear, I'm looking at an old oil painting. The scene it depicts, the caption tells me, is from seventeenth-century

Sweden, but for me it is a glimpse of what has just played out here on my own plot.

The brushstrokes show an evening kitchen: the lamps glowing and the sides of the room dim. A young woman with a linen cap and apron stands in the foreground wearing a look of anxious incompetence—it's the moppet (sharp eyes, bad at sweeping). She looks deferentially and fearfully to the woman who sits to her left: a figure whose face I know despite its being turned away in the painting. Her greying hair is practical, a little wayward, wiry and full, and she holds herself with power and contentment, a could-be-unleashed-any-moment energy and a tiny hunch of the shoulders that speaks of new stiffness. This is the body of someone fully present in their life, a life that has been quite the thing.

Here she is—Joane Newman—or *a* Joane Newman, at least: sitting in front of a basket of white eggs and holding one to the light of a candle. I zoom in on the cracked oil paint's surface and study the curve of the side of her face, the flame illuminating it at the very moment she sees the red veins. The start of life. The sign of a good biddy. The proof that all is well, though nothing is certain.

Now that I have seen the painting I am not certain, Joane has put paid to that, but sure nonetheless. This painting is enough for me to feel sure that Joane Newman and I told a true story today—becoming more, not less, true because some was made of her and some of me. I have held and candled eggs, Joane held and candled eggs; women held and candled eggs and many other things besides.

I'll walk this land to look for those women. Land that is like sky—made of invisible things denser and more expansive than the distracting sparkle of stars. Light bends around these women's stories but like the event horizon scientists, I sense them and believe in them. Like Joane, I will bring them to light with nothing more than a candle in the dark.

PART TWO

SUMMER
2019

May

MAPMAKING

t is finally warm and dry enough for us to walk the children to school across the fields. We tell them the plan and Arthur's face becomes a little pointy-chinned circle of anger and misery. He tenses his body and then releases it repeatedly in a jerky explanation of how unreasonable we are being.

He feels things deeply, this one. His husky laugh is generous and frequent, his concentration and interest in things is deep and wide and he matches this with regular quick flips to furious—a place he has the stamina to stay in for quite some time. There was an eighteen-month period when he was angry about breakfast every day. I thought those start-of-the-day rages would never end, but they did, of course; in that slow way children have of not letting you notice or mark another something that has gone forever. Every gain in parenting seems to come with a loss that takes awhile to understand.

Eventually the four of us leave the house together and as the children open the gate, any thoughts of hating walking vanish. They run to the top of the field with the goats leaping alongside, thrilled to see their playmates so early in the day. It's the kind of morning that puts a daisy-and-buttercup filter on everything. I pull on Jared's arm when he's midway through scrambling over the fence and kiss him, loving him for making the forty-minute round trip a priority. I am very into the idea, but it often feels like too much of a bite out of my day. I watch the three of them head off down the hill and see them stop after the first stile to watch a startled heron desert his fishing spot and fly off over the woodland of Devil's Hole.

When they are out of sight, I head back to the garden. The old roses—a collection of cerise *Rosa rugosa*—are in flower near the kitchen doors. They've finally recovered from the inexpert prune I gave them during our first winter and their scent is something else, like the Turkish delight of my seven-year-old imagination. I have been meaning to make syrup from their huge hips every year since our move, but the years have passed and as yet the syrup has not materialized.

Though I should be inside getting ready for a phone call, I can't help pausing by the flower bed that I've been working hardest on. I've planted groundcover plants such as lamium to fill in the gaps and please the bees, removed a mangy-looking rhododendron (which would have killed the goats with a single bite) and added things I love: salmon-colored lupins, white cosmos, and ranunculus. It is a wonderful wait for them to fill out and bud.

As I do a whistle-stop tour of the garden this morning, I see there are two varieties of lettuce ready to harvest and that tiny pears are forming on the trees we planted late last autumn. This is the first year that I've managed to work on enough areas of the plot to feel like I am beginning to get to know it. I have noticed that the ground by the front door is particularly dry, but a couple of yards away the slight slope means it's damper. There's a spot in the east-facing bed where the wind whips over a wall, thwacking the leaves and stems, and I realize that this is why nothing does as well there.

Slowing down enough to notice these things is the goal I know I should be aiming for. Yet it is not easy for me to hold on to it when everything else crowds in. This is why I walk the plot and set it in my mind every morning and night, trying to feel a part of this place—a kind of a paradise.

Once a week we've been dropping the children with friends and going to marriage-counseling sessions, trying to understand why we have moved so far apart and, we hope, to find a way back before it is too late. We are sitting on the familiar sofa again now, where it has quickly become clear that our smallholding, the way of life I thought we'd agreed on and moved here to pursue, has become a problem.

Jared and I have told the counselor about many things: our childhoods, the best times, the difficult things we've faced together and apart. I have gotten used to talking like this because I was seeing a therapist of my own until it became more urgent to see one together. My first trip to her office came a year after our move here. After the first intense spring and summer on the plot, autumn had brought a slight letup and I didn't have more than a vague inkling that there were plenty of jobs to be getting on with, even in cooler weather.

Despite the reduced workload I still felt overwhelmed and anxious into winter and, one January evening in 2018, I found myself telling my good friend Clare that I was absolutely fine, but I couldn't remember when I'd last felt happy or proud or looked forward to something. Everything was a slog—even arranging to see her for dinner had seemed like a chore. I told her that every little thing took something from me and left me lessened. But she shouldn't worry, I had followed up quickly, seeing her face. I wasn't stressed or sad or anything like that, I just felt wrung out and tired. A dishrag that needs a wash. I laughed as I said it.

Five years previously, I'd knelt alongside Clare as she birthed her 11-pound, 4-ounce baby on the floor of her living room. In moments of pressure—situations of stress, emergency, and intensity—I am lifted up to a calm and solid place of overview and smooth competence. When someone really needs me, as in the extremity of giving birth, I come into my own. My wide focus compresses to the sharpest of points: the person, the need, and the best response. For most of Clare's labor that need was for nothing more than a security blanket. She was doing beautifully, all was going well, and I would have been only another body in the way, so I'd sat on the stairs, tucked out of sight, but letting my presence be felt.

Then there was a slight shift in her breaths and though nothing had changed, I knew everything had altered for her. She was thinking back to her first baby's difficult birth and beginning to panic so I went quietly in to her, crouched down and said, "This is nothing like before. You are doing this. He is not stuck. This is normal and everything is going fine."

Sometimes we need someone to notice our distress, meet us where we are in our heads, and not wait to be told—refuse to be brushed off. I met Clare where she was in her panic that day and three minutes later she was holding her son. Five years on, over dinner, she met me where I really was and said, "Do you think you might be unwell?" She asked it at first and then it became a statement: "I think you might be unwell." Before she'd finished the sentence I realized I already knew it to be true.

The next morning, in pajamas and through tears, I tried to deal with it, whatever "it" was, wondering how long it had been incubating. Since the summer; since the move? Since before the move? Forever? I saw the doctor and filled in the mental health questionnaires that were emailed to me. Signed off work, I diligently downloaded meditation apps and joined an exercise class, wanting to use the time I had on things that would get me back to normal as quickly as possible.

SSRIs and beta-blockers were offered as partial solutions to the anxiety and depression I was told I had. The doctor looked a little annoyed as I declined and I almost relented, not wanting to be difficult. But I couldn't ignore the impulse to really understand what was wrong before attempting to fix it. Taking the medication felt like putting a bandage that might not fit over a wound that needed exploring and flushing out before stitching it up properly.

She offered me four free half-an-hour phone-counseling sessions but, knowing I needed more, I found a nice therapist and used money we couldn't spare to attempt to puzzle it all out with her in weekly sessions. I made painful choices: took an unpaid sabbatical and then left the job I had spent the past five years making. I did brave things: telling people I loved things they didn't want to hear, that I didn't want to say, but that had to be said. I asked for help against all my instincts and asked again when I didn't get it. Through gritted teeth I repeated the line that I had anxiety and depression, trying to believe it and find the right cure.

So this morning I tell our shared counselor, while Jared listens, that 2018 was twelve months spent recovering from 2017: telling myself I was taking it easy, licking my wounds, making smaller plans for the future so that I could avoid whatever burnout, whatever edge of breakdown I'd been teetering on.

I try to explain that in some ways last year has helped: the daily panic has eased and I feel clearer when I open myself to the land rather than fling myself at it. Though I don't have enough words for the nuance, I attempt to explain that despite all this I am still daily on the verge of drowning in my life and I can't understand why. The small sofa enlarges as I speak. It elongates further when the therapist quietly points out that while I touch my husband often he has not reached out to me once.

Yes, I say eventually. That is how it feels. The closer I press myself to the land—the surer I am that it contains the answers—the further Jared feels from me. The session ends and we leave, placing this new paradox on the car dashboard where it vibrates ominously as we bump over potholes, juddering along with the growing realization that these sessions might be making things worse.

Noise is too much for me: chatter, the kids arguing in the background, radio, the dishwasher being emptied, the cats meowing, the rooster crowing. A dropped knife floods me with adrenalin and one of my children creeping up and shouting "boo" makes me scream so loudly that they cry. I need gentle birdsong (not the shrill chirps of frightened fledglings), open spaces, and no one to need anything from me—including myself.

Night has gone and midway through this new day, to help with the mix of resolve and instability that always descends after counseling, I am busy breaking up long-dreaded administrative tasks by reviewing my chaotic research notes. In addition to a pile of papers and books dipping in and out of the broader history of smallholding and home-steading history, I have another pile with a narrower focus: my land, the local area, and its people. I want to understand how, when, and who cleared this particular part of the forest, who built this house, and whether it was always intended as the smallholding I want it to be now.

A series of Land Registry plans and old Ordnance Surveys is my current preoccupation. These tell me that our house and those of our two westerly neighbors were built between 1920 and 1939. Today I've been granted online access to the local tithe map: a nationwide survey, conducted in 1839, that might show me what was there before. I open the emailed link excitedly, spend a few minutes searching for the right segment, and then open it to find a huge trapezoid with the number "405" handwritten on top.

This angular shape is the original pasture that today's three parcels of land were made from and its name was Church Hams. I spread out wider and see much of what I know. Roads, woodland, and the familiar footpath to the village that cuts across Victor's land—three acres of grazing that I can see now were once perfectly named: Footway Field.

There is a lot contained within these flat and brittle documents: fingers on the paper, wobbles in the lines, lives hidden in the ink. So many stories, so many other maps to find and so many links between the broad brushstrokes of trend and policy that I have been trying to make sense of, and the evolution of this one small place.

My piles of paper and stacks of books are jumbled now; the already messy filing system disturbed by my need to look at all lines of inquiry at once. There is something interesting in the big picture here—it grabs me even more than the detail and the stories—but I can't tease it out when everything is so chaotic and cluttered. There is too much information and I don't know what matters and what can be set aside to let the important aspects stand out. My head is thick with thoughts. I'm pushing something heavy in a wheelbarrow with a very flat tire and it takes so much effort to travel even a small distance. I squint and give myself a shake but I can't fling off the mental lethargy that has descended even when I turn back to my work.

I work through my to-do list, checking things off slowly now that the research has muddled me until a loud bleeping makes me jump. It takes a second to remember what the alarm is for but then the memory comes. It must be nearly 2:00 PM. I set my alarm for quarter till the hour that Jared and I have appointed to deal with the greenhouse that I couldn't pass up when I saw it about to be junked as a neighboring house was demolished. Jared was enthusiastic too; checking with the owners, arranging for our neighbor Harry to pick it up with his trailer and promising to make the fixing up his project so I can get on and grow things in it. Today we'll start on a glazing renovation job for which we are woefully underqualified.

In our couples therapy sessions it has become clear that the tasks that the smallholding, house, family life, and work necessitate are playing a significant role in our discord, and we are a month into attempting to use a weekly schedule to counter this. On Sundays we sit down, see what lies ahead for the week, and set aside dedicated time for the regular, periodic and occasional jobs we need to do. The hope is that this will stop the bigger tasks from being forgotten, the smaller things from piling up, and will play a role in reinstating us in the role of partners on the land. Though the schedule might tell us to pressure wash chicken coops, plant out wildflower plugs, or, this afternoon, to fix up the greenhouse together, for me it says something far more fundamental. It is a plea and a promise which says: be here in this place with me, work with me, see what I see, see me.

I pull on work clothes and, on a whim feeling nervous about all that's caught up in these tasks, I take the maps with me as I go outside. I walk through the smallholding to the shed. With the maps in my mind as well as on my desk I see my land as shapes, lines, points, and edges. I consider the boundaries. On one side oaks, willows, ash, cherry, and maple trees form a straight-ish line of maturity, suggesting that this division of land has been a physical reality for some time. On the other something different: a hedge, some overgrown conifers, and a whole load of dubious-looking sheeting propped up by metal posts—a much more recent partitioning that matches the lines drawn on the later map.

My land is the map brought to life—a living plan whose texture soothes. A variety of tree bark, the surprise of holly, softness of lichen, and a tingling nettle sting: I reach out and touch all I pass, using my senses to take a load off my thinking brain. My gaze flicks from ground to maps until a glimpsed sliver of something stills it. There's a picture printed on the back of a thin book I didn't even mean to bring out with me. My hands meet its shiny red cover and I walk to the wooden table so I can put down the little pile in my arms and pull this, whatever it is, out. The book slides out of the clump of maps and once it is facedown on the table I see the back cover image is itself a map. This one is older, from 1729 according to the notes inside the book, and the undulations visible even on the low-quality scan suggest the original is made of something thicker than paper as I know it.

As I focus in harder, patches of red, green, and yellow reveal themselves to be fields and roads near my land. In between them there is nothing but blank spaces. The relationship of one area to another, the link between places, not deemed important enough by the landowner who commissioned it or the mapmaker who created it. This is what I need today: a map with clear priorities. Not too large, not too small, and no extraneous sections. Just the important parts—enough to find my way—and show me which is north, south, east, and west.

I try to orient myself now using the compass drawn on the scanned map's left-hand edge and spread all the maps out on the table to see where one ends and the other begins, where they overlap or contradict, and to look for the story they tell as a collective. Closing my eyes I breathe into them as I did with Joane. I take the energy left within me and direct it into the paper, stretch out to collect the bits of myself that were abandoned in the therapist's office and send them the same way too. The ink boundaries become three-dimensional. The maps grow up as land around me and without leaving the orchard picnic table I set off to journey through them.

I walk north at first. A recently divided pasture with three bungalows, pigsties, barns, and sheds springing up on this and the neighboring plots. Now I spin and look south, hopping from Ordnance Survey to tithe map and the scene rewinds: boundaries disappear and the trapezoid of pasture 405, Church Hams, smooths itself out. Over the pen-line fence of our southern boundary I see Footway Field, and when I turn back to the north, a small building housing a manger and half-full water trough has assembled where our house has dissolved.

I'm about to explore this building when a sharp beeping startles me enough to make me gasp aloud. My second alarm, set for fifteen minutes after the first, and intended to make sure I am where I said I would be at the right time. Quickly I gather the papers, place a brick on top of them and move quickly to collect my tools, trying to hold on to a little of the meditative sensation of my journey despite its abrupt ending.

When I reach the shed I'm confronted by a mess of pots, canes, tools, and bottles of organic seaweed plant food that instantly undoes all the good work my little walk has done. I'm in the shed but I can't remember why. Panic rises. I must remember. Why can't I? My processing speed slows: a more extreme version of what I felt earlier when the research piles spread themselves out too messily in the shed of my skull.

It is too quiet, and I stand for a moment unable to do anything. Then, as I often do, only half-jokingly, I start to mutter. "What am I doing? What am I looking for? Who am I? What's my name?" As I hear my own questions, a recalibration happens: the greenhouse, glazing rubber, the schedule. I'm back and I find the roll and some scissors, head to the greenhouse, and start stuffing the black strands into the grooves on its panes. My body is tired from today's mental exertions and this fiddly work is not my forte on the best of days. I have to keep stopping and watching an instructional YouTube video to work out what to do next.

Where is Jared? He isn't here and I need him—he's better at this stuff than me and the whole point of this is that we do it together. But I don't want to remind him. One of the ideas behind this schedule is to stop me feeling like the asker, the nagging interrupter, the bad guy who feels guilty about needing something. He's supposed to be here already. It is written on a piece of paper in the kitchen, confirmed in the online calendar, and we set a reminder that might as well be a promise.

Ten minutes later, surrounded by shreds of glazing rubber that just won't go in, I send a terse text. I don't want to feel this bitter and angry about something so trivial. Everyone forgets things and I long to be a happy-go-lucky free spirit who doesn't notice or care. Almost bigger than the upset I feel toward him is the knife-in-belly reminder that I am not that free spirit but a mean old control freak who needs a schedule to live and taps her foot on the ground impatiently when others dare to fall out of line.

Since this plan was put into action Jared has forgotten that it exists with such regularity that something within him must be resisting it, whatever he says. It is only a few days since the last forgetting and the upset it caused, so this feels sharp and deliberate. I wish the evidence of something so fundamental to our problems wasn't caught up in such a boring, stupid life detail, but it is and the tension of big feeling and the supposedly small issue pulls at me as it always does.

Five minutes later—more than halfway through the hour before the school run that we have allotted—he appears at the door. His face is studiously stripped of recognition, camaraderie, or apology, waiting for me to be annoyed and setting out his defense. I'm not annoyed—this is so much bigger than annoyance. Yet the mismatch between how deeply I feel, how he is acting, and the petty picture it paints instantly exacerbates the internal argument.

This schedule solution has already slid over onto the problem pile and I am trapped in it, in myself, and in us, again. I try to hide the deep and wobbly sadness I feel about this stupid greenhouse project but I fail. My words land short and bitter on the already dry ground, I do most of the talking and Jared becomes more dismissive and defensive and then completely silent. He will not or cannot see what I see and I am desperate for him to.

I should let it go but I can't. It feels as if my very existence is contingent on proving that my version of today is real. My voice comes out sounding wrong and it sounds like the voice of the annoyed, critical person he thinks is speaking.

I know we made the schedule together. I know I spilled out the most fragile parts of me in front of the couples' counselor so that Jared would see why it was important and wouldn't forget. Yet he has forgotten and it makes the story I've told myself about everything twist into an untruth. If my existence relies on proving my version is valid, then I have failed. I do not exist. I totter, I wobble, and fall.

In this dark, frantic, and angry place all the things I know to be true and good have flipped to lies and loathing. I'm tingling with adrenalin and must get away from Jared to dissipate it safely without saying or doing anything I will regret. In the shed I pick up the axe—whose exact location I know despite the mess—and raise it up and over my shoulder and then down hard on the pile of wood and old furniture waiting nearby for the bonfire.

It feels right to do this. To take the hate and channel it into splintering a half door and rotten dollhouse. I'm breaking things again, yes, but at least they are things we don't need, that aren't me, and it helps. Then Jared rounds the corner; asking what I'm doing, telling me to put the axe down, saying that I will hurt myself and demanding that I stop. Another solution becoming a problem.

Is he right? Is this wrong? Or am I just not allowed to be angry—even out here, alone, taking it out on the trash? There is only one option left: to run away. I retreat inside to the bathroom so that at least there are no spectators for whatever happens.

I sit down on the toilet seat and, as I do, I have an odd sensation, one that I have been feeling too often of late. Like putting my foot down where my brain has told me there will be a step but meeting air instead. A tiny difference of no more than an inch unbalances me entirely because it exposes the gap between reality and the constructed world in my head.

I know I should be sitting on the toilet's avocado-green lid, but I can't work out if I've actually connected with it or if I'm still moving through the air. My feet don't feel solid against the linoleum either, as though I've misread its level too. I don't know whether I am safely still or falling; stuck, trapped, holding on for dear life or sailing through the air to something better and freer.

Just last week I parked my car, turned the engine off, and felt it roll forward into the one in front. I braced myself for the impact while reaching for the handbrake to try and stop it and discovered the brake was on. No impact came but the sensation of rolling forward and away from the place I had tried to park did not stop.

Hiding now in the bathroom, I keep crying in an automatic response to what feels like being left alone again but which is presented back to me as me being unreasonable and critical. I flick my head to try to get rid of the increasingly familiar thoughts of jamming sharp things in between the bones of the back of my hand.

These disturbing visions have increased since we started the couples therapy, triggered as I attempt to explain a need that feels obvious and existential and find it dissipates through the air in the counselor's office. In our weekly slots I've tried to tease out and trace the reasons why the schedule feels important, and how all the promises and mismatched forgetting are making me feel as if the story I've told myself about everything is untrue. Talking in these sessions, spilling out the most fragile parts of me, is not helping. It feels as though I'm pulling out every one of my hairs and each of my fingernails, laying them on the mug-ringed table in front of us, and then watching the air we disturb as we walk out of the room blow them through the open window.

My instinct now is to reach for the stability of what I know about Joane Newman, but she feels too far away from this moment of unpredictable movement and energy, a leap I can't make today.

I pace a little and bang my fist against the mirror half hoping it will break. My sweater is on the floor first, then I chuck my overalls down; I'm hot, sweating. My brain was too slow earlier, now it is too fast. If I were to plot myself on a graph I'd be a series of sharp-pointed peaks and troughs. I should be better at flattening myself out, find a way to be gentle undulations or a nice steady line instead of these aggressive triangles.

I play myself out as shapes and soon the triangles and curves remind me of those I saw outside before my second alarm cut me off. I let myself return to the map world, finding that with the smallest amount of attention the landscape of the plot's past appears like a pop-up book behind my eyes. From my now invisible bathroom I walk past the livestock shelter that predated our house, through the gate, and head out along our road to the west, demolishing houses and inserting open fields and woodland with my gaze. My footsteps beat a rhythm against the tithe map's dried pulp and my highly activated nervous system becomes a little less frantic with every step. As I walk the line of Mabel's View—where I sometimes find myself while out for a run, cursing Mabel (whoever she was) for the steepness of her relentless incline—I feel disoriented and unsure where to go next. This autumn sunshine of yellowing paper is a better place for me than that bathroom floor, but it is not quite right. This is not my map. Gates move into the places someone else's pen has mandated, and there is nothing beyond the strip of trees over there—a gap has been left where I want detail and beyond the windmill in the distance there is too much going on, distracting me unnecessarily.

Land changes and maps don't. A single, static map won't be enough for me, will it? There is nothing available that lays out all the unknown things ahead. If I knew how to make a map though, to revise it over time and keep it updated according to my purpose, to include only what is most important at the time, perhaps I would never wander off course. What I need is to find someone to give me the tools to make my own maps.

The world turns a little faster. I shift along the road and back another century as a red, green, and yellow filter is applied to the landscape of the back-of-book map. It is 1729 here, and a man moves in the near distance. He stops often, making notes, sketching, and staring at the landscape as if it were—because it is—his job.

It is not the first time that the Mapmaker has come to this village. Nearly thirty years ago, newly apprenticed to his uncle Francis, he picked up a heavy pouch of tools and followed the older man to chart a local estate. Now the former apprentice has become Master Hill, a revered professional in his own right. He is returned to these parts at the call of John Bridger, a Canterbury man who wants to record land he has inherited and set his weight down firmly upon it with a topography of future rent payments owed.

The Mapmaker likes to work alone and no one carries his bag today. He feels it pull at his shoulder as he decides where to draw the field lines, the sun deepening the scores that are beginning to divide his face into a series of irregular shapes. He is used to the looks he gets as an intruder in this village of only sixty dwellings and happy to stare intently at the things its inhabitants no longer see. Accustomed to choosing what to include and what to set aside, he takes his time deciding how best to erase the movement of life from this scene. Later, sitting by the light of his window, the Mapmaker will choose a palette of green for the land, yellow for roads, and red for roofs. In the places where ditch, thicket, and broken-windowed shack are of no interest to his employer, he will leave the paper blank—the gap acknowledging the distance between what exists and what he has been paid to see. The measurements he takes for those who pay him are acts of simplification—constructions of necessity, lies of a sort. They help others but they also help him to cope with the weight of the world's complexity.

The Mapmaker is also an artist. I know it from the flourishes on the finished document's cartouche and from the way he looks at me here on Mabel's View as we pass with a nod. He sees it all, even if he doesn't add it to Bridger's plan: homesteads and holdings, hens pecking, children playing, people at work in the fields, lovers in the shadow of the hedge, paupers' hollow cheeks as they walk past an abundance of food, stories in every millimeter. He has drawn them somewhere even if their outlines are not visible on the finished paper copy. They are what he takes most notice of and he draws them in his own time, in his own mind, and with his own inks.

He is above me on the hill now—the Mapmaker, the artist—but he turns, as do I, and we look at each other. Something has changed. My view of the world has altered as if I'm a slightly shorter height than usual my usual, and there's scratchy fabric against my legs and a weight in my arms. Who am I? I know who he is—the whole village knows who he is—not much is missed by the gossips and fussocks. But he is not of this place so he shouldn't know my name, especially as I myself don't seem to. The Mapmaker looks at me and mouths something I miss. I step toward him on unfamiliar, aching feet and this time I catch the words: "Mary Turner."

I know it to be true, now that he has reminded me. How did he know? This Mapmaker with his intense stare can't have fathomed that I am just come back from the Churchwardens and Overseers of the Poor of this village, nor that this baby, warm and safe in my shawl, is the bastard of John Smith and that I am shamed and called draggle-tail, hedge whore, game pullet—turned out of doors and spat at ever since my belly grew big.

He has no way of knowing that I am trying to throw that shame down and trample it toe to heel with every step. He didn't witness my moment of righteousness today when the wardens told that scrub of a man he must give me one shilling and sixpence a week for his child's bringing up. He can't know what it took me to believe I could win.

The Mapmaker does not know me, yet he sees me. He is here in this place with me, he knows that I won, he knows I might never win again. The eye that takes me in is kind and keen: I fear and want his gaze alike. This man has a face like a mirror and in it I see myself: the determined angle of my chin, the gap between my lips, and the way I pull myself up out of the clay with every step as if it might claim me.

He looks at me as if he wishes he could make me a map. One to follow into next year, when I will have to put my baby in the ground, and beyond, to when I find a way to move my mouth into a smile again. He looks at me again as if he knows that a single, static map is not what I need.

I hear it then, metal landing on stone and then he is striding away from me as I turn toward the object that has fallen from his bag. A few steps and it is in my hand: round, made of brass, and engraved with marks I don't understand. As I look up he turns once more, too far away for words, and I don't know if he sees what I am holding. I'm not sure if knows he has dropped it or if he let it drop on purpose for me to keep—this thing that fits in my palm with arrows that spin as I turn. Pointing me toward something, pointing something toward me. A way to map my own course.

I want what it promises. I want it. I am going to keep it and believe it was a gift. Quickly I tuck it in my shawl with the baby and carry on my way, not looking back in case he notices or changes his mind, and then turn along Brooke Street past Brooke Farm, alongside Church Elms and stop at the pasture of Church Hams, where the cows graze. I check no one is looking and pull out my new treasure and hold it up to where I am going—Footway Field, through Devil's Hole to the village. One arrow points to my path ahead and to a snakelike symbol at the circle's edge. I draw its shape in the air with my finger: a little curve up and then turn, a curve down and then turn again: S. The smooth movement of these arcs comforts me as I shift the slight weight of my child and set off toward where the arrow points.

Mary Turner walks out of my skin and out of my field now. The map world loses its dimensions and I am left to imagine her as she takes the cut of the footpath and then beyond the point where the scan of the old document meets the edge of the page. She has taken the shortcut, but I think the Mapmaker will reach the village first—propelled by his longer strides and regular meals. He knows how to navigate the landscape without the compass that Mary must now learn to use. The Mapmaker needed his tools but the artist didn't, and it was the artist who let his compass fall once her greater need caught his attention. Like Mary, I choose to believe it was a gift. And though her need is greater than mine, I want him to give his compass to me and choose to believe he would. I need to find my own compass though and learn the skills of mapmaking myself. I can and I will. But I want him to come back too. I want him to show me what is important and how to make the world simple, then complex again.

I just want him to put his arms around me.

I just want him.

I have wanted him since I looked at the brilliance of his inks, since he faced Mary and me on the eighteenth-century slope and saw our every atom. But really I have wanted him since before all that. From the moment I read that, of all the uncommon first names he could have had—at a time when everyone was called Thomas, Joseph, or Richard—the *J* in Master J. Hill stood for Jared.

June

I DISSOLVE

There is a lone patch of dark brown tiles just outside our bedroom. Until now I have never managed to work out why it exists among the expanse of wooden boards and carpet. Its function has become very clear today. With the cupboard open, and the other doors shut, this is a very defined space in which to exist. An enclosed cube with a cool floor to lie on, curled up on my side, as tight as I can make myself: an anemone corm, an honesty seed, a speck of brown from a spent foxglove's spike.

I don't know how long I've been here or why I'm crying and thinking about implosion. Implosion: the opposite of explosion, when the weight and pressure of matter causes something to collapse into itself or the space it occupied. A brutal crushing that happens from the outside in.

I know that the last thing I did before I lay down was to use my last bit of clarity to text Clare and ask if she could come because maybe I need to go to a hospital. I don't know why, though, or what they could do there. I don't know where Jared is right now. I don't know anything . . . but I'm here in this cool, dark void and I pull the door closer to make everything shrink in further still.

The visions of stabbing myself with scissors in the fleshy part of my hand, of hanging myself from the thin metal beams in the garage, are a constant loop of silent film. I have no idea how to switch them off or get up. I don't want to get up. I don't want to do or be or think.

My phone buzzes and after a while I look at it. Clare has rung and then texted. She can't come now, but she will tomorrow. She tells me to get Jared or take a taxi to the hospital if I need to. Shall she ring someone, she asks? Her texts are blue rectangles of worry that slide onto the screen again and again and again. I don't know. Maybe she should. Maybe I should. I half try to do something but suddenly the last fight goes out of me and I give into the downward drag. I focus on a ball of fluff in the corner and feel myself getting smaller, heavier, and at some point I close my eyes.

I am walking in the garden I know best, though I don't see it as a gardener would. I don't spot the plants that need watering or notice where the bittercress is taking over in the herbaceous border. For me this place is a series of paths, hills, and hiding places. A playground: full of color and places to chase, laugh, and ride a bike or to sit in the shade with a book. This garden is planted with dens and lost kittens and I don't grow anything here but myself—taller each year despite my mother's pleas to stop and agree to be bonsaied like the little trees we look at in the place my father calls the Satanical Gardens.

I step away from the back of the house onto gravel and then a sloping lawn where (before my mother got to work on it) there was a view of nature's best attempt at taking back what was rightfully hers: the ruins of a formal Victorian garden. I ignore the obvious sunny route across the lawn, down stone steps and under the rose arch, and instead walk along the shady laurel-covered path: a place for whispered games and secrets. The shed I pass has been castles, caves, and prisons, and is now full of rabbits. The original two were supposed to be female, but somehow they have become 140 little furry bodies that have me supplying half the pet shops in Birmingham and discovering that I don't know how to say I am overwhelmed.

I hear my just-into-adult-size feet crunch along the paths that my mother uncovered like an archaeologist. Not long ago all this was hidden by a waist-high celebration of spiky, stinging weeds. But since my mother was pulled to this place by goodness-knows-what, she has worked on it tirelessly; unreasonably late into the evenings, forgetting to stop, forgetting to feed us, forgetting to feed herself. She has tamed it; levered roots out of walls, hefted stones, and dug and dug until the garden was remade according to the plans in her head and the instructions left by 150-year-old walls and specimen trees.

It's ordered and beautiful here now and—in this, my favorite part of the garden—there is a rose arbor. I break into a run on seeing it, skimming the grass as it drops down sharply and ends, forcing me to jump into the darker world of a woodland dell. Down here the ground is damp and carpeted with ivy and wild garlic that flavors every game of hide-and-seek. The trees are crowded close and I sit on one of the rotting trunks and look up to the steep bank beyond the fence where the old railway line runs. As ever I am rewarded by a view of the little palm tree. It grows in a curve of rocks and transforms me, even though I'm supposed to be done with this sort of thing by now, into a castaway on a desert island. I stay here for a while chatting with the Victorian palm as I always did in this childhood of a garden—the garden of my childhood.

I don't remember when I woke or how I got from the floor outside my bedroom to the kitchen, where Jared is looking pale and worried. I don't really remember what happened over the past days and hours to get me to whatever new low point this turns out to be.

This is what I do know: The children are away, I don't want to go to the hospital anymore, but I do need *something*. I know that I have been trying to tell Jared—for days, for months, for years—that all is not right, but I must have said it wrong. Though he is capable of dealing with this reality in staccato bursts, he can't or won't retain it and neither can I.

I do remember that we have been fighting and that I have been spinning out in turn. I remember that I've spent months shyly arranging pieces of myself in the couple's therapy room as if they were fragile, finely tuned instruments that could help us find our way. And that I am a fool because the things I laid out were neither beautiful nor useful. They were hideous, twisted things instead. Every conversation is evidence of it—my awfulness—and I'm forced to see, smell, and taste it again and again.

I don't know much, but I do know that I keep trying to turn it all around—but that every feeling betrays itself and me at some point. I have become a war; opposing sides caught in each cell and folding me in on myself while ripping me further apart.

My head is full of self-destructive thoughts and though I do not want to do awful things to myself, the more they play out behind my eyes the more I am afraid that I might. This way of being cannot continue, and right now I cannot see a way to stop that isn't tangled up in the garage beams.

I have been volatile; sitting down and making a to-do list, feeling energetic and positive one minute and entirely overwhelmed the next. I remember that at some point, perhaps today, I went outside and started pulling up the plot by its roots—choosing the things I loved, that were hardest to germinate, the plants I had been most looking forward to watching get taller, grow flowers, and spread. I pulled up foxgloves, alliums, sweet peas, and larkspur. I pulled up the lettuce and carrots and ripped out the dahlias before they could flower. I wrenched the cosmos and cornflowers from the soil and yanked out the pale calendula that were ready to open. Last of all I pulled up a pink lupin, two years' work, the suggestion of color on its first flowers making me smile every time I had spotted it through the window.

I pulled it all up anyway and chucked it on the ground and then ripped the green and sweet-scented mess up with my fingers and screamed. I wanted to reach right to the center of the earth and burn the skin off my fingers. I wanted to bury myself in molten rock at the world's core and feel it consume me.

I am crying again here in the kitchen as I try to piece all this together in front of Jared but become all the more confused. Fury at something—many things—and hatred, at everyone, including myself, pours out as a Morse code of thoughts and worries, everything in little disjointed piles and no logical route between them.

This place was supposed to give us what we needed, what I needed. It was going to be a thing of purpose, happiness, but somehow it is wrenching us apart and pulling my hinges off. It's good, it's bad; I'm good, I'm bad; I need Jared to help me, he is the problem; I am the problem, I hate myself; I want to go home, this is home, where is home, I don't have a home, I am the home. What a fucking mess of a home this is. I need to see something beautiful. I need the ranunculus that was squashed. I need the lupin I just pulled up. I need to destroy something else. I need to stop. Stop.

I am incoherent, but I tell Jared to move the scissors and then somehow he finds out about the self-annihilatory thoughts that I have kept from him until now. We sit with this at the crossroads of panic for a few minutes while his face moves through bewilderment to fear. Neither of us speak. I don't know what he is thinking. My brain skates over everything and lands on nothing. The world undulates around me and everything is blurry except the points of the knives.

Then a bleat. Amber's distinctive dinnertime call—all high pitched, unnecessary hysteria—breaks the quiet, and her goofy, goaty face intrudes itself between the intrusive thoughts. She is a very funny-looking goat and her daily pretense of desperation is always funny too. Humor diffuses horror and thoughts of her are helpful. When Jared returns from feeding her, I find I am just about calm enough to begin to talk about what we do now.

It is a different day. At least I think it must be because it's late afternoon again and I am in a different place, wearing other clothes, my body smelling clean and my shins, when I run my hands along them—pressing to check if the bone is where I left it—are smooth and hairless. Yes: We are in London, it is tomorrow, and this is our friends' house: cool, light, and uncomplicated.

Somehow we are going to a party tonight. We should have canceled because it was impossible for me to go away for the weekend when I couldn't even get from the kitchen to the bathroom. Canceling seemed impossible though too. We had friends relying on a weekend of house and animal sitting while builders ripped their house apart. I couldn't leave them in the lurch or face staying and hosting all five of them. And, though he insisted it didn't matter, I knew this evening was important for Jared and his work.

Instead of canceling we are here and, though I feel like an invalid, the most fragile, saddest parts of me have been scooped out and put in a paper bag, on hold until Tuesday after the bank holiday when I have promised Jared and Clare I will see a doctor. I'm walking the path of least resistance; taking a crazy kind of vacation from my life.

Jared tells me it is time for us to go out. I am like a little girl—doing no thinking for myself—so I don't check the time or the route. I just take off the pair of sheepskin slippers I'm wearing—a birthday gift Jared has given me earlier than planned—put on my going-out shoes, and check myself in the mirror, surprised that someone this absent even shows up.

There I am. Here I am. Who am I again? I don't have much of a grip on myself but I like what's reflected back as I look at this woman. She's wearing a 1970s dress with fluted sleeves and it hits her in all the places it should. She turns one way and then the other, a fluted swoosh of a person that a little makeup and a scrunch of her hair has turned into pretty. She opens her arms wide to show off the huge winglike sleeves and I watch as she becomes a butterfly and the butterfly becomes me.

On our way through London my senses are working harder than ever and my skin feels prickly with excitement and nerves for the evening ahead. I feel mad, completely crazy. Like I might try to balance on the handrail of a bridge or take my clothes off and walk naked through Regent's Park reciting poetry. But I quite like it. Nothing matters and everything is bright and sharp and a little off-center. There is desire too. In a place other than the smallholding, I notice the muscles of my husband's upper arms under his suit jacket and I want them around my waist. I want him. I just want him.

We drink champagne at the party, as if it's the kind of thing we always do, and as if there is something to celebrate. I feel light, lovely, and find I have things to say, intelligent questions to ask, and a laugh that comes from somewhere in the evening air. After an hour or so, Jared and I are at opposite ends of the garden and I am entertaining a circle of older men, waxing lyrical on the joys of keeping goats. I am enjoying being an oddity: twenty years younger than them, a bumpkin dressed as a princess and I have their rapt attention. One, the self-appointed elder, introduces me to everyone else as "goat girl" and I smile and twirl under the strings of lights that weave through the trees. Then I see Jared through the bodies—his eyes flicking toward me often. I look at him and see someone I remember. Someone I love.

Then he is next to me, his fingers lingering on my back. I notice how he smells, spot him look at the angle of my chin, the gap between my lips and the rest of our night is mapped out by the look in his eyes and the way his hands find the narrowest part of my waist and press gently, my ribs moving up to make room for him. As he leads me away, instructing me to eat and watching to make sure I do, he tells me that the men I have been holding in my goat-girl court are some of the most famous artists in the country. But I don't care about them because tonight he is everything I remember and all I care about.

After lunch the next day Jared and I walk across the London park to a community garden sale. The people here, almost all a lot older than me, are clearly my people. I buy cilantro, peppermint, a zucchini plant, and some peach-colored verbena with the twenty pounds that the friend we are staying with has lent me and that she will refuse to let me pay back.

As we walk back through the park, Jared and I talk. The plant sale has brought me back to myself a little, last night brought us back to each other, and the comforting sound of the stream flowing through the trees has loosened my protective grip on my thoughts.

"Do you still want to do this?" I ask him directly, wanting to know if he has changed his mind about the smallholding life. "Should we sell the house? Move somewhere smaller? Give up?" He does, he says. He values the space and the freedom and he likes where we live. He does want to do it, he wants to stay—though maybe not as much as I do. But, he adds, he doesn't think he ever wants anything as much as I want everything.

We talk, without recriminations for once, about feeling as if we are in a trap. We have to work hard to pay for all this, but in working hard we don't have time to make progress on the land. This makes me more anxious and then I need the outdoors all the more to help soothe me and then there isn't enough time to do the work to earn the money. We run through our options: downsizing, borrowing money, one or both of us getting full-time jobs, starting this all over again somewhere cheaper. It feels like a relief to have a conversation in which we agree that there is a problem that isn't one of us and we try to solve it together.

The path takes us past a playground and talk turns to Arthur and Sofya: what they get from the plot, the things they have learned, whether another move would be good or bad for them, whether selling the animals would hurt them as much as I imagine.

"I can't make big decisions right now," I admit before we turn back onto our friends' road. "Neither can I," replies Jared, hinting for the first time at what I have known for a while: that he doesn't feel so good either. "We can't move; I couldn't cope. Not now anyway," I say, and so we agree to just hold on. We will keep going, make no big changes, make no life-altering decisions, but dig in and hunker down. It comforts me more than it should to have set a goal that requires only that I stay where I am and do as little as possible.

Decision made, I relax into words that tumble out of my mouth like a waterfall. I speak without knowing quite what I'll say, needing to hear the thoughts aloud to know what the point I'm making is. "I thought we were doing something new and radical when we moved." I laugh at my silly, slightly younger self. "I just copied my parents didn't I? They moved to a garden and made their life in it and so did we. How were we so oblivious?"

The park's stream softens the silence that follows this thought and we cross the bridge that takes us back to where we are staying. I think about patterns and how easy it is to set off along a path set out for us by those who went before without even realizing it. Each generation thinks they are making a new discovery but often it's just another version of the same thing, made new only by ignoring what is already there.

"It's like the Men of Kent," I tell him, and he raises an eyebrow, having no idea what I'm talking about. I carry on excitedly, spotting this new pattern that comes from my latest reading. I've been trying to trace Joane Newman's family back and forth from her lifetime and have ended up, as I often do, going off on a tangent.

Swimming around in 1635, the year she was born, I found a passenger list from a ship that sailed away from Kent, out of Sandwich harbor, on a perilous more-than-two-month journey to Massachusetts. The *Hercules* left England that year with over a hundred souls on board. Shoemakers, servants, men of standing, their wives and children. Some were Puritans fleeing persecution. Some were perhaps as interested in money and power as they were in God, but all who set out on that 3,000-mile journey were leaving a land of problems behind in search of somewhere shiny and new.

They sailed to make a New England on a "new" continent, believing it untouched, fresh and ripe for the taking. They weren't following a pattern. There was no past. This was somewhere novel and untainted. Unimaginable.

"Can you imagine, though?" I ask Jared, stopping outside our friends' front door to finish my thought. "Leaving Kent for America on a ship, in 1635? When hardly anyone else has made the journey. When you might well die on the way. What did they imagine America was like? Could even begin to imagine it? Weren't they terrified?"

But I have to stop there because it is time to go on our own journey. I pack my clothes into the small suitcase with a bellyful of jittery nerves that seem more fitted to a two-month ocean crossing on a seventeenth-century boat than an hour on a rather reliable train.

My butterfly dress is inside out on the floor by Jared's side of the bed—a walnut-colored whip of seventies nylon. I pick it up and smooth it out, holding it to my face because it still has last night and its suspension of time in its synthetic fibers. Then I pack it away, along with the butterfly version of me, knowing she is in there: fluttering, twirling, drinking champagne, and taking her dress off in the moonlight because she wants something and for once thinks she deserves it. There is something of her I am going to want again, but there is a voyage ahead to contend with first.

It is hotter here than in London and the air that hits us as we step off the air-conditioned train is vacation-in-the-Caribbean-thick. I stumble onto the platform. My steps are shaky and they wobble me through the crowd as Jared leads me in the right direction. As soon the train left London the nervous jitters became full-on, raging seas of anxiousness. I am remembering how unwell I am.

As I get out of the passenger seat in our driveway it seems to be hotter still. Zips of adrenalin move through my body as everything I've set aside for the weekend reappears now that I am back. I begin to walk around the lawn, trying to get out of my head and body and into the soil and the air where it is less fractious.

There are so many butterflies today: peacock and red admiral, common blue, marbled white, small white, and orange tip. My nemesis, the cabbage whites, are there too. A few have found a gap in the netting and are fluttering ominously above the kale, probably having spent the weekend doing their worst.

I love the butterflies but I do not love the caterpillars; even though every piece of beautiful, bird-feeding, garden-racing butterfly DNA is already there in the brassica-munching creature that will soon hatch from the eggs I'm sure have just been laid. My kale will give each caterpillar the strength to grow and then, after a couple of weeks, to hang upside down and spin a silk cover and then a brown chrysalis within. Hidden inside, it will dissolve itself almost entirely (surely it must be excruciating?) into a lumpy liquid of potential. Out of this soup it reconstructs itself as something unrecognizable, yet exactly the same.

The caterpillar-turned-butterfly will emerge four to six weeks later and hang down once more, pumping the liquid leftovers of an old body into its new wings to strengthen them. Finally, when quite dry, the butterfly will take flight over the plot that it spent the first part of its life crawling over on its belly.

I can't remember how to be a butterfly and though I wish I could crawl—so much contact with the earth would surely be soothing—I don't feel strong enough to pull myself along. Instead I keep walking, turning ninety degrees to the south, where I find the children giving each other pedicures on the grass as the babysitter departs. They run to me and I hold them, squeezing them too tightly because the skin on my bare arms is numb and barely registers their touch.

Over the tops of their heads I spot the first white poppy wriggled loose of its casing. *Papaver nudicaule*, "Champagne Bubbles," has waved petal edges, a spindly stalk, and a warm yellow center. Its felt casing is less decorative but quite a feat of engineering. I spot it as it rests mole-brown and discarded nearby. A perfect oval, split down the middle and gradually pushed up and off by the opening flower. I pick it up and slip it on the end of my little finger, show it to Sofya and Arthur, and together we wonder what it would be like to be accordioned up and sealed within.

Once the children have gone back to their game I continue my tour, looking for something, or someone. My senses are open to more than flowers now. Every fiber of me wants to slip through these difficult hours into a different time or place and find a moment of learning, connection, or just plain old distraction. My walking becomes almost meditative and I no longer think consciously about where I am headed. Every now and then I let my route register, finding that I have been drawn back to the pond over and over again. I attempt to think myself into someone else's story; working back through my research, summoning the outline of Joane and Mary, and when that doesn't work, trying to feel the cold heaviness of the compass in my hand.

But all I do is end up back at the pond, glancing and then looking away from the water repeatedly, when I find only my own face looking back. After another loop I force myself to stop and look—to really look. This land seems to lead me to things for a reason and there is only so long I can resist. I feel the electric pull that I am getting to know. There is a woman's story here after all. I crouch to be closer to her, to the water's surface, and I disturb a little clod of clay that drops in, making ripples across my reflection face.

I close my eyes. I breathe out and give into what I see inside. Somewhere I have been once before: shivering alone in a clearing, just out of a tin bath with skin red raw from scrubbing. The wind is cold. I have to walk to keep myself from freezing. I walk and walk until I can't walk any farther because I'm at the edge of a pond looking at my reflection in the not quite frozen water. The ripples change my face from beautiful to hideous and back, again and again.

I do not want to be here. I do not want to look at this. I asked for another story, a slip away into a different world—something new and untainted. I have been given my own story instead.

My eyes open at the realization. Everything is staccato, a disjointed slideshow that moves too quickly. There is no pond, just a mirror reflecting the me of four years ago: slightly rounder cheeks, less freckled face, and a backdrop of the seaside house where Arthur was born. I see myself at my desk with projects, emails and reminders flinging themselves at me relentlessly. The carousel spins and I'm crouched on the floor next, playing with my round baby—trying to be present but feeling many things pulling me away. Spin. I'm arguing with Jared before picking up wallpaper scissors and cutting my long hair into jagged, chin length slices because I don't have time to wash it and he doesn't understand. Spin. I'm sitting in our seaside townhouse garden; noticing it for the first time and half recognizing, half remembering that outside, closer to the earth, is something that might help temper the increasingly frenetic pace of life. @T:The seaside house of four years ago fades out and everything spins faster and for longer. When the scene stills I see myself at just seventeen years old. I've made it to the front seat of the youth orchestra. I'm sure the conductor knows that I mime all the hard passages—and most of the easy ones too—but the players behind can follow my accurate bowing technique and so it doesn't matter that I am only playing the air half a millimeter above the strings. My contribution to the beautiful layers of sound filling the concert hall is a fixed smile and a pantomime of arms. And I am enjoying it, but I find traces of the woman with the scissors here too; she is paying the closest attention to absolutely everything, making a huge effort to play her part, and the stakes are higher than makes sense.

A small jump and relief comes as the late-spring air rushes at my teenage face. I'm galloping a horse over the Birmingham country park where I spend most daylight hours when not at school—the nights now taken up with boyfriends, parties, and review for exams. I don't care about the three flies I've just inhaled: This is a place where all my jangling pieces knit together.

We slow to a walk and take the path that traces the brook that—if I knew how to ask the question—could tell me a story of the winter water meadows that were here before picnic tables and local government signage. I feel light and full of potential. The drop of my mother's shoulders as she disappeared happily into the garden taught me to take myself outside to feel whole, as did the contented clarity of my father's expression when he returned from the mountains—cuts on his hands from the rocks, blisters on his feet from the boots.

This is an antidote to the effort of the week just gone, the frequency of my body's vibrations slowing as the leaf-dapple hits. I feel brave enough to see if I can jump the horse right over the brook and land on the other side. I steel myself, collect her to a canter, prepare to fly over the water, and then my body jolts, everything tumbles, and I thwack against the bottom of the ditch. As up and down reveal themselves to me again, I move my fingers to my face where pain is beginning to spread across the crisscross of stone slashes on my right cheek and eye socket. I am fine though—I really am. This is the kind of injury that feels like a badge of honor, each scratch a sign of membership of a club I want and need to be in.

The pictures from the past come faster now. My hair gets blonder, my face rounder, and my knees scabbier. I'm nine and sitting with my classmates writing my own school report as we have all been tasked to do. I take it very seriously, even though I am at the top of my class and have nothing to worry about. My writing is deliberate, slow, and neat; remembering to punctuate and evaluating myself unsparingly in every direction between each full stop. My hand grips the blue pen tightly and the muscles ache with the effort. *I will improve . . . I will try harder to . . . I will not . . . I am going to try very hard . . . try hard . . . try harder.*

Images scroll swiftly. My first year of school, drawing every picture exclusively in shades of purple until they decide to take the purple crayons away. Fighting with my Granny because I want to see if I can float on the water in the lake like the geese do and she will not let me. Crawling through a field of sheep with doughy toddler legs, loving the smell of the grass and trying to eat it. Then just warm, dark colors and shapes before I land back in the now, by the pond and looking at the face of thirty-six-year-old Rebecca and seeing just how much she has forgotten.

The teenage me who picked herself up and limped to the tree stump to mount the horse again saw the simple truth that the land was a place to come to balance the effort of the rest of my life. Yet even she'd already forgotten there was a time and a way that required less. If only I could remember what it was.

I had also forgotten that I was already breaking long before we moved here. That our life in the countryside was supposed to be an antidote to this, replacing problems with something fresh, simple, and new. But I hadn't considered the big flaw in my plan. I thought it was the lifestyle, the work, the pressure, the town, the loud neighbors, the concrete that was the problem. But they were not the problem. The problem was me.

If you are the problem, then no matter where you go the problem will come along for the ride. Whatever dream you follow, whatever supposedly virgin territory you travel to, and however many times you tell yourself that it's unblemished: If you are the problem there is no escape.

No escape: I've seen to that. I've been hard at work since our move digging the problem of myself into every bit of my new life. I've been baffled as to why I felt worse and not better, but I see why now. My reflection, my problem, is shown to me relentlessly here. It is reflected in every window, dug into every row of potatoes, and hatched out with every chick. I followed a dream of a simpler life and found myself locked in a complicated nightmare: eyeball to eyeball in a staring contest with the original disaster of me.

The next day, the doctor's waiting room is quiet and sparse but I can barely open my eyes as almost anything triggers a chain of anxious, interconnected thoughts.

I hear the consulting room door open and force my eyelids apart to see the doctor who looked at my cut leg in the spring inviting me in. He's about five years older than me with an open and straightforward face, and he listens as I stammer out how I'm feeling. I'm agitated, trying to keep still, calm, and reasonable in this medicalized place of being still, calm, and reasonable, but it is hard and embarrassing and really, I want to curl up in the dark space under his desk.

"I sometimes wonder if I might be bipolar or if something else is fundamentally wrong with the way my brain works." I get the words out, feeling sick at the taste of them. "Sometimes I have all this energy, I'm unstoppable and I can do all these things at once, really fast, and then it keeps going, like a whirlwind and I can't stop it. Then other times I'm so muddled and I can't manage, so confused and angry and upset. I don't understand it."

"What would you like to happen next?" he asks. I haven't prepared an answer to this open question that feels like a gift, but find I know it anyway. "I feel like there's something underlying this and I want to know what it is. I don't want to take medication until I know what's wrong." I wait for his response, knowing that last year the other doctors were very keen to medicate me. "I agree," he says and suggests a referral to a psychiatrist. This is the thing that I didn't know I wanted—to have an expert help me look at the problem I have become. I feel relieved to be en route to getting an answer. The doctor writes up a referral and explains that I'll get a call from someone from the secondary mental health team to triage me over the phone, and I am grateful to him for treating me like an adult and supporting my decision to try to puzzle it out further.

"And in the meantime?" he asks before I leave. "What are you going to do to cope?"

I tell him I have felt more comfortable over the last couple of days when I keep myself firmly in the present moment, not thinking beyond a few minutes ahead and slamming an internal wall down as soon as I stray from that. He approves of my plan to do more of this until the help comes.

And the land, I tell him this with an actual smile. I am going to work my land.

July

A PURITAN LADY

The first psychiatric nurse calls one afternoon out of the blue. The house is full of children playing and I've been trailing through it like a beer-drunk snail, making looping, illogical tracks as I offer snacks, checking that none of the school friends is climbing on the well, spot a weed to pull, and then duck back inside to deal with the laundry. I am trying to live without much thought, not letting myself dwell on my past or future and no longer making plans or lists that would hold my line through the day more steadily.

The ring of the phone shocks me from where I've ended up: reading a book of poetry in the quiet of the bedroom. I answer, wondering how many people are available, with no notice, to have this—the most private of conversations. My surprise itself surprises me. I have been waiting and anticipating this triage appointment to decide if I am unwell enough to warrant psychiatric help. It is fine for a little while to be just the 20 percent of a person I currently am: an automaton who is not allowed to stray from the bubble of each moment, but I can't really work like this or be a friend or a nice mother or even be relied upon to buy goat feed before it runs out.

My hands and arms are shredded from the work that caught my eye yesterday: clearing brambles and nettles until my back screamed. My fingers are stained with soil from sowing foxglove seeds too. Sowing is allowed, but I don't let myself consider where

I will plant them if they germinate. I have to leave next year alone for now.

I have tried to retreat into books as I did as a child but reading has been harder than usual. Novels are too long for moment-to-moment living and almost any full-length book prompts too-expansive thoughts and ideas. Scraps of my self-curated research list are what I'm making do with, along with volumes of poetry. These books sit in stacks and teeter on the edge of windowsills and tables where I have abandoned them when the next thing called.

I am awkward as the nurse starts talking, not sure how to be, and struggling to find something to mark the page in *Mercies*, the book that I'm reading, before I put it down. I tear off a magazine corner and place it between page thirty-eight and thirty-nine to mark "I Remember," the title of the Anne Sexton poem I do not want to forget to go back to.

I say, "Hello," and, "Fine, thank you. How are you?" holding my mobile as I do on a work call, as I do when speaking to my parents or Clare or booking a visit from the vet. But this is not a light social chat or a meeting that I was sent an agenda for. So I lock myself in the most faraway place I can find—the bathroom—and try not to see that my knees are shaking.

I talk to the nurse and he is kind, gentle, and human. He calms me quickly, asking what it's like to live in the countryside and mentioning an aunt who used to live nearby. His questions delve into my symptoms, my history, my family, the support I have, and what I feel I need now. I'm speaking with a quieter voice than usual to stop phrases such as "intrusive thoughts of hanging myself," "almost high, mania?," "feel like I have disintegrated," "stopped driving, stopped working, stopped leaving the plot unless I have to," from making it to anyone else's ears, perhaps to keep them from mine. I wonder whether I'm half inventing these things, exaggerating them as some sort of attention-seeking ploy. Then with the same intensity I wonder if I'm vastly underplaying it all.

Between answers I focus my thoughts on the view from the window because my brain can't be trusted with even a few seconds of roaming alone. The garden has laughed in the face of the destruction I thought I had wrought upon it last month. It has recovered much faster than I have. The plants I stuck remorsefully back in the soil before we went to London have worked their severed roots back in already, as evidenced by new leaves just beginning to bud.

The nurse draws the conversation to a close after forty-five minutes saying he agrees with me and my doctor; it doesn't sound like a clear-cut case of anxiety and depression and there might be something else going on. It would be a good idea for me to be referred to their psychiatric team. He tells me that he'll be putting the referral through and that it will be a few weeks until I'm offered an appointment, describing where the clinic is and reassuring me that they will do their best to help. He ends the call, lifting one weight from me and putting another with a slightly different shape—the shape of what it is that's wrong with me—down in its place.

For my birthday Jared bought me an annual ticket to Great Dixter—the famous garden designed and made by Christopher Lloyd. Along with the children's gift of seeds and a tool for harvesting apples from high branches, it was the perfect present and we have just returned from our first visit. Having not really left the plot since London, the world went from a very small two-acre patch of breakfast, lunch, and dinner, interspersed with digging, to a global wonder of color, opportunity, and plans that ricocheted off each other and split into ideas containing promises, pressure, and the great bigness of the future.

I ran from one area to the next, delighting in the garden and trying to explain to Jared why it was all so good. The famous meadow, first planted by Lloyd's mother, was loose and beautiful—buzzing with insects, the odd gladiolus providing a hit of magenta and all boundaried by the safe formality of architect Edwin Lutyens's yew hedges. Now I feel a little like a prisoner might when returned to jail after day release: sadness, constraint, frustration along with the relief of limits and familiarity.

As I return my nice clothes to the closet for I-don't-know-how-long, I notice the Anne Sexton poetry book I cast aside when the nurse called and ease it out from where it has been half hidden under a coffee mug and a letter from school. The cover is simple: a black-and-white photograph of the author, sitting in front of her typewriter but turned to look directly into the camera's lens. The Anne who looks out of her book at me is darkly coiffed and made up, wears slacks and a plain white shirt with studied casualness, and holds a cigarette that's almost part of her hand. The way she is positioned is a confusion of long-limbed, relaxed slouch and self-protective hunch.

Only partway through dressing I sit on the bed to read the introduction to the volume because her photo has turned her from a vehicle for words into a person I want to know. "Some called her genius. I called her Mother." The first paragraph's last sentence is a slap and I look at the name of the person who wrote it, Linda Grey Sexton. These are the words of a daughter who was nineteen when, in 1974, her mother, who had wrestled with mental illness for decades, put on her fur coat and went out to the car, where she would die by suicide.

"I Remember," the poem that I did indeed forget to pick up after the nurse had finished, was written twelve years before her death. I turn to it now and I read again of invisible beetles beginning to snore, of grass "tough as hemp" and a world without color. It doesn't seem enough to leave Anne's words in my head, so I read them aloud with her beautiful, sad, tired, brilliant eyes behind mine, making my own story of the bare feet she writes about, worn since the twentieth of June, and alarm clocks they forgot to wind.

The poem ends before I am ready and I circle back through the last nine lines again:

> the sun blew out of sight like a red picture hat and one day
> I tied my hair back with a ribbon and you said that I looked
> almost like a puritan lady and what I remember best is that the
> door to your room was the door to mine.

A little alert lights up in my head—this is what I wanted to remember when I first read this poem. I open the door from my room and walk through it to Jared's room—the kitchen—where he is standing at the counter preparing dinner ahead of time. I watch him, I remember, he looks up, and I kiss him, then move on to the task that the poem has prompted: a puritan lady of my own.

"The Men of Kent" who left for New England on the Hercules in 1635 were easy to find. They paid for the ship or their passage; made up new names for the prairies, rivers, forests, and shores they landed on, and secured their claims over time with deeds covered in traces of who they were and what they had done. Thomas Bridger of Faversham; John Lewis of Tenterden; and Thomas Besbeech of Frittenden: just a few of the puritan men whose land was once close enough to mine to call them neighbor.

They packed their names and the names of Kent itself and traveled away from here to label Massachusetts with them. New Kent Street, Scituate; Brattle Street, Cambridge; New Ashford, Berkshire Country—all so-called for places I could walk to from here. Yes, there are a surfeit of puritan men from the *Hercules* to study, but a puritan lady is proving harder to find. There are women on the passenger list but many disappear during or immediately after the voyage, and beyond an occasional birth or death date there's little to go on. I attempt to follow Anne Sexton's ancestors back in hopes of a coincidence but meet only a nineteenth-century dead end.

All I have are their names. I type them, arrange them on the page, and read them aloud; trying to remember someone I have never met and making a poem from their syllables:

Anne Besbeech,

Susanna Heywood,

Anne Richards,

Agnes Starre

Comfort Love

The letter comes ten days later. The envelope is addressed to me but the "Dear . . ." inside is a name I don't recognize—an unknown doctor at my own doctor's office, perhaps. I skim the letter, the black type blurring as I look for something meaningful.

After a list of the referral criteria for the secondary mental health service that reads like a reprimand, it says: "Following our discussions the decision has been made not to accept the referral at this stage as we feel that the patient does not meet the criteria for secondary care services."

But I have already been successfully referred, haven't I? I spoke to the nurse who said it was necessary and that I would be getting an appointment. He even told me where to park. So I go back to the top and read the page again, slowly this time, to see what I must have missed. There is nothing different in the second read—just the same flat refusal of help—but on the third look I do find something. Following the "yours sincerely," there is a single text box with a border. It is quite small, but it has "cc: Rebecca Schiller" written inside. Within this box, in this letter that came in an envelope with my name on it, there is almost nothing for me except this: six bald digits of the suicide hotline's phone number.

I have been busy shutting myself down for weeks, dipping into feelings only by eating poems like candy from a bag when the craving hits. The upset is there, I know it, but I've blocked the path of awareness and it's hard to feel it properly. I sit and read and reread.

After a while, Jared comes in and I hand him the already creased paper. He is angry, confused on my behalf, and looks a bit scared— scared for me or scared of me? His fear finally activates a real response. I am furious and as he is the only one here, I am furious with him. I rage as he tries to help, to offer his arms or a plan, but I shout at him to "fuck off and leave me alone." I tell him that I don't want him and don't need him, that he never helps me. It is horrible and unfair of me despite the pieces of truth and past experience in what I am saying.

Why do I resist help? It's not a mystery, now that I have this letter with its denial of my reality, refusal of aid, and the offer of nothing but the hotline number, printed like a dare. Better not to ask or hope for help then. Better not to wait expectantly, like jelly in the jar, for someone to stick in the knife and spread me thinly before screwing the lid back on.

I continue to say horrible things and wait for Jared to go. It usually works but this time he refuses to leave, remains calm and doesn't react against me. My eyes stop bouncing around. I force myself to look into his face like a mirror, seeing his fear and through it the something frightening I am being. His overwhelm is etched there too and its confirmation that I am indeed far too much. But his expression has another dimension to it; one that ebbs and flows but never quite disappears. It is caught in the groove between his eyebrows, smoothed over the scar near his ear, and glints in the shine at the center of his bottom lip.

The black tunnel of Jared's pupil—a void only made so visible because of the ring of hazel glow around it—emits particles that make their way toward me. They hit my skin and though it tries to act as a barrier, they tunnel and burrow into me. I have no choice but to take the bombardment as these pieces of my husband smash into pieces of me and release something warm and good.

He steps forward and I accept his arms, saying that I am sorry, that I need him, that I am glad he didn't go. With my head in the place above his rib cage any last resistance is broken down. When I look up my eyes meet his and I see it for what is: the substance that has been battering, softening, and filling me with what I needed. Of course—it was obvious. Of course—it is love.

The second psychiatric nurse rings ten days later, just before a friend is due to pop in. Again I hide in the bathroom, this time talking to a brusque man who, from the start of the call, seems unimpressed. Perhaps he's annoyed that, after I showed up and cried all over his tidy consulting room, my doctor challenged the psychiatric team's verdict and demanded they consider me as a patient again. Or maybe he's always like this. Either way he doesn't listen, anticipates, interrupts and then minimizes everything I say until I loathe myself a little more and am grateful for his condescension.

"You're a journalist, a writer—yes?" he asks crisply, and I am surprised by his tone. "Yes," I say, wondering why he makes me feel as if it's a secret, and a dirty one at that.

"Yes, I've googled you," he comments. "I hope you don't mind." I do mind, very much, but I laugh and say, "Of course not." Which is what I am supposed to say. He goes on to tell me that he's read my recent work and it seems as though I'm coping and I start to wonder if maybe, because I managed to write seven hundred words for public view, I am. He interrogates me about whether I was sexually assaulted as a child or whether my husband abuses me now. I say no and he lets the "no" hang in the air for a while before saying very definitely, "I can put the referral through again, but it will be rejected. You don't meet the criteria, there's nothing here to refer you for."

"How about some CBT?" he offers, like when my kids ask for an ice cream and I suggest an apple instead. CBT: Cognitive Behavioral Therapy. It is something instead of nothing though, and as by now I think I should be grateful to lick the mud off his shoes—giant time-wasting baby that I am—I say yes and goodbye and thank you in an over-the-top way.

In the kitchen, my friend, who has no idea about any of this, is waiting. I blurt it all out to her and her expressions cycle swiftly through interest and surprise to concern and then wariness as she takes in my red eyes with their purple shadows, the clothes I've creased and stretched by pulling at them and by the pause-snatch of my breaths.

A few days after this call, I am on the hunt for bricks to hold down some weed-suppressing membrane when I notice that, though it is a little late, there are still enough flowers on the elders to make cordial. With nothing lined up yet to help me get back on track I am still forcing myself to exist in a state of limbo, picking things up and putting them down at random, finished or not.

Part of me is unburdened by this meandering way of life and I have to stick with it for now. There will be a waiting list of at least a couple of months for the free CBT treatment. As my earnings are down I can't afford private treatment and will have to wait for at least a couple of months for this service that I've paid into all my adult life through the UK's national insurance scheme.

I see the flowers on the elders, forget about the bricks, and shout for my daughter. She and I have a newish tradition of making elderflower cordial together, but last summer I missed the small window between elderflowers not-yet-open and elderflowers all-gone-over. This is a spur-of-the-moment making it right.

We scramble through the rubble in front of the hedge and Sofya picks what she can reach and puts the sickly-sweet smelling flower heads that I hand her from higher up in a bag. Inside we wash them gently, stripping off their leaves and stems, and then placing the damp umbels upside down to dry. This evening I hope I'll remember to find bottles, sterilize them, and check we have enough sugar, lemon, and citric acid. Tomorrow, if she reminds me, we might assemble the mixture and infuse it for twenty-four hours before straining through muslin. For now we have done all we can and Sofya runs off to play.

I see the post has come with a letter for me. Inside are the results of an online questionnaire that I was asked to complete by the local CBT provider to work out how unwell I am. There's a long preamble, which I skim, and then the part with the score, which I make myself read carefully:

Your Patient Health Questionnaire (PHQ9) score was 13, indicating moderate symptoms of depression and your Generalized Anxiety Disorder (GAD7) score was 19, indicating severe symptoms of anxiety. Your CORE (Clinical Outcomes in Routine Evaluation) score was 24, indicating moderate to severe levels of psychological distress. You reported some concerns regarding risk to yourself. You stated that you have intrusive thoughts of harming yourself or suicide. You stated that you have no plans to harm yourself and that your husband is supportive and you also receive support from your doctor. You agreed should your symptoms worsen you would contact your doctor or use the helpline numbers provided. You have been accepted for CBT and a practitioner will be in contact with you when an appointment becomes available.

The words pull at me, the end of the letter not seeming to match its beginning. I look up the scores because I want to join the paragraphs together and find the link between them. Twenty-four points. Despite completing this questionnaire a couple of weeks after my lowest dip, when I had squashed my distress and blanked myself out, I only snuck under the arbitrary line between moderate-to-severe and severe psychological distress by a single point.

This is not how it is supposed to be. The mismatch between how I thought it was and what seems to be the case stretches the world away from me in two directions. I know the next scene in this story. I'm back in the state I was in last month—much worse than twenty-four points. If I remain in this room looking at this letter any longer I'll return to wherever that horrible place is. It takes a huge effort to redirect, but I make myself put the letter in my desk drawer, where it nestles with the old Post-it notes, broken pens, expired debit cards, and unopened bills. I push the drawer shut forcefully, to make sure the bad things in there know to stay put, and as I take my hand away the metal handle snaps and cuts into me. There's no pain but the gash turns from white to red and drops of me leak out onto my clothes and the carpet below.

I huff angrily to the bathroom in search of soap and a bandage, wanting to stamp my feet because nothing is going in the right direction. Now this, on top of everything else. The small clock in the bedroom next door ticks aggressively as I clean myself up. Everything is annoying and the tap drips audibly after I turn it off, the ticking thrown off its beat by the syncopation of the water drops hitting the sink.

My hand stings, the noise is too loud, and everything in me wants to escape but I don't know which direction to go in. I dither, trapped on the spot and looking for a way to get back to the skating-the-surface living I've been practicing. I focus on my breath. I think about the good things: the children, the animals, Jared, and his love.

Love. Comfort Love. I remember her name now from the *Hercules* passenger list. A servant of Thomas Besbeech, she was recorded as boarding the ship in Kent but is not on the list of those who disembarked in New England. Did she take a new name, was she forgotten, a runaway, or was her dead body wound in a sheet and rolled into the Atlantic? Which direction did Comfort Love go in?

The air becomes thinner as if I am at altitude and time seems to speed and change direction. There is a story here, a woman. I am collecting them like charms on a bracelet. A pain much sharper than my cut hand bites and I lean into it, sensing an opening, feeding it with pieces of myself and, when it is big enough, travel through.

The sun has blown out of sight. Love, loyalty, blood, waves, death: All four are ticking and dripping all around me in the dark muddle. My thumb moves to my cut and presses hard to release a little more blood. She is in there, the puritan lady, caught in the liquid sap of me.

The view dips, rolls, and stabilizes to a place with moisture in the air and a woman coming into view. She is hazy but looks to be the same age as me. Her hair like mine too—yellow and brown of corn and hazel as chosen by the sun when it lands. She is not Comfort Love though, far too well dressed to be a servant. This is someone else.

I feel nausea rise as the ship moves through the choppy sea. Breathing deeply to quell it, I look around for Comfort, for evidence of where I am and who this other woman is as the scene becomes clearer and everything from the wood grain on the deck's boards to the sound of the waves is settled crisply into place. Using all I see as a needle and adding thread made of what I know and how I feel, I stitch up the moth holes in time until I have the whole of it.

This is Anne Besbeech whose name was not on the *Hercules* manifest despite being wife of Thomas, mistress of Comfort, and mother of four daughters who were all listed there. I see the six of them standing on the deck near to her. At the back is a young woman with plainer clothes: At last, here is Comfort. She is a watchful person and as she darts forward to pass one of the girls a shawl she reveals dark circles under her red eyes and rounded shoulders, burdened by the heaviest of weights.

Comfort busies herself with the family but Anne does nothing. Though the four Besbeech girls are tearful their mother just stands there and gutters like an oxygen-starved flame. I wait for her form to settle into the scene and do some mothering, but she remains transparent, useless. I don't know who to look at or why nothing here makes sense.

Then I spot it: the mismatch between how I want it to have been and how it really was. Is this really how it happened? Both Anne and Comfort seem to hear the question, but it is Anne who shakes her head in response and grips the ships' wooden rail looking this way and that. The deck under our feet lurches independently from the swell of the sea and the three of us slip down; through the cabins, the tiller room, the cargo hold, and flow into the ship's underside before emerging into a quiet, candlelit chamber where Anne's form is sharp and distinct at last.

It is 1634, eleven months prior to the *Hercules*'s departure. Before me is a scene of husband and wife, their bed, and blood that won't stop flowing. It is Anne who lies in the bed bleeding. Her skin is grey and I can sense her heart in my own chest; it beats with last-ditch vigor as the rest of her body switches off. She gives a listen-hard look in my direction when she finds me, here in the corner where I sit unseen by her husband but noticed—and I am pleased when I see her—by Comfort Love—the servant who moves in and out of her mistress's room like the tide. "Promise me . . . love . . . daughters . . . you will always." I hear only some of the words from Anne's dry lips but all of Comfort's reach me. "I promise. I could never forget." She gives her short answer solidly and bends down to touch her cheek lightly against Anne's.

Thomas's face is pressed into the bedcovers seeing nothing, his nose squashed against Anne's thighs and his right hand lays on top of both of hers. Anne speaks in a soft whisper to him now. "Thomas, take your face up from the bed for I have need of your strength. I knew I would stay with you as long as the dark night persisted and, though I wished it to last forever, it could not. Day has come and death approaches near."

He looks up: a face puffed by shock and anticipation of grief to come and I want to comfort him, make everything OK and so, I see, does she. Thomas takes out an oval pocket watch and examines its face with relief. "No. The night persists yet, my love." He says it gently, but firmly. "You are not called by the Holy Spirit yet, and hours may turn to years before He summons you."

"It is for me to say, husband." Her words are cobweb thin and he and I strain to catch them. "It is morning: look! Daylight moves faster than the hand of a watch that needs winding." Through the window, the confirmation: a view of hills in the east meeting glowing sky at the horizon. The puritan man flicks between the surety of his puritan watch, his wife's pallor, and the sky, as if they are a sum that doesn't add up.

She is resolute, helping him over the ditch that separates how he desperately wants it to be and how it is. "If I could stop drinking from time's vessel I would. If I could quench the thirst some other way, I'd spend my life in this moment. But I know not how. I sip seconds, gulp minutes, and drain the hours and morning has come; the sun is rising. I must submit."

He sinks into her again, pain rampaging in one direction and denial raging just as hard in the other. "Take up the psalter." She looks to the nearby book and then to him, repeating her request. "Read me the Psalm!"

She is not to be refused; her heart slows now with every beat. Yet he can't seem to pull himself up. Comfort strides into and across the

room, takes up the book herself, and hands it to me wordlessly. "Why
. . . ?" I start the question but answer it myself almost immediately.
Why can't she read it herself? She doesn't know how.

The room is made of the gentle rip of pages turning, of ragged
breaths, and small sighs as Anne guides me to the psalm she needs. I
skim her annotations in the book's margin as I search for it: snatches
of who she is: questioning, faithful, and melancholic; torn between
her faith and the paradox it makes when paired with her desire to
steer her own life. This is a woman of feelings and thoughts deep and
wide, squashed by the time she lives in, pulled apart and put together
by love.

I start to read now and it doesn't matter that I'm not a believer;
her faith is enough for both of us. Soon Comfort joins in with these
words that she has heard often enough to repeat from memory.

> Therefore we will not fear, though the earth be moved;
> and though the hills be carried into the midst of the sea.
> Though the waters there of rage and swell:
> and the mountains shake at the tempest of the same.

My voice falters on "waters" and is submerged entirely by the surge
of feelings at "tempest," but Comfort's comes steadily to replace it.
They whisper to each other, some things I am not meant to hear, and
as Thomas sits up at last, Comfort takes the psalter from my hands
and puts them in his, their eyes never leaving Anne's.

As the puritan man reads on, the puritan woman's love fills the air
like smoke: swirling, imperfect, dangerous, but thick enough to hold
so many contradictions together, at least for a while.

"The waters *are* raging, Thomas—salted by your tears. I would
stay, but like the swallows must before the leaves fall, I will go. 'Tis
the season for it. Do not hold on." She looks up and around the
room. "Do not hold on." We all strain to catch her words. He looks

at her hands between his and releases them and, with a flutter, all is quiet.

The room darkens and Anne and I sink down as one—through wood and stone, seeping from soil to river and finally out to sea. I sense her grief, her desire to have those she loves and trusts with her. Her need for them to stay together, to do as she had hoped. If some of her has gone to the place her faith promised, plenty is left behind to feel all this. Death doesn't play by the rules either of us knew: She is still here, still a person, though contained by an ocean, not a body.

Above the sea's swell is split by the *Hercules*'s wooden hull as it sails out of Sandwich harbor for New England—an eastward start on a westward journey. Thomas, their daughters—her family—stand on the deck looking back at the land they think they have left Anne in, as it shrinks and disappears. Comfort is at their sides doing as her name suggests, as she promised she would with no one to do the same for her.

Grief grabs both Anne and me at the sight of their faces, and we are both seawater, ready to crystallize as salt, ready to become a warm current or a strong rip. It is not fair. It has never been fair. As ever Anne points out what she knows to be true but her voice comes only as foam on the waves, wishing she could have said what she now knows while they could hear her. "I am not back there, loves. I am here: in the tides, in these waters that rage and swell. I will always be here: at the end, at this new beginning. And I remember that in the beginning . . ."

The volume dips and my fluidity changes to something fleshier and more familiar. I flail in the water, my lungs needing air that will come when I leave but not ready to until I hear the end of her sentence. "I remember . . . in the beginning," the puritan lady speaks directly to me now, trying to pull the memory of what she wants to say through the closing gap. "In the beginning was . . . the word. And the word was . . ."

She cuts out: Jared and the children's voices, the tick of clock, and the drip of my tap. We have run out of time and I am in my room, not hers. In my body, in my life, with afternoon light landing on a book of poetry and no ship to be seen. Where is Anne now? I look at the eyes on the book's cover, then at the mirror. Hair tied back, I have the look of a puritan lady too, and as I see myself I remember.

I was never there for Anne; I was there for Comfort. Two women both erased from history but one removed a little more because, as a servant, she was noticed even less. I think of Comfort trying as hard as she could to be everything to everyone and getting on that ship to make a terrifying journey. Why did she promise? Why did she care so much?

Then I remember something new. The sound of Comfort's sheet-bound body as it hit the Atlantic's water. I remember the sensation as she spread through it. I remember the sound of Anne's voice, delighted, devastated at being reunited by death: "Comfort?" I remember that it was a name she had spoken with secret tenderness before. I remember the warmth as the two women finally muddle and mix.

I remember. And what I remember best is the end of that sentence I never heard. And of course—it was obvious. Of course it was Comfort. Comfort Love.

In the beginning was the word. And the word was: love.

August

EYE OPENING

This evening, while putting the goats to bed, I see that the Victoria plum tree is ready for us to begin picking. Nothing tastes as good as these plums warm from the tree. I pull one down, splitting it in half to check for little worms and, finding it clean, pop it in my mouth. I close my jaw around this taste of the harvest season. I haven't brought a basket out, so I stuff the two large pockets of my denim skirt with as many ripe fruits as I can and then use my T-shirt to make a bowl of sorts for the rest, exposing my stomach to the evening air. We'll eat some tonight, put a bowlful in the fridge, and Jared will make the rest into batches of jam and sauce stored in precisely sterilized jars, sealed with wax disks and labeled AUGUST 2019.

I'm not the only one out harvesting tonight. The sound of farm machinery comes from all directions. Combine harvesters, tractors, and trailers stacked with bales of hay drive past with increasing regularity. At this time of year I see the long, hot days our neighbors work—sixteen hours from first light until the darkness falls—and often into the night with lights shining and at race pace to get the crops in before the weather turns. The village butcher, whose flocks run near our field, tells me he hasn't had a vacation in twenty years and that tight margins mean the days of paid help are long gone. He does it almost all himself—on top of being in the shop butchering and serving. Victor talks to Jared about the low price of meat making a mockery of the care he puts into his animals.

Our yield requires much less of us and yet I've still not managed to stay on top of our crops. Making my way through the summer in this—part forced, part organic—short-term meander has turned down the dial on my agitation, but it has left me without a way to ensure I've watered, thinned, fed, and protected the garden as I should. The enormous squash vine has one miserable fruit and the pepper plants are only just in flower now—far too late.

The soft fruit, however, is doing well—happy to be left to its own devices. Jared and I have found harmony in the fruit cage where he is king; naturally more suited than I am to the detailed, methodical work of picking berries from the branches that I nurtured earlier in the year. I love seeing him go out every evening, often with the children in tow, to fill bowls with black currants, red currants, raspberries, the beginnings of the damsons, and blackberries from the hedges.

I take the plums in to him now and then begin collecting the Discovery apples. They are perfect fruits: white flesh shot through with pink, and it's worth risking a sting from one of the wasps feasting on the windfalls to gather them. I fill my basket, throwing most of the damaged ones into the field for the delighted menagerie but stomping on a couple this side of the fence as a treat for the littlest chicks. They squeeze through the small gaps and peck vigorously, happy that the bigger birds can't follow and drive them away.

Eight days later and Arthur is toasting marshmallows over a fire we've made in the field. I am trying to enjoy our family cookout but I can't shake a back-to-school feeling as the reality of the next season looms at the summer's end. There are only two weeks of the children's summer vacation left, and once they are back in the classroom, it has become clear that my summer of recovery will have to end.

Jared is struggling after leading the charge of late and, though he doesn't say it, he needs me to step up and take on much more, and soon. Going from where I was in June, to now, to where I need to be to do that—in just a couple of weeks, with no outside help—is going to be hard. I am trying to acclimatize as slowly as I can, gingerly reaching out to the wider world again. Earlier today I sent a few emails, a tentative response to a request to speak at an event in November, and made myself compose a long-overdue reply to a friend. Just that small step toward normal has altered the gentler rhythm I have worked so hard to fall into. Everything is moving a little faster around and within me. I like and am thrown off by it in turn.

As the flames crackle, I check the buckets of water we have to hand, just in case, because it is very dry at the moment. The temperatures have dropped from recent record-breaking levels, but it's still hot and it has hardly rained in months, the news telling of a spate of countrywide crop fires as haystacks and bales overheat and combine harvesters malfunction.

These fires are nothing to those in the Amazon that Sofya, delighted by the kids' newspaper subscription she's been given, is telling me about. According to her concerned words, an area the size of the UK is now burning in South America. She brings good news though too, snickering as she tells me that scientists have discovered a type of seaweed that makes cows fart less, but putting on her serious face to explain why that might be good for the planet. One country, she goes on (Indonesia, I find out later) is banning people from cutting down trees, but everyone, including her, is very cross with the president of Brazil for his part in that country's forests' destruction.

A little later, with the children quiet in their beds, I am getting out of the bath thinking of the heat raging in the Amazon and of other forests being lost, that are already lost. So many are gone already, and though plenty of us take moments to feel upset or worried we don't often let ourselves face up to what their loss really means for us and the planet. I am very cross too—with the president of Brazil, with many others for all that has led to this moment, and especially with myself for not doing more these past few months.

As it is still light-ish, I dry myself and put clothes on instead of pajamas. I take my anger and frustration, my impotence and the push-pull of my thoughts—don't think about this, you aren't ready; think about this, you have to, ready or not—outside to where they can't bounce off the walls.

Something is shifting within me and I need to try to understand whether it is good or bad. The sky is darkening but there is no moon yet. I'm on the lookout for it because the past 48 hours have been full of news and social media alerts me that tonight the sky will welcome the Sturgeon Moon. I've never heard of this August moon before but with the media starved of content while politics takes its summer vacation, it has now been put front and center in my mind.

The oldest oak tree whispers in a language I find I am fluent in as I wonder where to go. *Come here! I know the answer. I know what you need. Don't turn away, even when it's hard, especially when it's hard.* Under its branches I consider the months to come. I haven't yet reached the top of the CBT waiting list, so none of the promised outside help has arrived and it would be logical to remain in the summer's holding pattern for now.

Work and real-life pressures are already intruding and making this harder. If I'm to continue coping in this way I'll have to go in harder, build the walls in my head a little higher: put down my research, ignore the whispers from the land and the past in case they take me out of my constricted comfort zone.

There are aspects of this new approach to life, forced to flow from one discrete thought and action to another, without plans or goals, that fit my temperament better than the way I have learned to live. But the effort of constraining myself is becoming a burden. As the days go by it takes more from me to force myself to dam the divergent streams of energy, ideas, and thoughts that usually pull me through life. Without understanding if and how to disentangle the good from the bad—without knowing how to sort old from new and better from broken—I have declared *everything* off limits.

My head is so full and I want to get above it, past the branches and into the clear sky, where the Sturgeon Moon will appear. Such an odd name for a moon—and a fish. Do we even have sturgeon here? With the tree as a research buddy I spend a few minutes learning about this prehistoric fish, critically endangered in the UK, giggling at the little strands near its mouth that look like a 1970s mustache.

Moving from fish to moons, I read the Greenwich Observatory's list of names for the twelve or thirteen full moons of the year. Wolf, snow, worm, pink, flower, strawberry, buck, sturgeon, harvest, hunter, beaver, cold, blue. Beaver? These moon names must be very old or new because beavers became extinct in the UK in the sixteenth century and we didn't reintroduce them until 2001. The list has poked something in me. It doesn't sit right. I was expecting old names handed down across the English countryside from druid to peasant to desperate editor of too-empty newspaper, but that is not what this list seems to be. I click more and find an irritating vagueness everywhere I read.

The names are translations of indigenous American terms. Apparently, in August, the sturgeon in the Great Lakes and Lake Champlain were plentiful; April saw an abundance of early blooming prairie wildflower (it doesn't say which), so this moon earned the name "pink" and in March, the worm appeared in the newly thawed ground giving this spring moon its moniker.

Which indigenous peoples though? When? And what were the actual words they used, because it wasn't "sturgeon" or "wolf." How and why did moon names follow the same path as Anne Besbeech's children but in the opposite direction? Where are the words Joane would have used when she looked up at the full moon each month?

The people before her, those who made the first dens in the Wealden forest, would have needed to refer to the moon as they saw through new holes in the canopy.

I wrap myself around the oak, finding a place where the moss has grown to rest my cheek against it. I am hugging the tree now, feeling my pulse against it, and taking something from how solid yet alive it feels. Tree hugger: an insult which becomes, in my mind, a wondering. I type, press Search, and wait for the links to load, expecting a tale of hippies and highways but finding eighteenth-century India instead. I read about the maharajah of Jodhpur and the new palace he wished to build near the village of Khejarli by felling swathes of nearby *khejri* (acacia) trees.

In defense of the sacred forest a villager, Amrita Devi, wrapped herself around one of the trunks; 363 villagers soon joined her, hugging the trees despite the soldiers' threats and continuing their embrace as the axes fell beheading both humans and acacia alike. On hearing of their sacrifice the maharajah relented, gave up his palatial plans, and turned Amrita's hug into a legal protection of the khejri groves that still stands today. Would I be that brave? Would I take the easy or the hard way?

That's the bigger question too. On the surface I have to choose between the easy and the hard way forward from here. *Easy* is keeping things small, light, disconnected, focusing on the good, refusing to see the difficulties, being still, doing less. *Hard* means facing up to things, uncovering, looking for the truth, persevering, feeling the weight of responsibility, pursuing ideas, failing, and trying again. The trouble is that this kind of easy feels hard to me and hard, though not easy, is easier to reconcile myself to and live within.

Easy is pretending and pretending requires a lot of effort. It would be easy to stay confined here and see this tree only as shade and future firewood, yet it is so much more to me than that now and it would be harder still—impossible really—not to pay attention to it.

Hard is truth that throws off pretense even if it feels like cutting off a limb. The hard way contains so many directions, so much potential energy, and it both lightens and burdens me.

The moon will hang low in the sky tonight but I don't need its light to see that I'll be broken by the difficulty of the "easy" way. I am the hard way: That's the way it seems to be for me. The world catches the light in so many places and my eyes dance to keep up with the glimmers. There's a pattern on the oak, made from the ridges and cracks that emboss the trunk: a circle inside a rough oval. I look at it and it looks back: an eye. My hand moves to press gently against it and a ripple of energy shocks me like an electric fence. My other arm moves out instinctively for balance and, with hardly any warning—but just as I find I am expecting—a woman steps effortlessly out of the tree and into the luminous space between my arms.

We face each other and I take in her agelessness and skin tinged brown and ochre—and green. She doesn't seem to mind my stares, staring right back, almost defiantly, a quarter smile on her lips. Her hand goes to my cheek and I feel her touch, as though it contains something of the electric pulse that stung me a few moments ago; it is damp and springy—a balm.

"Anne Dadd." I don't mean to say the name aloud. I'm not sure I do say it aloud, but she seems to hear the words and tilts her head in response. Another Anne: this time a seventeenth-century widow who lived in my village in the 1650s, and about whom I read two pages last week. In 1657, just as the fervor for hunting witches seemed beginning to cool in England, she was accused and stood trial as a witch for the murder of her neighbor's wife and two-year-old son. She takes my hand, puts it against the eyelike pattern on the tree, and I see Anne Dadd in that nearly four-hundred-year-old prison cell: dark, cold, and full of coughs and hopelessness. She is not like the rest of them. She is different, other, with a lightness around her and power within so palpable that I snatch my hand back reflexively and the prison vision fades.

I had presumed she was accused falsely—of course there were no witches. She was an older, vulnerable widow, the witchfinders' classic target. Yet clearly she is not of this world or that one and—I can't help but think it even though I don't want to—perhaps she really is a witch who turned against her neighbors? As soon as the thought forms I can see she's heard it. My red cheeks are grabbed between her thumb and fingers and she pulls me roughly to her, close enough to taste her mineral breath

"I am no murderer." Her voice when it comes is a waterfall, a thunderclap, a nightingale. "I am no witch either: 'witch' is the wrong name. A falsehood that men with closed eyes stuck over truth. 'Hag' would be better choice, if you remember the holy title it used to be."

"Anne?" I make her name into a question and she tuts at me, disappointed again. "Anne is the wrong name too." She's reveling in this story, enjoying the chance to spin it out with pauses and illustrate the word with extravagant movements of her hands.

She sits down on a nearby log, patting the place beside her. I hesitate but then I am there in the space next to her and it is cool, yet comforting, like familiar slippers after a long day.

"This is a year of discovering secrets. They are coming to the surface like bones for you. Here, let me give you another." Her hand presses an acorn into mine before continuing despite my unsure face.

"My name is Agnes, my mother was Agnes, and her mother too. An Agnes might hide behind an Anne if she has to, but it is nothing more than an enchanted mirror conjuring what we want them to see. We cannot live fully within that name, for we straddle the hedge that keeps men from the world and the world from men.

"One foot is always outside: rooted deep as we walk the enchanted places: a gift and a duty. And so we hold on, though it is harder and harder to grip. We keep the old ways, guard the old words, know which herbs heal and which kill, and look for signs of what has gone before and what will be.

"It is not witchcraft, child." She is in my head again, I can feel her earthy fingers rummaging in it. "It is not sorcery or devilry of which I speak. This is how the world is and always has been, and if, like me, you are an Agnes, you see it and can only ignore it at great cost."

She pauses, leans closer and, in a whisper that whips like wind in my ear, she delivers her punch line with quiet relish "And you are like me. You are an Agnes too."

This strange monologue is made all the stranger for how natural it feels to hear it. I am an Agnes. It makes sense. She chatters on quietly, stroking my hair and calling me lost daughter, her voice moving from outside to inside my head as she continues what is clearly a lesson.

"I could hear the ruffets of woodland speak when I was a child but it was my mother who showed me how to listen. There was much I could see already but it was she who taught me how to open fully to it. Now I will teach you."

My mouth is dry with anticipation. "Let your fight between within and without cease, for the world is not made of distinctions."

"But . . ." I start to question her and she cuts me off. "Rest awhile. You think too much and it tangles you further in the ivy vine that already squeezes too hard. Let me fill you with old stories and old words, for they will take the space you fill with all your fanteeging." I look puzzled but she doesn't explain the odd syllables. "You know what it means. It is there already." And when I think again, I find it is. *Fanteeg.* An old Kentish word for fretting.

I listen as Agnes renames the birds: the robin becoming the ruddock and the blackbird with his glossy "bloomage" the blackie. Soon, even though the moon is rising, we see the chitty wren and hear the wobbler in song. "It is the Weed Moon to me but it goes by many other names too," she explains, answering the question I asked before I met her. "*Temezowas, Weodmonath, Tahma Mua, Aranmanoth, Heyannir.*"

The eighth full moon rises over weeds, high grass, and dry seed heads as she tells me that the seeds must be harvested by hand or beak or wind. "You know this already too, daughter, for you have always had your eye a little open though not often or wide enough." She starts shouting a little now, frustrated by my lack of understanding. "Open your eye properly, girl! Not those eyes." She loosens her grip and stands up. "The other one—the other eye—the one you see me through."

She is agitated and paces in the moonlight and I see her more clearly. It is the patina of bark that colors her skin, her feet root with each step, and it is as much tree as woman that places her lips on the center of my forehead and kisses it. My head cracks open. Knowledge flows in from everywhere—an ice-cream headache—I keep eating despite the pain, because it is pleasure too.

When the inward rush slows, I see she has moved away and is standing by the oak trunk. "Don't!" I am afraid to go forward without her. I still don't know how to do it—to be an Agnes in a world like this.

"I am not going. I was always here." She touches her forehead and I feel it on mine." You have always known it, don't pretend." And with an affectionate, scolding shake of her head she steps back into the air and the tree.

For a minute or two I am too dazed to move. Then what Agnes has woken in me propels me and, by the Weed Moon's light, I go to the clump of *Nigella damascena*, cut the dry stems and place their seed heads in a bowl. Nigella—a plant with a woman's name—which has many other guises too. Love-in-a-mist, bride-in-hair, hair-of-Venus, lady-in-the-bower, ragged lady, spider's legs, Jack-in-prison, devil-in-the-bush.

I loosen her seeds and hear them hitting the china with a musical chink; pennies in a wishing well, rice on the floor, acorns on the hard ground. The first plums are ripe enough to give off scent and the sound of tractor engines working late doesn't quite cover the chirp of a cricket in the long grass. The past is here in these strangely familiar movements. An obvious purpose—something my fingers were meant to do. Knowledge hidden from me and now escaped from my DNA thanks to a kiss from the past—something I didn't know that I knew. Like the moments before my daughter was born and my body expelled her without my brain getting involved. Seeing my son's face for the first time and thinking, "Oh, it's you."

I set some seeds aside for myself and then, knowing I must give back as well as take from the earth, I open my fingers and scatter the rest in an arc that spans the summer's zenith before falling in light taps onto the ground.

The summer break is dragging, and after a fractious couple of days I am dedicating this afternoon to the children, hoping to be the patient and present mother I want to be. My plan to start the afternoon with bribery is already underway and their sticky fingers are holding Popsicles as I tell them about the exclusive "Chrysanthemum Club" they have just unwittingly joined. The club's membership is small (just us three, plus the cats as Arthur insists) and its focus is narrow: eating snacks and harvesting seeds to use next year.

Soon Arthur is at work putting the little black bullets of nigella seed and the grey/brown curls of calendula into envelopes while Sofya and I are trying not to giggle at his spelling of the latter's common name, "Marry Golds."

As the three of us start cutting poppy pods down, realizing too late that without their petals I have no way of telling which variety is which, I can't resist the temptation to try to weave a little of what I have been researching into our morning. Since Agnes opened my eye to seed harvesting and saving I have realized how much free seed I've wasted in the past, and I am now determined to know more and do better.

I've tried to buy organic in the past, to support small companies, and choose heirloom varieties, but all too often I've bought whatever was cheapest and quickest. Now I have made a firm promise to save the seed from our plants to use and share. This new rule is going to make everything a little harder at a time when I need my life to be easier; slowing me down with a new series of jobs to fit into the existing rush that makes me feel overwhelmed in exactly the way I am trying to avoid. Yet I am taking it again—this, the harder path, the extra work, all the extra ways to pay attention—because it feels like the only way.

With all the zeal of a convert I explain to the children that much of the garden-center seed is specially bred for huge harvests of super-sized fruits. They look impressed at this, as I have been in the past, but then I get to the punch line. We couldn't do what we are doing today with most of those garden-center plants because they, and their big-brother farming equivalents, have been cunningly designed to be sterile. There's no hope of a future crop, just a trip back to the cash register and a need to use more of the pesticides and fertilizers that eventually ruin the ground.

The afternoon slides past and before coming indoors to finish sorting our haul, we pick the last of the blackened foxgloves. I've been trying not to deliver an agricultural lecture during our precious time together but I've found it hard not to spill the contents of my thoughts out to the two people I most want to know these things. I've told them about things I've learned recently: of "freed seed," not owned by anyone—livings made from it, dinners had from it, bees dipping into the flowers that it germinated. I told them of American farmers who have been fined chunks of money simply for keeping and reusing seeds because they are owned by a company who make money by renting the seed out, and so saving it becomes a crime.

I keep forgetting my audience and using long words or jargon—"hybridized," "mixed farms," "industrial," "subsistence," "climate emergency"—watching their eyes glaze and wondering if they are still pretending to listen only because they are afraid of my volatility. I tear myself away from this thought because it makes the ground evaporate and all my worst fears assemble under my feet to taunt me.

Yet when I pull myself back to them now, the way the late summer hits their faces and lights up the world they know, they smile at me as if I have all the answers. We chatter about the things that matter to each of us. The way Amber the goat looks a bit cross-eyed these days and that Belle is growing a beard. How two plus two equals farts, according to Arthur, and at what age Sofya can have a phone. (When she's fifty.) They let me slip in nuggets that have captured my attention but which I've had no one to share with; thoughts of subsistence farmers, those whose land has been family-farmed for generations, for whom the benefits of breeding seed on the land in which it will grow are significant. Their seed has engineered itself and been passed from parent to child. Without it they may struggle to survive.

We take the poppy stems to the kitchen and sit together, splitting the pods and pouring their contents percussively into bowls, trying to keep the varieties separate. After a while the children start arguing—a sign they have reached their limit—and I tell them to run off and play. They are gone half a second later, leaving seeds everywhere and a metal bowl spinning slowly in their wake. I try to clear up, but the floor is so covered in little grey-black dots that it's futile. If I spilled enough water in here there would be poppies blooming along the grout lines next year.

Next year: I have to get through the coming fall and its return to everything first. Taking the hard way, trying to keep my eye open, even when the winds pick up.

I stop sweeping, crouch, lick my finger, press it against the tiles, and put it to my mouth, thinking of piles of leaves, of muffins and mud, and the Battle of the Somme.

PART THREE

AUTUMN–WINTER 2019

September

THE DEADENING CLOAK

The first of September brings a pear from the bare root trees Jared and I planted last year. Pears, we have discovered, don't ripen well for eating when left on the branch. Unlike most fruits, they sweeten from the inside out, so when the still-tethered flesh feels perfect to the touch, the inside is mushy and past its best. For a couple of weeks, I have been gently tilting the tree's fruits according to instructions from online experts who have assured me that this small movement will be enough to separate them from the tree. I have been losing faith fast though—tempted to give one a good yank—but I try one more day of gentleness instead and, as promised, the green pear, with a cloud of red on one side, finally snaps free.

We are still eating from the land, but the summer has never felt more over. I have a busy month of work ahead. It is time for me to open the smallholding gate, walk through it, and try to pitch myself back to the world as a proposition rather than a problem.

For now, with the pear deposited on the porch windowsill, I return to the safety of the field to shut up the hens. There is a change in the air—I need a jacket—and this new cool gives me a fizzy feeling in my gut. Some of it is excitement as I throw off the summer's constraints; there is impatience too: to be, to live, to do, and to succeed—and I am afraid too. It is hard to know whether I am ready for this. I feel much better, but that has been the way of things for the past few years and it's hard to trust my assessment when it has been so off before. With a few extra responsibilities piled on, and the unreal life I've been living over, I could be back to where I was in June in a heartbeat.

But instead of letting this merry-go-round whirl behind my eyes, I stop and take in a small section of the plot, inch by inch. Though I'm no longer shutting myself off to them, I'm trying to make my way through difficult things in smaller chunks and spotting a bee species I don't recognize on the field, scabious breaks the worry up nicely. The bee has long antennae, a yellow-buff head and thorax, and a dark, almost imperceptibly striped abdomen. Though it is a little late to see one, it's probably a male long-horned bee, which, I read, is becoming increasingly rare—perhaps because as solitary bees, their lonely lives mean they have no rabble from which to learn. Unlike the social species in the genus, the long-horned bee is less adaptive to changing environments and the new dangers this brings: They are more easily caught out.

This fellow flies off to his uncertain future and in his wake I see that my only "Café au Lait" dahlia has finally bloomed. I planted it badly, in an overly windy spot that gets too little water, but it has at last agreed to give me a single, odd-looking flower. As its name suggests, this dahlia should be a pale cream with the tiniest hint of milky coffee. Instead, this one's left side is stained randomly with a vigorous pink, while the right-hand petals are moon-pale to the point of glow. It seems as if all the pigment that should have been distributed evenly through each petal has been concentrated in one half—an uneasy split.

I linger out here as daylight fails, the weird dahlia picked for the vase but going a little floppy in my pocket. Night is coming earlier and earlier as we head toward the autumn equinox. Equi. Nox. The twice-yearly moment when the day and the night are as long as each other, in perfect balance—though I'd never thought about what the word really meant until I began to live for the times of year when there is more light than dark.

A few days later and I have arrived in London. The drive, parking the car, the train, the Tube, what to wear, what to bring, and how to prepare for a day of being "on" has scattered me across yesterday and this morning, each thing requiring my attention in a different direction and spreading it across the hours between thought and action.

Yet at least part of me has made it to the capital holding this large bunch of cut flowers—a gift for the host of the course I'm running today. Traveling with plants can be awkward: the glass jar that threatens to spill or smash, the top-heavy bunch that wants to topple, the barrage of elbows that might squash and bruise the petals.

I am always glad when I've done it though. Today's is particularly beautiful. There are seven varieties of dahlia: "Schipper's Bronze"; an orange one whose name I have forgotten; violet of "Blue Bayou"; magenta "Isabel," with her pom-pom-like appearance; the huge white "Snowstorm"; a little coral-colored mignon; and the ethereal "Dark Butterfly," all mingling with spikes of larkspur and the milky froth of cosmos. On the high-speed train, the other commuters respond to the bouquet with smiles. *Pretty flowers.* They don't know that I brought my garden with me as an amulet, a force field to protect me from the sensory assault and to keep my brain where it feels calmest.

At King's Cross station, commuters, hurrying for their Tube, flick their eyes to the green stalks and bright petals. I see their faces relax as they take in a slightly deeper breath. Here in the artificial light of the underground, as far away from the open skies of my plot as I can get in a single morning, the sight of flowers just picked from a country garden seems to restore everyone who spots them—just a little.

After twelve years living in London, I know the Tube drill well. I move along the platform away from the entrance, through which hopeful passengers stream relentlessly, and stand where I think the larger, double doors of the carriage will open.

As I wait for the Victoria Line train to arrive, I can't believe I did a version of this scramble almost daily. The station is scented with bodies, tired air, and machine oil, and when a train arrives it is impossibly full. Wondering if I can remember how to do this makes me too slow, and by the time my body reacts, people have already disembarked and a few new passengers have shoved their way on. There is no room, and so I hold back. Two minutes later another train arrives and, though I am ready this time, it's the same jostle and red faces. I have no idea how I am going to get on this train, and so I wait, hope, and look around.

There is a deadening cloak city dwellers put on before wrestling regularly with a busy city's transport network. It's stitched from numbness and offers protection from claustrophobia, strangers' armpits, and bad smells—the way opioids function in labor. You can still feel the pain, but you don't give a shit. It makes you impervious to anyone and anything, save the tiny gap you think you can insert yourself into and then do. Mind that gap and *only* that gap.

On my first train journey this morning I read the novelist Penelope Lively's book on gardening, in which she writes about the "noticing" that all gardeners train themselves to do. Here on this platform I spot how my own noticing has altered since I left the city behind and moved to a place that has honed my already-sharp senses to an even finer point. I have listened to Agnes, opened all my eyes, and I no longer blur everything to protect myself. Instead, my brain tries to notice everything and everyone.

The Tube trains pull in and out and I am no closer to boarding. Sheer awareness pulls me out of myself and then bounces back to bombard me. I try to direct it to the flowers instead but there is too much of everything else. The contrast between the petals and the platform jars. Maybe I can't do both. Maybe I have to choose.

The clock on my phone says I've been here ten minutes already and to distract myself from how much I hate even the suggestion of being late, I focus in on a man who is also waiting in the little crowd nearby. He looks a little like my stepfather-in-law: bald and smartly (though not chicly) dressed. Studious-looking glasses, suit trousers, the top of a white collar and blue tie emerging—not from a suit jacket—but from a high-tech, lightweight thermal vest. I'm sure he would call it a *cagoule*.

He's very trim, but not thin, in a way that speaks of exercise and competitive outdoorsy-ness. The man is in his late forties, perhaps early fifties, and would look self-possessed and in control were it not for the absentminded way he is chewing the cable of his earbuds: high-tech, good for running in, expensive. He chomps on them, his mouth opening and closing slowly, and I catch little glimpses of his tongue as it twirls the grey cable. He is not expecting to be noticed here but I see him nonetheless and I am embarrassed—for him, but more for an imagined me who has forgotten to keep tabs on what I am projecting into the world.

The cringe makes me turn away and a moment later I finally manage to squeeze onto a slightly less crowded train, using my back to shield my bouquet from the crush. As we pull out of the station a woman shuffle-runs onto the platform and trips on her too-big shoes. I tense myself against the tumble but we are in the tunnel's darkness before it comes. The breath of a smartly dressed man to my right makes its way to my nose. He drinks but hides it. A woman in her twenties sits across from me fiddling gently with a bracelet that spells out ELODIE; she is thinking of the softness of last night.

Farther down the carriage is a man whose demeanor and outfit demand a name: Expensive Suit Guy. He takes up three times the space he needs and is impervious to the shins of the older woman nearby against which his case bangs repeatedly, despite her winces and jaw clenches honed by decades of putting up with this shit. I'm pulled from imagining the perfect revenge by the man to my left who keeps looking at his watch and tugging his shirt collar: a job interview, I think, with a pang of jitters; we are stopped in a tunnel so he might be late. I might be late, I realize, my heart beating faster.

I can't do this. This noticing is too much. I'm pulled into these people's lives and I might miss my stop. The flowers are getting squashed, petals so bruised and creased that they are no longer a safe place to focus. And still the train doesn't move. I look up and there is the Tube map—multicolored lines and dots neatly spaced across the poster. I start to trace them, saying the names of the stations in my head: Aldgate East, Whitechapel, Stepney Green, Mile End, Bow Road—moving east along a strip of green and pink—places I know, places my friends still live.

The Tube map's usefulness is in its reductiveness. Like the deadening cloak I find I've lost, the design reduces interference, erasing the places, the friends—all but the essentials. This is what makes it possible for me to navigate the complex network underneath this incredible snarl of a city. Were I to use it to find my way aboveground, I'd get very lost. It's so far from an accurate representation of distance or direction as to be make-believe

Even down here it's only fit for use if everything works just perfectly. There's no stop here—we should be moving—but here we are, in the limbo of a tunnel, stopped in a place that doesn't exist. I should be reducing the inputs into my head but instead I'm seeing more and more, even here within something I've seen so many times.

I try physically shutting my eyes to shield me from it all but the map is alive inside my head. These eyes aren't what I need to close; it's the other one. I try to reverse what happened when I was with Agnes, looking without seeing and gradually reducing the journey to nothing but lines and dots.

Exactly four months after I lay on the floor and wondered whether I needed to be in a hospital—and ten days after my Tube journey—I am sitting in a room looking at a man and wondering whether this time help is really here.

The CBT I was promised has started and this first appointment comes not a moment too soon. My tolerance for the real world seems to lower each time I take a break from it and I feel it jarring me more with every passing day. I need this man to help me find a better way to reenter it or I'll have to stay cloistered on the smallholding forever, the bank overdraft enlarging and parts of myself atrophying with every passing day.

His name is Ben Cherry. He's younger than I expected, younger than me, I guess. I smooth my clothes as he introduces himself and goes through the "measures"—the results of an online questionnaire I completed yesterday and will have to fill in prior to each weekly session. Ben is a stranger, but his laptop has already given him a preview of me, turning my answers to the miserable little prison of each question's multiple-choice option into a chart of how anxious, depressed, and distressed I am.

According to these calculations I'm feeling dramatically better—at least when compared to the answers I gave in June. I start to explain that I'm feeling the beginnings of it all going wrong again and then trail off, not wanting to make a fuss or appear to be challenging the computer's version. We talk generally, then more specifically, and I try and fail not to read too much into his facial expressions and to concentrate on the plan we make to meet next week and start in earnest.

The "measures" make me want to burn the building down. Despite being the broadest brush, painting a picture so impressionistic as to be almost abstract, these numbers are the main thing that represent me here. They will steer the focus of treatment, be used to assess its effectiveness, and time will be called on this help when they judge me to be fixed.

Yet I like the man charged with all this. He treats me like a person—one with a working brain—and puts just enough of himself into the room to remain perfectly professional while making it clear that he is a human too. Ben clearly cares about helping me and gives his time in a relaxed way—as if he wasn't hemmed in by all kinds of systems policies, funding restrictions, and pressures. He is trying hard and so am I. This is what I have been offered. I take it with both hands and decide to make of it what I can.

The morning has been one of bustle and best-laid plans colliding to make a muddle. I am busy ensuring that muddle doesn't spread out and stop me keeping a promise to Sofya for this weekend. We are going to make rose hip syrup. The hips are already shriveling on the bushes, and though I'm supposed to wait till the first frosts have come to pick them, the recipe I've found assures me an overnight blast in the freezer will do something similar to the flavor.

The coming weekend has too much stuffed into it, so I set a reminder and a second reminder, and check to make sure I have all that I need. The old *Rosa rugosa* look like they'll give the best crop, though tricky to pick. Searching for tips, I skim "traditional" plant remedy websites which speak of witch brier and eglantine and find my way to a video of Kristina Hook, a Wampanoag tribal leader. She picks rose hips from bushes at the side of the road; plants that look identical to mine, handling them by the leaves so as not to damage them.

As she picks, Kristina talks about how she and others of the Wampanoag people of Aquinnah continue to dry rose hips for tea (which is medicine) and make them into jam (which is food), instructing us to take only what we need and to use all of what we take. The camera zooms in for a tight shot of her expert fingers opening the hip and pointing to the seeds within as her voice tells of next year's roses.

I'm jolted. I've never thought of roses as growing from seed because I have only ever propagated by making cuttings. I've seen their seeds, and their existence is obvious now that I think about it, but as I have never had to collect or plant them, seeing has not turned to noticing.

Aguinnah: the word contains breath and movement. A town at the western tip of an island in Massachusetts. Martha's Vineyard, I've heard its name spoken in films, so-called for a woman whose very existence has withered, starved of light by the shade her explorer relative cast until no one remembers which Martha she was. *Noepe*, "dry land"—the Wampanoag name that turns the word for this island into a symbol on an undrawn map.

I flow east from the roses that grow along the shore near Aquinnah to Massapootoeauke, a land of the great blowing of whales. Surely the *Hercules* would have passed near it just before reaching its New England dock. Then I go on to Sequinauk, "early summer land," the name tethered to a time of a year, revealing the invisible map to be a calendar too.

More seeds that I failed to notice until now because I hadn't realized they had anything to do with me. The year 1684, the year "my" oak started to grow, which I went back to in relief thinking that nothing there could be my fault. I was wrong. Though *fault* is not the right word, 1684 *is* to do with me, though I have not been taught it, or if I was, I didn't listen.

In my English childhood "Indians" were cartoon figures at war with cowboys on the screen. My country had neither and so neither seemed real to me. *Pilgrim, pioneer, frontier, reservation* were cartoon words too. No matter that many of the pilgrims and pioneers were *from* my small island; there was no cultural resonance—they and their actions made no impact.

I start to make another timeline by laying out pieces of paper on the floor: 1684: a meeting in Albany between the English and indigenous leaders; land rights at the top of the agenda. The Indian Nonintercourse Act of 1790. The Indian Removal Act of 1830. The Homestead Act of 1862. The Allotment Act of 1887. The Indian Reorganization Act of 1934. The Indian Claims Limitations Act of 1982, the year I was born.

I lay these American events and legal acts out against my other timeline, the one that revolves around my own Kentish plot, and stand on the guest bed to get the widest view, and to try to spot in which places they overlap. One line of searching, keeping, protecting, and holding on to an idea that I cherish, the idea that humans need the land. Another line of theft, deliberate severing, and coercive removal of people and land. As I look the two lines blur, slide, and overlap. To have land in the way I understand it, someone has to take it; whether from a forest, a people, or both.

I'm balanced almost on one foot with the physical effort of trying to see so much and find a way to make it hang together, when the door opens abruptly and Jared bursts in to tell me we've missed a parcel delivery. Pulled so suddenly from a place that took such effort to reach, I wobble and splutter crossly about being interrupted as I try to orient myself. I nearly had something just then and now I can't even vaguely remember what it was about.

The parcel. Shit! I extrapolate the issues this delayed delivery will cause across seventeen different planes of consequence and see that this small thing could screw me in a vast number of ways. Jared tries to reassure me with solutions, and though his words come with good intent, he hasn't noticed anything that's affected by the delay. For me the missing parcel is important, upsetting, and big; to him it doesn't really exist and the space between our different realities is a place I get very lost.

I'm on some twisted new version of the journey I just made on the bed to that expansive place, but it isn't OK to go that large for something this small. It isn't normal to see and feel all this in something as dull and everyday as a delayed parcel. The intrusive stabbing thoughts dulled over the summer, but they are coming back now, interspersed with visions of myself hitting the floor in sweaty repeats of punishing push-ups. Between imagined push-ups I try to shut that other eye as I did on the tube and glimpse the clear, straight lines of its map instead. Dot. Line. Dot. Line. Don't change lines. Stay with the Dot. Line. Dot. Line.

I see Jared's rigid face and I try to turn his pupils into the circles of stations, reducing the interference, and removing the context. These are just places to stop, to rest, to open the doors and let some air in. A nice straight line where one little thing leads to the next in measured, sedate steps.

A week has passed and I'm walking away from my latest CBT session. I have not yet remembered what it's like to live in autumn and winter, so the rain takes me by surprise. A few steps away from the building and, though my head is drawn in like a turtle, as I haven't brought a coat or an umbrella, I am already drenched. Attempting to embrace the wet, I walk as slowly as I can bring myself to and look at the sky, fixing on the drops as they drill down and land on me with a splash. I always feel out of place here in the center of the town ten miles away. The crowds of people, shops pumping music, the smell of lunchtime and so many stories up in the air ready to fall on me. Looking at the rain helps tune the cacophony out and get me back to the parking lot.

Ben started our session by saying he wanted to give me a provisional diagnosis of generalized anxiety disorder. I could see his point then and can see it now as I walk across the asphalt to my car. When Jared drives he parks in the closest or least expensive place. I do not. I have left the car here, in the first lot I parked in the very first time I came to this town, on every subsequent visit, no matter if there are places closer or cheaper.

On the first visit to any new place I'm vigilant and bracing myself against the breaking of as-yet-unknown rules. The consequences of a misstep in a parking lot, perhaps becoming trapped at the barrier, arguing with the operator via a crackling intercom, shouldn't feel so life-or-death. Yet they do, and the part of me that sees this scenario feels the assault of it acutely and works hard to avoid it.

It isn't that I lose my ticket often and I've never driven the wrong way or gotten lost within its system of barriers. Parking fines are a rarity for me. But I worry that they might happen and it took a lot to drive on through that worry on my first visit. Even more to take in and remember all the things that would prevent me from making a mistake. That's why the second, third, and fourth times I visited the town I clung to the familiarity of the first parking lot. It was hard-won.

Ben told me earlier that he's not qualified to draw official conclusions but, as procedures dictate that he needs a framework through which to help me, this diagnosis (that is not a diagnosis) could be a helpful place to start. He pulled up the relevant page on his laptop and asked me to read a description of the condition and I did, recognizing the smack of anxiety in the strict rules I have made for myself around something as neutral as parking my car. Yet before the end of the first paragraph, I knew it didn't fit.

Though I was aware of how much more complicated I was probably making this for Ben, I couldn't stop myself from telling him that this didn't add up. Yes, I told him, I do worry and overthink, but I'm often also opportunistic, adaptable, brave—foolhardy, even. If I decide to do something, I push ahead quickly without much thought of consequence getting in the way. Doing the right thing often compels me to act even if it means doing something risky and exposing. If a perceived injustice was happening to me or someone else in that parking lot, I'd drive right through the barrier that I'm so worriedly respectful of in normal circumstances without a thought if that's what it took to defeat the injustice. The bigger the challenge, the more I am up for it: like upending our entire life to move here based on little more than a whim and the notion that it would all work out OK.

I explained that the anxiety I feel is different. It impacts only certain areas of my life and exists in the things I have been told are small, mundane basics of being an adult human: housework, planning for holidays, the way other people view my appearance, the house, the laundry pile, getting behind on picking up the leaves, or updating my computer software.

He listened and looked a little puzzled. I felt bad. I should just accept the framework. Maybe nodding my head and not thinking beyond someone who knows better is part of how I fix this problem. But I can't yet leave something alone if it doesn't feel right. So I told the confused-looking therapist that this anxiety is not generalized at all—it is very specific, though to what it is specific eludes me completely.

When the rain stops for a while on the last Sunday of the month, I nip outside to move hay from the garage and notice that the house's stucco is covered in crane flies. Not a small cluster, but hundreds of them everywhere. A crane-fly pilgrimage for which I have no explanation other than the forecast for high winds, which has had me battening down the smallholding's hatches.

I tie up a few roses while I am out here and spot that the hollyhock in the drive has gone to seed. Each flower that turned into a pod has now opened like a cup and the circular seeds are arranged on their sides in a ring, each slotting perfectly into its matching groove like a slide in a projector. It is a beautiful and practical arrangement that I now destroy in the pursuit of more hollyhocks.

As I broadcast the seeds randomly, I am delighted to see the "Black Jack" dahlias have finally opened. They have steadfastly refused to bud all summer but tonight their maroon-black flowers contrast as planned with their coral-colored neighbors that have flowered continuously and extravagantly since early July. These different trajectories have annoyed me—unable to complement each other if they aren't open at the same time—so I am glad that now, radiant, if a little late, the two finally overlap.

I take the last of the seeds to the driveway beds and as I pick my way I spot a flash of purple. Daisy-like flowers on tall stems—asters—something I've had on my to-plant list but were already here if only I had looked and seen them. Do I notice too much or not enough?

I store the surprise and joy of these flowers and come inside bringing an armful of logs with me. It is the first time we've lit the fire for months and the room starts to smell of burning dust, the residue of the summer giving in to the flames, disappearing up the chimney and entering our lungs—becoming part of out there and in here.

There are still days of warm weather and blue skies ahead and later I will go out in the dark to pick raspberries. But it is time to fill the wood stores nonetheless, to collect kindling and get ready for the coming season. I'm already thinking past autumn to winter and it seems like the right thing to do. Bad or good, right or wrong, Ben Cherry–approved or not, I can't wait until we're freezing to check we have wood. This life on the land acts as an enabler to my screwed-up brain, throwing me out of the approved timeline today because of the need to be two steps ahead tomorrow.

October

RIOT/PROTEST

Fall brings fungi to the plot. The October garden has come up in a sudden rash of mushrooms and toadstools, and though I'm far too much of a wimp to fry some up, I wonder whether they are edible and stop to take pictures of the ones that look as if a fairy could be along any moment to lean on them.

I am outside giving myself a pep talk by focusing on the ground where, as well as the shaggy ink cap, fairy ring, and sulfur tuft, there are so many foxglove seedlings growing; some self-sown and others helped along by me. These little reminders of next summer make me smile despite the sick soup of worry that has been creeping up my body since my last session with Ben.

Somehow I'd managed to make myself forget the all-consuming sensation of being physically ill with unspecific agitation and its buddy, following close behind, disappointment, directed at myself for feeling this way again and still not having pinned down why or how to avoid it.

I finish my walk and return to work still feeling a bit hopeless in spite of all this new growth. Some of the reasons and triggers are obvious. Our bank balance has dwindled while I couldn't work much over the summer, and though I'm not ready to, I've pitched myself into projects that might overstretch me but promise to pay the mortgage.

The house bears every sign that I should not have taken my eye off it by going away. Mess everywhere, cold too, because the portable radiators have not been brought in from the garage even though the temperature dropped. Every vase I'd filled with flowers for my family before I left turned to a stinking mess of sludge that no one else seemed to see or smell.

I have CBT again tomorrow and I must be at that stage in the process where it gets worse before it gets better. No pain, no gain. I try not to stack these things one on top of the other and to instead be kind—to myself and to my husband—but I feel sad and tired and let down. There's an iceberg between Jared and me out there, and here in my work from a crappy email that gives me extra work.

I let myself warm up by opening some mail and flick through the very first issue of a local history journal that has arrived like a savior while I've been gone. The lead story's headline is RIOT IN THE VIL-LAGE: DISCONTENT IN THE SUMMER OF 1838 and as discontent is such a good match for what I've been feeling, I permit myself ten minutes of soothing reading about riots before getting on with the email reply.

The article is written by my favorite local historian, Joane's really great-granddaughter. She's pieced it together meticulously with hand-drawn maps and diagrams showing the reader how this older version of our world maps onto the now. It was 1838: the time of the rural Swing Riots in England, when cold winters and bad harvest, combined with new machines, low wages, and unemployment, led to widespread poverty and unrest.

Over the previous decades our parish had gradually partitioned once-common grazing land to make gardens for paupers who struggled to feed themselves and their dependents—once again, a patch of earth for cultivation given as a solution to numerous problems. Some people grew vegetables and some built houses and by the time the land was surveyed for the tithe map, sixty-five households were named as owners of these little plots.

In 1838, against a volatile national backdrop, the rich landowner decided he wanted those gardens back and attempted to evict the families whose survival likely depended upon them. Was it a riot, then? Or more of a protest? An angry mob with ringleaders, threatening violence, throwing stones, and subverting the law on several planes as the records of subsequent court proceedings suggest. Or families bound together by desperation and principle: Daw, Dunster, Wanstall, Cobb; refusing to leave their meager eighth, sixth, or quarter acres; protesting the assault of the powerful on the rights of six, seven, eight, or nine lives per plot.

A riot or a protest? Two interpretations, two takes, two different impulses, and two outcomes. The families won and lost: sent to court, found guilty, but then granted the land in the end. They got to keep their gardens but not their children: a swathe of the rioters' young people boarded the *Cornwall* and set sail for a new life in Australia the following year. Forty out of forty-three of the immigrants' passage was paid at least in part by the parish officials. "Help" coming in the form of an eviction notice of another kind.

Fridays have become my Ben Cherry day, so I am here again in this strange mixed-use office reception room with people waiting for job interviews and others, like me, trying to look as though we are here about the administrator vacancy instead of a state-funded mental health intervention.

Inside the room, Ben tells me he has been talking to his supervisor and they have come up with a new provisional diagnosis. I'm both pleased to be a special case and horrified to be a hassle as he sets out a different model: clinical perfectionism. I sit up a little straighter—I'd rather be a perfectionist, even a crazy one, than someone with a generalized worry about being alive, though I'm pretty sure this in itself reveals something terrible about me.

Ben explains what clinical perfectionism means: a person who sets impossible standards and then gets little pleasure from reaching a goal because they assume achievement means the aim was too modest. He describes abject feelings of failure and then complete demotivation. There's a refusal, apparently an unconscious refusal, to do things you aren't naturally good at and a punishing cycle of working harder and harder, setting tougher targets: all the feelings of failure without the balancers of success. Something of this rings true but it is not perfect—and yes, I tell him, I absolutely see the irony in that.

At home after my appointment, the words *clinical perfectionist* are taking up too large a space in my thoughts. They aren't right. This isn't it. I can't seem to help muddying the water but I don't want to carry on feeling like fifty-seven square pegs trying to fit in one dainty round hole either. Why am I resisting this; insisting on seeing problems that probably aren't there? Maybe it is nothing more than ego: thinking I'm too special and unique for a label. According to me I don't have anxiety—generalized or otherwise; I'm not depressed; and now I'm resisting clinical perfectionism.

Evidently I'm such a clinical perfectionist that even a diagnosis can't meet my exacting standards. I should give in. Stop declining the gift of help just because I don't like the paper it's wrapped in. I want to give in, but how to do it? It seems impossible to switch off the thing that's stopping me from being sorted out when it is the very problem I need help with.

This conundrum is becoming a weapon made of myself and pointed at my own throat. I attempt to get away from it by walking down one of my usual paths of relief. Outside I look for the color of the leaves but see nothing but my failure to get round to raking them up. An escape route to the past is my next try, but I am welded to the now; some mean or sensible bit of me shutting off those synapses. All there is: a hall of mirrors, each glass showing another ugly, distorted reflection of my face.

The internet is a last resort—a way out via the search for John Wanstall, who left my village in 1839, after "rioting" to defend his family's land, and sailed for Australia. John Wanstall: the hollow sound of fingerprints on the keyboard ricochets off the walls, and I try to hold the thoughts of where he might take me in front of my eyes like sunglasses.

I don't know why I am so compelled by the idea of finding out what happened to the rioters' children, why I've spent hours drawing instantly illegible family trees on the backs of unopened envelopes. It feels essential to pin down these individual component answers so that the big picture will make sense. The screen is too bright. I look at the wall but find it papered with an endless view of the worst of me. So back to the screen again, where finally I see Wanstall's name on a record. A letter waiting for him at an Australian post office means I have found him and it is so much more relief than it should be.

One last check on another family history site proves one click too many, though. This John Wanstall is twenty years too young: I haven't found my clue after all, and it starts to feel like a conspiracy. I can't leave it like this, I can't bear to have this loose thread irritating and itching at me. *Of course you can't*, sneers my head-voice. *You're a clinical perfectionist. You need everything to be perfect.*

I need to stuff something else between my ears so I can't hear it. Not John Wanstall, but Australia in general should be fine. What do I know about Australia? I interviewed a midwife awhile back and learned about how indigenous women in some remote areas were forcibly removed from their homes and their families to hostels. They spent weeks in these unsafe places before giving birth alone with only a machine for company.

"On country": that was the English translation of the way that many women wanted their babies to be born. A concept so important but based on an entirely different understanding of what is to be human, that I couldn't grasp it.

Across the globe to Canada: a project I researched before our move here led by indigenous women bringing birth back to indigenous lands. Its impact was startling: as more children were birthed "on country." (to borrow the Australian phrase), addiction, suicide rates, and domestic violence dropped across the whole community. With needs met rather than dismissed, a bright-enough light was finally shone on supposed failures and deficits to reveal that they had always been expressions of trauma and pain.

Bad guys: the people who took the land and then pathologized the people they took it from for responding to the hurt they had caused. John Wanstall: fined for his protest and hauled up in court as ringleader and rioter by another set of bad guys. But Wanstall did go Australia, even though I haven't been able to trace his movements once he arrived. And on this new continent he's the bad guy, the one taking land. He so quickly becomes the oppressor, not the oppressed.

It's too confusing. It doesn't work. Nothing will line up and I'm back at bloody Wanstall again. *You want it to be perfect, eh, perfectionist?* sneers my head voice again. *Perfect? A perfect bitch more like, can't even be kind to her husband when he's depressed. Selfish cow, incompetent, stupid, weak, bitch.*

I put my fingers in my ears needing to drown it out and "LA-LA-LA-LA-LA" isn't working. What else have I got? Homesteading. Yes, the people whose vocational labor is infused with meaning of their own choosing. I like those guys. Click, click, read, click.

I'm moving fast to limit the time between thoughts through which the voice could slip. Abraham Lincoln, offering 160 acres, by way of the 1863 Homestead Act, to those who could claim it and pay a modest fee. Signing it over to them officially if within six years they could "prove u" on their claim by clearing the land, building a house, growing crops, or raising livestock.

A good guy, a good idea. "I am in favor of cutting up the wild lands into parcels, so that every poor man may have a home." Who could disagree with that promise of equity? A chance for brave people, poor people, to level up. And they suffered to do it: covered wagons and thousands of miles: heat, snow, wind, death, and determination. Building houses out of tree trunks, lives from dust.

But there's a problem here as well. It's only a good idea if you ignore parts of the story: the layers of inequality, the unfolding consequences, the severing of indigenous people from land, the exploitation of the land itself. And I'm back in good/bad, right/wrong, either/or, and the acerbic tones of my inner voice get louder with every failed attempt to decide which is which.

I feel a surge of rage at this article, at myself for spending time on it; at needing this nonsense, at needing the stupid therapy, at thinking we could live here, be parents, stay married, and grow our own fucking broccoli. *Don't.* Another part of me is trying to speak up. I can't go back in time to June and March and 2017, but I can feel it pulling me. Time traveling, even though it doesn't exist.

I have stay here. Now. Learn the rules. Be focused. Rules. I need rules. OK. Rules. What was I thinking about? Time travel. Yes. I move swiftly back to the computer before I go wrong again. "Impssible time tr4vel," "tme travel rules," "timetravel existence?/": I type the phrases into the search engine full of typos, hurrying to use this search for proof that time travel is nonsense to filibuster my cruelest inner voice.

I want an internationally acknowledged expert to pop up and show me the error of my ways but instead I read that some scientists think it is theoretically possible; something to do with black holes again. Now I stumble on the information that there's a giant black hole right at the center of our galaxy; a ceaselessly sucking thing eating the fabric of . . . what? What is it eating? "What do black holes eat?" Click. Keep clicking. Read the answers. Spacetime? What is "spacetime."

Physicists have squashed the words *space* and *time* together to make something else—as if each weren't confusing enough by itself. Click: read, watch; click: read, watch: a video with a cartoon monkey moving toward a black hole, full of concepts it would take me months to understand sufficiently to allow me to take the big slurp of cool, refreshing spacetime that I long to.

"The faster we move the slower time passes." *The faster we move the slower time passes. The faster we move the slower time passes?* What the hell? I understand each individual word. I know what the sentence is saying. Yet that doesn't tell me what it means. How can time slow just because we move fast? What does that look like? How would it feel?

This is the opposite of the authoritative expert grounding me with facts and rules. I'm back in the physics lab at school, my teacher giving me an extra lesson. "I don't believe in physics." It pops out of my mouth in a moment of frustration and he looks heartbroken and outraged like Peter Pan hearing a child say they don't believe in fairies.

But I didn't believe. It didn't exist for me. I couldn't understand physics in the way I needed to in order for it to become solid enough to have faith in. Learning the work-arounds and faking it for the exams wasn't an option. I had to do it right or I couldn't do it. *OF COURSE YOU COULDN'T!* The critic in my brain is shouting and taunting me now. *You are a clinical perfectionist. You are a clinical perfectionist. And the funniest thing is that you're so awful precisely BECAUSE you're trying to be so great.*

I flip: pick up the books, maps, notepads, and magazines—all the research materials I have been collecting—and throw them at the wall, the hardcovers denting the plaster. I tear flimsy printouts into as many little crumpled pieces as I can.

Then I look at the computer. Expensive, essential, bought with money I earned from overworking in 2017 when it all went wrong. I am so tempted to pick it up and throw the screen against the wall, hear it shatter, and see the chunk of plaster its corner takes out of this ugly room fall to the floor. If I could pick myself up and lob my body at the wallpaper and revel in how broken it is as it slides to the floor, I would do it.

What an ugly mess. What a stupid, ugly, fat baby of a mess I am. I slap my own face as hard as I can and then do it again and again. The slaps become punches that I hope will leave bruises. Why am I such a mess? For nothing, for no reason. Because I am awful. Because I am shit, pathetic, spoiled. Nothing. I am nothing. A mask hiding a great big void. A human cover-up trying to be perfect—what a joke.

I have the smoothness of the computer screen in my grip, and I could do it. I want to do it. To give up. To smash it into the window and hope the momentum carries me to the moment of collision too.

I look up, considering it seriously, and my reflection looks back at me. At first she is just a hall of mirrors of awful, and I might as well go whole hog and be the person I fear I am. Then the sun moves, lighting up the dirty marks on the window's glass. Small handprints and smeary finger pictures overlay my reflection and at the center of my red-faced, wild-haired window-self: the mark of a pair of lips. I pause: a kiss on my forehead is not something I can ignore.

Perhaps the monstrous thing—a mob-me, an angry, violent awful me to be hated and vilified, corrected, punished, rehabilitated—could be seen in a different way. I shouldn't pay attention to the impulse to make sure I understand every possible interpretation. Needing to get everything right is exactly the kind of thing that got me into this state in the first place. But I look at my reflection and feel the cool of that kiss on my skin again and I can't resist.

The monster turns to hag, the hag to Agnes, and Agnes to me. A riot or a protest? Good guy or bad guy? Oppressor or oppressed? It depends on whose side you take. I am both sides—all sides—and it's hard to know whether I am screaming at injustice or if I am the injustice. It is too much. Though I have loosened my grip on the computer and the vicious inner voice has piped down, it feels like a surrender rather than a victory.

In the first hours of the next day I wake feeling sick. The rest of the very early morning passes in an up-and-down from bed to bathroom where I alternate between sitting with my back against the cold porcelain of the basin and my head in the toilet bowl. At seven I am back in bed exhausted, and Jared asks Sofya to do the animal jobs. She runs back in to tell me of the first frost, her cheeks pink with cold, her thick winter coat still washing-machine clean.

Everything feels awful and heavy, and now that I am alone in the room I search for a way out. A possibility, a gap, a fissure in this horrible morning but there is nothing here. No old words, no old ways, no forgotten women. No space. No time. There's only now and here. It's probably better this way. How it's supposed to be. How I'm supposed to have seen the world all along.

My eyelids fall again and again and eventually I stop resisting the only escape route I have. I sleep: on and on, all day and through into the next night. I can't move as I sink further down into a thick, dark place. It's warm in here and even when I try to open my eyes they close again by themselves. There's no need for food or drink. I'm a stone covered in moss radiating the heat from the day's sun back into the comforting darkness.

On the few occasions that my consciousness bubbles up, I remember that this is exactly how I used to feel as a teenager. My mother called them my "blonde days." I would seem ill and, despite not having any concrete symptoms, would spend a day or two in deep sleep, barely moving. I needed rest so much that my body used to turn itself off periodically and lie fallow for a while, just as it is doing now.

I seem to only have three brain cells still working, but even so I feel a question coming. Why was I so exhausted as a child? My "blonde days"—why did I need them then, why do I need them still? I start carving this into the central pillar of my mind but the blackness invades again and I am switched off.

October is nearly done and I have been tracking the weather closely; the daily temperature forecasts are a gardener's friend in autumn and spring. Though the tender plants have survived the first frost they don't have long left. My overwintering seedlings are housed in two plastic rabbit hutches to keep them safe from cats, birds, and soccer balls, and the deep trays allow me to bottom-water them as needed.

Today, after heavy rain, I spot a big flaw in my cobbled-together system. Without drainage holes in the trays, the rain has collected and the geraniums hate it, as do the echinacea, and they have expressed their hatred via almost instantaneous death. I watch my mind begin to make this small thing into the first of many sequences of interaction. But it is a half-hearted attempt and surprisingly easy to stop. I'm distant from everything at the moment. Just a person over there somewhere who knows that things happen, perhaps even to her.

The clinical perfectionist would look for the flaw in her seedling plan and when found she wouldn't rest until she'd turned whatever was at hand into a temporary solution—all the while working on the grand plan for something more permanent. She knows that if something about this setup doesn't change, I'm going to have to laboriously empty the tray of plants whenever it rains, tip the water out, and then put everything back in. She knows there is no way I will remember to do this regularly for the next six months and she doesn't like any of that one little bit.

That uptight, overcontrolling, anxious perfectionist woman has to have everything fixed—now. She sees and hones and works away at grand plans: a greenhouse with all its glass, a cold frame, outdoor taps exactly where they are needed, hooks in the place her hands reach for the shears or the watering can.

She puts too much time, effort, and importance on all this. It tires and worries her and she can't seem to gain perspective. I am cutting her off. *She* is over there making a fuss about nothing and *I* am over here, working on the good-enough way, with Ben's help. Everything is fine over here, where it isn't the end of the world and nothing is perfect. I can ignore the seedling's wet feet. Solving a problem by letting my thoughts spread out instantly around it is a problem in itself. I don't have time to spend an hour rooting about in the shed like a mad inventor turning bricks, sheets of plastic, and old radiator brackets into something that will solve our lack of equipment and inexperience for now. The right way is to let go of this small thing.

A carrion crow shouts its loud and rasping caw and I look up to see a pair flying over the field toward the village, their shadows following the path through Footway Field. My forehead prickles, as I realize it has been doing since I spotted the water in the tray. *Ignore it.*

There's a brief internal tussle with a voice that tells me to open my eye, but it floats away to "over there" too. That other eye doesn't exist and the delusion of it is tangled with my faults. I don't need to think about plants or crows or find meaning everywhere as if the world was full of signs. I don't need Agnes. She's a figment of my imagination. I've forgotten the Agnes word for carrion crow because it was never real, never necessary, never a good idea.

No woman has emerged from the past since I started seeing Ben Cherry and that is good—good enough—a sign that I am making progress. They always pop up when I'm overwrought. They are my brain trying to desperately answer questions, make a pattern, find a way to fill in the blanks, and have a perfect picture of everything. They are expressions of my perfectionism. A good-enough way might be not to bother asking the questions at all, or at least to be content with a neat list of facts.

I don't care that it feels odd and wrong to be so removed from myself and everything else. I don't care that the rest of the seedlings will die. I don't care that my feet move strangely over the waterlogged grass as I return to the house; something not-yet-blunt-enough within raising a classic over-the-top objection in one of its tried-and-tested ways.

Sofya is busy getting ready for Halloween—her lack of skill with the face paint turning her witch's costume into something truly terrifying. I've been keeping an ear open in case she needs help while I order seeds for next year's crop. My latest homework is a new rule (that's not a rule) about breaking my rules and so I'm not sticking to my resolution to only use what seed I've saved and not minding that I haven't had time to save all I'd planned.

Ben and I landed on this approach after I explained I'd challenged myself to buy no clothes during 2019 and was now borrowing Jared's coat and socks until January 1, 2020, when I was allowed to replace my worn-out essentials. As I spoke it sounded ridiculous even to me. More ridiculous still, that as we talked about how being less rigid might feel, I had to admit that the first feeling that came when I thought about breaking my own rules was terror.

We agreed that I would try, despite the worry, and I always do my homework, even if it's hard. It has been an absolute and unbreakable rule of mine, which, I am realizing, is also an issue. I've become so accustomed to the pursuit of perfection at any cost that I want to be perfect at not being perfect. I don't know how to break my rule without setting another unbreakable rule. It's a head-scratcher that I'm trying to just muddle through.

I've got tomato seeds left on my list of things to buy before we go to the village for trick-or-treating, and I have just come across a cultivar called "Paul Robeson": "a big dusky red beefsteak Russian heirloom tomato with cult status in the US." The description of its complex juiciness and "luscious smoky sweet and tangy flavor" makes me salivate, but with disappointment I see they have sold out. *It doesn't matter*, I tell myself, keeping the bitter little voice at arm's length. *Just have a quick look for another supplier and if I can't find one I'll order something else.*

The screen fills with pictures—some of tomatoes, but others of an African American man from the 1940s or '50s, singing into an old-fashioned microphone. The first link below the images is entitled WHY SOVIET RUSSIA NAMED A TOMATO AFTER AN AMERICAN CELEBRITY. I really want to go on this tangent and explore the weird link between this man and tomatoes that I can see shimmering in the distance but I'm not sure if I'm allowed to follow the impulse. Perhaps this is her, the perfectionist, at work. She's the one who needs to know everything, straighten it out and tidy it up no matter the time it takes or how hard it might be.

But it could equally be the perfectionist's voice forbidding me to read on. She's the one who sets impossible standards and insists I keep to pointless rules, and maybe if I don't allow myself to read this article I'm just putting on a hair shirt of her making. Dissecting myself like this has me so full of doubt that I waver: not a state I can safely remain in for long. The heavy safety of feeling flat and far away threatens to lift and I look at the beautiful fruit burnished dark red–green and decide to let myself bite. It is, indeed, juicy.

In 1898, when our plot was just the easternmost strip of the pasture called Church Hams, Paul Robeson was born in New Jersey.

Paul's father was of Igbo heritage but born into the brutality of slavery. The decades between his birth and Paul's had changed the world, though not, it would turn out, nearly enough.

As our house was built, Paul graduated from law school but his legal career was cut short by daily racism and he pivoted to acting and singing instead. His wife, Essie, worked, bringing in the dollars that got them through the harder times, until his performances earned him celebrity status.

The "Paul Robeson" tomato isn't complex only in flavor. It houses the story of how he craved the freedom promised by a society that said it was carving up the wild places to give every poor man an equal chance, but how he instead found a racist system that took his entertainment and held his dignity down.

Somehow his dedication to and need for civil rights is where the tomato enters, stage left. Inside its flesh are the visits he made to Russia, the hero's welcome he received, and his growing love for that unlikely motherland, thanks to its promise to dismantle the systems under which he had suffered.

In Siberia, an unnamed Robeson fan bred the most delicious tomatoes that grew perfectly in their challenging climate and acted as a buffer to the poverty that Soviet propaganda promised was a thing of the past but wasn't. Loving this tomato as they loved Paul Robeson, these Siberian growers gave it his name. A story of love, hope, ideals, and fruiting. A story of contradictions, hypocrisies, brutalities, and disappointment. The two-tone of the fruit's skin: hope and ideals meeting injustices, genocide and corruption. I let myself see that both stories are true, both are false, and each extends far beyond the name of a single plant. The tingling starts up on my forehead. I feel more alive than I have in a while.

By 1989, as our house's previous owners carved the date of their latest renovations into its mantelpiece beam, Bill McDorman, an Idaho seed saver, traveled to Siberia through a widening gap in the iron curtain. He was on a covert mission to smuggle out some of its legendary tomato varieties. Robeson himself had been twenty years interred in Ferncliff Cemetery, New York, but his tomato had been growing on quietly in Siberian gardens; keeping people alive—with more than food. McDorman returned home to the USA without the Paul Robeson tomato, but with sixty other tomato varieties secreted about his person and a lasting impression of a society where keeping and sharing seed remained an awful and wonderful necessity.

A year later it snowed on our plot in a big way. Flakes fell in Washington, too, as George H. W. Bush vetoed a civil rights bill and, in the last months of the USSR, Perestroika—the Communist Party's radical reforms—allowed Marina Danilenko to start a business with her mother. The collective farm was dead, but she was alive and quick enough to become the owner of the first private seed company in Moscow. She gathered seeds from farms and backyard growers, selling half a million packets to eager Russian gardeners. In 1991, as the borders opened, Marina traveled to America to meet friends of McDorman's: Kent Whealy and Diane Ott, who cofounded the Seed Savers Exchange—one of the largest nongovernmental seed banks and the first to use the English word *heirloom* in relation to seeds.

Marina handed over 170 varieties of tomato seed, including a packet with "Pol Robeson" handwritten on it by her elderly employees. A gift from a regime that had spoken of equality yet delivered the opposite to a country that talked of self-determination but had, for Paul Robeson and millions of others, been built on exploitation.

The tingling on my forehead is almost burning as I read the names of other varieties that migrated from one huge country to another once-enemy state: Czerno Krimski, Siberian Giant, Azoychka. I continue to follow the tomato vine back from Russia and find myself walking through the Alyawarra people's homelands, east of Australia's Alice Springs and seeing *akatjurra*, small bush tomatoes, drying in the fierce sun before being rolled into balls and stored against lean times to come. I try to pronounce words of Nahuatl, the Aztec language: *tomohuac* ("swelling, roundness, fatness") and *atl* ("water") that became *tomatl*. I see the Spanish discovering a "new world"— an old world, of course—and turning the fruit they claimed to have discovered into *tomate*. From there, I find the Spanish role in the genocidal Atlantic slave trade and go on to discover something of the horrors of modern slavery used to bring some tomatoes to our supermarket shelves today.

Jared knocks and I stand up feeling dazed and lost in ruby spheres, worried that I have been here for days and missed Halloween entirely. He says it's only been half an hour though; there's no rush apart from within myself. I'm not sure how I've fit all that into only thirty minutes.

The faster we move the slower time passes. I guess it is true whether I understand or not.

We walk through the village with a little group of friends and the aid of many flashlights. The clocks have been turned back, the sun sets at 4:30 PM and, as there are no streetlamps in this little place, night means darkness in a way it hasn't in my life before. We use our flashlights to cross our own plot when we get home, too, because the driveway lights broke last year and haven't yet been fixed. And that is fine. It is fine. I tell myself it is fine again and again and that the rising panic jostling with numbness is fine too—part of the process of learning to be different. My thoughts rage like rapids in a river after too much rain. I went down that wormhole, stuffed too much into my head again and now all I see is imperfect things and patterns. Just when I was doing so well.

At 10:00 PM I burst my banks all over Jared. I tell him through in breaths that don't reach my lungs that this is all my fault. This smallholding that we cannot afford and do not have time for. I thought it was a reasonable goal: good for us and good for the world, but I can't be trusted anymore. I just repeat the same mistakes again and again, though I am trying to do better; even setting myself new rules is breaking the new rules and so I keep screwing up.

I can't be trusted; yet I'm the one who has to work out how to make this situation better. I'm not allowed to make strict rules anymore but what's "not allowed" if not a strict mandate? The impossible puzzle comes out all disjointed and I can see I am losing Jared. I should stop but I don't because it doesn't make sense. It doesn't match up. I can't leave anything like this; misunderstood, unfinished, partial. Of course I can't. *Stupid. Clinical. Perfectionist.*

I subside eventually, exhaustion providing the stopper I couldn't find myself. We go to bed in silence and I lie awake listening to the tawny owls call to each other. Her *to-whit* is followed by his *wooooooo* every single time as they hoot their love song across the dark sky.

I do not wonder if they are sitting in the old oak, or what Agnes calls them, and that is fine too. The part of my mind that wants to fill itself with the old words and old ways has been excised. I am a dishrag, wrung out and grey and ready to be washed. It is for the best. It is fine. It doesn't matter. This is not perfect but that is the point.

Was tonight a riot or a protest? Who cares. I have given in, stopped resisting, and I am done with both.

November

IDEAS DO NOT FALL
FROM THE SKY

en Cherry is trying his best today, as ever. He wants to move us on from thinking about the overarching problem he believes I have—clinical perfectionism—to looking at more of the specific ways it has infected my life so that we can begin to tackle them. He has drawn something called "a worry tree," and we are laughing like old friends about how CBT loves a diagram with arrows. "Arrows?" intone the CBT gods, "That'll fix 'em! Draw a few more!"

I settle down as he explains his diagram, which represents a process for dealing with worrying thoughts. At the tree's tip is the worry and, after noticing it, I am supposed to follow the arrows through the branches and down the trunk, deescalating my panic by finding out what it is I am anxious about; whether it is real or imagined; if I can do anything about it (and if so, when?), and then make a plan of action with one thought flowing into the next.

There are a few useful things hanging from this sketch's branches, but mostly it is giving me the urge to laugh. I try really hard not to— these sessions are gold dust and this man is one of the golden people in my life right now; trying to help, giving generously of his effort and time. A giggle pops out despite this effort and then I shake my head as I smile. He looks at me quizzically. "Ben," I explain, "I don't need a worry tree—I *am* a worry tree." But he smiles then, too, and laughs before asking me if I can say a bit more.

This process you've drawn—I do it naturally, I explain; about everything, all the time, almost constantly. I admit that I am not very good at the letting-go-and-moving-on part, preferring to find as many routes down the arrows and ensure that every scenario has been covered. However, I do know how to process worry, how to make a plan and tackle it and then move on to the next scenario and then the next. The rules we talked about last time are part of it all, along with other mechanisms I have for planning and organizing.

Ben invites me to lay these out: how I deal with a big and busy life: lists, apps, reminders, self-imposed deadlines, discipline, and rules—the sort I'm supposed to be easing up on. Without these strategies I explain that I fear there would be chaos and it's up to me to keep the tangle at bay. "Would it really be chaos, though, without all this?" he challenges me. "And why is chaos something terrible?"

He asks if my friends' houses are ever messy, whether they forget things and if I would judge them for it, showing with his questions and my answers that, once again, I'm wasting so much energy and time on something as foolish as holding back a perfectly adequate life.

We agree on an experiment. I will consciously let go of the reins a little, abandon some of this overplanning and overworrying and give up on some of my systems. I sit in the waiting room after the session and spend a few minutes turning off notifications on my to-do list app, squashing the urge to set a reminder not to set reminders. The room is full of other people talking but I am further away than ever and don't hear them as I busy myself with letting go of the clutter I don't need in order to discover that the chaos is all in my head.

The days have closed in like little vises and the darkness has expanded to fill hours that in summer were daytime. Everything is a rush again and a fight against the night. The first hard frost came last week, too, and, within a few days of suspended silver mornings, the dahlias and nasturtiums—all of the annuals that had been beacons of color against a general slide to grey and brown—turned to mush. I must pull them up and dig out the dahlia tubers, but not today.

I know that this is when I should be finishing off the outdoor jobs that were started in September because any work I do after the intensity of spring and summer and before the ground turns hard will be a gift to myself next year. Rebecca of 2020 is bound to need help, but I have had neither the time nor the energy to spare for her and most of these jobs haven't even been started yet.

They could hang over me now on a twirling mobile of guilt, and maybe they are, but I don't look up and so I don't see them. These neglected chores aren't life or death, and until all of me believes that to be true I am going to refuse to see them even if it means blurring my eyes to nicer things too.

There is one project that I have not fallen behind with: planting the wildflower bulbs that have been waiting in the shed until the ground was soft enough, which today it finally is. These small shriveled things in paper bags will, I hope, give me native springtime flowers like snake's head fritillary, wood anemone, bluebell, and wild daffodil. I'm planting non-native flowers too: large crocus, nodding Star of Bethlehem, and camassia, though only because I ordered them in an excited flurry and forgot to check where each originated. Choosing native species was an important part of this project and the old me would be frustrated with myself for rushing and messing up. But they are here, and I will plant them and they will do—and that is that.

I'm using my new *hori-hori*, a Japanese tool with a fluted blade—like a long, narrow trowel—serrated on one side and, in this version, with a handy scale of depth marked on. It is already my favorite thing: light and strong, ergonomic and sleek, and there's almost no job I can't do with it. Around the grass I go, scattering a mix of bulbs at random and driving the hori-hori in where each falls. With a wiggle left and right, I make an opening of the correct depth, put the bulb in roots down, and press the clay back together to seal it.

There are hundreds of holes to be made and so this will take me a few sessions. Once I'm done, I'll start the next phase: using a rake or—better still if I can stretch to afford it—a rented scarifying machine to expose the soil under the thick grass. Then I'll scatter the meadow-making seeds: yellow rattle that will parasitize the vigorous grasses until, given time, they recede, leaving space for a diversity of plants to self-seed.

The vision of this future meadow keeps me going even though my hand is aching from gripping the hori-hori tightly, my back and knees are sore from crawling, and my clothes are wet and muddy.

The last bulbs I plant before going inside are camassia. I bury them a few inches under the soil that flanks the path, in the hope of making a walkway of their flowers. I can see them in bloom now: bridesmaids in indigo dresses, throwing their petals over us as we walk to the front door.

November is not my favorite month; this is not my favorite time in my life; I didn't even mean to buy some of these bulbs. But I am planting them and after a couple of hours of direct contact with my land, the dark glasses I've been wearing to the world and how I feel about it lighten a little. I let myself feel it and then slam the safety shutters down again.

The house has slid to its winter state of mud-daubed, drying coat-covered dinginess and we keep the fire going day and night, as much for cheerfulness as warmth. I am sitting close to it, flanked by cats, filling in a timetable. The paper is divided into seven days, each with a slot for every hour from 7:00 AM to 10:00 PM. I'm supposed to use it to loosely keep track of what occupies me each day. This is part of finding reality rather than aiming for perfection. Many of my anxious thoughts and controlling ways are connected to fitting things in, getting things done, remembering and prioritizing in a busy life on a busy smallholding.

This timetable may reveal that I don't have as much to do as I think, or that I'm wasting time trying to do everything perfectly, or I'm simply doing the wrong things. It's another tool to help give me perspective and shake me from my perfectionist obsessions.

I really, really dislike doing it though particularly as the timetable doesn't seem to work for my life. On some days I need it to start earlier and extend later, and the uniform size of the boxes forces me to use tiny handwriting in an attempt to fit in all that that hour contained. In others, there's just a blank or only one word: "dinner," or "goats." To help, I have started a complimentary set of notes on my phone, initially as overspill when the hour's volume was too great for the timetable's container, but swiftly morphing to something more.

These notes are now where I keep the sorts of thoughts, research, and ideas that used to clutter up and confuse my head. After a week of trying to shut myself off from them entirely I realized that was a step too far—I was making a rule again. Though I'm worried about going off on research dives because they seem hardwired to the problems I have with letting things go, easing up, and not sweating the small stuff, I know not to ban myself from things.

The notes are the compromise the good enough way to deal with this paradox. I'm not allowing or forbidding myself, but I'm not flowing completely freely either. It's too soon for that given the pathology lurking and leading me astray. Instead of getting lost hopping from link to link in an attempt to pin the world down perfectly I jot facts, thoughts, and topics down in a bullet point list. Each point separates naturally from the last and when I press save and archive the note it is done—over and finished. Setting things out this way takes the edge off, and I think it is working. Though I feel as removed from myself and the world as I ever have, it has been a while since I let myself be led down ten different paths to end up crying on the floor. Longer still since I distracted myself from facing up to what I needed by fancying myself in some sort of time-traveling conversation with the past.

The fireside is warm, so I stay here doing some of the research my meadow making requires or has prompted. I am trying to think in the bullet-point notes I make as I go along, each point distinct and separate from the last.

- Pros and cons yellow rattle: Reduce nutrients for goat grazing?

- At what point plant considered "native"? No consensus.

- Camassia: Native to many parts of North America's sunny prairies

- Camassia bulbs: Cultivated as food crop by many indigenous people. Some dug up and roasted, others return to soil.

- Willamette River, Oregon: Rock-lined pit ovens found there had been used from 8000 years BP to 140 years BP (BP = before present).

- Kalapuyan and Clackamas people: Cultivated/harvested/ cooked camassia in Willamette Valley.

- Kalapuyan word for "fresh" camassia: *di'p*.

- Willamette River was named *walamet*, meaning to "spill or pour water," by Kalapuyan people.

- Harvest sites destroyed/damaged by settlers particularly those with hogs. (Hogs = pigs.)

- 1843: approximately 1,000 European pioneers headed westward toward Willamette. Over next 25 years, 500,000 settlers traveled the Oregon Trail.

- Military force used to remove indigenous people after "skirmishes" (?) to what became Grand Ronde Reservation
- Cheryl Bryce, knowledge keeper of the Lekwungen Songhees First Nation people: reinvigorating the practice of cultivating, harvesting and cooking *Kwetlal*—camassia—in the meadows/hills of Meegan, Canada,

As I finish typing "Canada," the cat's *meow* distracts me and softens the bullet points of my thoughts for a moment. Instead of pressing Save and moving on, my mind hops along the notes from first to last, noticing the escalation from practical questions about grazing my English meadow to pioneers and contemporary Canadian camassia harvests. The journey these bulbs made to my plot is complicated and I want to understand it, I need to understand it, but . . . just in time I catch myself following the over-the-top thoughts. I'm about to throw the phone down on the sofa cushions and back away from it as if it's an unexploded bomb when I have a better idea.

I don't have to stop, I just need a new topic. This is all too loose and wide and I know there is danger in that wide place. I think hard about what topic is just about interesting enough for me to want to read around it, but absolutely, definitely not so fascinating that I will get lost in it and demand to know everything. The answer appears quickly: physics. And, OK, black holes and spacetime didn't serve me well last time, but that's only one aspect and there are forces and particles and all those precise mathematical things. A little book called *Seven Brief Lessons on Physics* will do for now, and I order it quickly: a clean, little, neat place to begin.

The month has moved on and though it has been raining for a week, I have finished the meadow bulb planting between downpours. The sky is grey today but not ominous, so I head out with my rake to try to clear the grassy thatch and expose the soil beneath before broadcasting the yellow rattle seeds. After a few scratches it is clear that the tiny window between clay too dry and clay too wet has already closed. This is ooze now and I won't achieve anything other than churning up a mud pit. More than 15 ounces of yellow rattle seed—costing the equivalent of a really good week's worth of groceries—can't be sown.

I should have been more organized and thought all this through instead of charging ahead (like I always do) as soon as the idea entered my brain, but I didn't, and that's that. End of story. I decide to keep the bag of seed in the cool of the shed over winter, to mimic the necessary frosts needed for germination in the freezer's drawer, and to hope for the best with a spring sowing.

I want to add a series of reminders for myself to make sure this happens, but the thought of Ben Cherry's homework moves into view: Shed the shackles and free myself from the lists. Accept the mistake and don't give it another thought.

I wake on the back foot, reaching for the lists I'm not supposed to be making. The busy month is catching up with me before I've even arrived in the day. In order to resist the urge to lay all that's swirling in my head out on paper I stare at the leaves being blown down and around instead.

With the glass as a barrier, I can't seem to contract my focus and direct it at the autumn scene, but it's different when I step outside. I pick up a fallen leaf and notice where it is smooth and how the veins make ridges I can run my fingers along. With this leaf in hand I am immersed and for ten calming minutes I might as well be a leaf; lifted, tossed, and dropped as the mass of orange and brown on the ground evaporates and solidifies at the wind's whim.

My nervous system stands down an alert level or two and I dig straight into work, not yet used to relying on myself to remember what is important today but finding something freeing there as well as unsettling. After a while I am deep in setting up a new page on my website for a brilliant idea I thought of an hour and a half ago—my brain zipping excitedly away from the early-winter dark.

My phone rings. The number is not one I recognize, so I don't answer, and a minute later I hear the buzz of a text. "Are you still OK for the meeting? Can't get hold of you?"

My stomach goes over the humpback bridge of horror. There's no name on this message and I haven't saved the contact, so I open my diary—nothing—and search my emails to find a clue. It's only in my recently switched-off app that I finally see the quelled reminder to do something important, with a woman who is paying me, forty-five minutes ago.

A full-body clench and cringe made of shame, panic, and a level of terror I can't explain takes me over. I look for my arm's-length approach and try to get back to it, keeping tight focus on the practicalities: texting her back with something vague that I tell myself is not quite a lie (but is) about a family situation and phone reception, giving huge apologies, and offering to reschedule. I can't admit I forgot and that I am so ashamed of this forgetting that there is no way I will pick up the phone and call.

Thankfully the woman is understanding and so I put a new time in my diary for next week and try to let it go. I have been the worry tree, the worry is dealt with, and now I should move on. I hear Ben Cherry's voice in my head. My experiment was bound to be challenging but everything is fine. There is no disaster, no imagined chaos made real. I do not need to fall back on those systems.

I make coffee, watching the grounds move inside the French press as I wait for the water to draw enough caffeine in. It's early and I'm slow to shake sleep off. There's a lone white rose in a stem vase in front of me and I stare at it wishing it had a scent so I could smell it while I wait. *Rosa rugosa* is the perfume I like best. I yawn.

Rosa rugosa, native to here, there, and everywhere.

I pour the coffee.

Roses. How old are roses?

Rosa hilliae: a fossilized rose leaf found in Florissant, Colorado, and named for Charlotte Hill.

Charlotte Hill: homesteader, 1849–1930, married at thirteen. A life of land, fossils, mothering, death, and the Persephone butterfly.

I drink the coffee.

Alice Day Pratt, author, *A Homesteaders Portfolio*. Single woman, self-described "Old Maid" school teacher, filed in 1911 on 160 acres of land in Post, Oregon, Crooked River Valley.

I drink more coffee.

Post is three hours from Willamette.

I wake up, shake my head to take myself out of it, and start to type all this into a new note.

The end of the month brings a vacation day for the children and brings with it a bird's nest blown down onto the gravel of the drive. The four of us have spent a happy hour examining it and trying to work out what bird it belonged to—a mistle or song thrush, we even-

tually decide. The nest is a master class in haphazard construction—
the mud I have been complaining about, turned into an art form.

We marvel at it: moss, paper, grass, and even the blue of a cheap
plastic bag, and we listen to a recording of the mistle thrush's song.
I want the children to grow up recognizing the sounds they hear as
individual voices, not just a monolith of tweets. We protect the things
we have relationships with and they are going to need to be protec-
tors of this world.

When we have committed the bird's notes to memory, Sofya and
Arthur run off and I set the nest aside on the ground. It is a struggle
to find any feelings at the moment but I think there's contentment in
this moment, like I might be a good mother. I let that rare thought
flood me as I collect everything we've strewn around, including my
phone—silenced to better concentrate on our outdoor fun. There are
three missed calls and two text messages. The first reads, "Hoping
you are still OK for our rescheduled meeting?" I can't bring myself
to read the second.

Fuck! I say it out loud. The meeting I missed last week was rescheduled for—oh god—an hour ago and I have forgotten again. It
was in my mind this morning—and I even let myself set a reminder
on my phone. I thought about it at lunchtime, but then we found the
bird's nest, and as that dimension is so different from the one where
the meeting exists, the latter vanished from view. The sick feeling has
returned at double strength and I try to push it down, along with the
empty dread spread across me.

I am so embarrassed, but I need help with this mistake. I force
myself to tell Jared what's happened, and before he can give me any
advice, Sofya, who has been listening, pipes up. Do I remember the
time I forgot to go to her school play and how she looked for me in
the audience but I wasn't there?

Yes, I remember.

Forgetting my daughter's debut in a play was an awful thing to do, but she was in another play three months later and it was a chance to make amends. I thought about the second play every day that week, crushed by her serious little face asking me not to forget this time. As she went into her classroom in the morning I told her about "breaking a leg" and said I would see her that afternoon.

But it was Friday, and Fridays were the one day where I didn't do anything apart from look after two-year-old Arthur. So, once the different dimension of Friday got going, my thoughts were only on the relief of having nothing to do and nowhere to go.

The school hall was in a compartment of my brain accessible through a wormhole that only became visible when I drove to pick her up. Children were coming out in costume, holding hands with proud-looking parents and I slammed on my car brakes instinctively at the sight of them—an emergency stop in the road seemed the only appropriate response.

For a second time in three months, my six-year-old had said her lines, hopped, skipped, and tried to smile while she scanned the seats for her missing parent. She and I both cried all the way home.

But, I have told myself, *this was an aberration*. I have never forgotten a play or assembly or parents' evening before or since—let alone two in a row. I am organized. I don't forget meetings—not one, never two—because I put everything on my list, mark it in my calendar, my reminders; I write it in marker on a sticky note if I have to. These lapses do not happen to me because I have systems to stop them and, usually, when a nice man isn't drawing arrows that instruct me to let go, I hang on tight. In the event that my knuckles are too sore from clinging on, I have a backup system. The bullet points and diary entries run in a constant ticker tape across my thoughts. I don't forget because I hold it all in my head—everything, at all times—and try really hard never to look away even if it is exhausting.

Ticker tape and blonde days: a cause and its result. The missed meetings and plays and the exhaustion I feel just thinking about them makes me pair these traits of mine up for the first time this afternoon. The sun is setting—a full seven minutes before four on this last day of November. I collect the bird's nest on my way inside. As I move it from one hand to the other, I feel a hole in its bottom, concealed by a thin layer of moss that makes the base look solid when it is not.

However many hours the thrush spent weaving the mud, the roots, and ribbons of plastic together, this basket would not have held everything it needed to. One little egg might survive, two, even, but the weight of the four or five eggs that these birds are compelled to lay would have split the flimsy platform, made known the hidden hole, and turned those futures into a splatter of yolk, white, and shell on the earth that finally broke their fall.

Open your eye! The words hit me on the forehead like a rock. Pain. My hands go up to press against it, mineral breath fills the air and I run into the house and lock the door.

I try a bath. It doesn't work. A glass of wine. That doesn't work either. My head is throbbing and I can hear Ben Cherry in one ear telling me that everything is fine, that it is normal to forget things. I am feeling anxious because I am an anxious person. I just can't bear that I made a normal, little mistake and that's why something is jumping up and down in my head insisting that I make sense of it, work it out, and fix it.

There is nothing to fix apart from my wonky view of the world. All I have to do is distract myself until my feelings and my headache pass. I need something bigger than them and I land on my newly arrived physics book.

I pick it up and start to read. At first I'm just floating over sentences without taking them in but within a few pages I realize I've made a terrible mistake. I have chosen precisely the worst book about physics for my particular purpose. I need a textbook: didactic, confining, precise. This one, written by Carlo Rovelli—a physicist who loves poetry, I should have known (maybe I did)—is all links and spirals, swirls and rule breaking, and I love it. It is bad for me but I love it and I can't stop.

Within ten pages, my phone is out, my computer is open, and I have so many tabs open. I need to understand this, all of this, and despite Ben Cherry screaming at me I keep going. I make notes but the bullet points are gone, replaced by hyphens and numbers that allow for the links I want to see. There are whole paragraphs of barely punctuated notes and a pattern emerges without my even trying to see it. With every new word and click it is reinforced.

Stephen Hawking, quote: "It is the past that tells us who we are. Without it we lose our identity."

1. Parallel lines can cross if they move through curved spacetime.

2. Space moves like the surface of the sea.

3. Superposition: Something that can do opposite things at the same time. Imagine if you could spin both clockwise and counterclockwise at same time. We can't, but the hydrogen molecules in our bodies can. An MRI machine works because of this.

4. Quantum physics = fundamental rules of the universe. The hidden things that happen there are "so very strange that we wouldn't believe them if they were happening to larger objects."

   • Quantum mechanics: Nothing is ever stable, and everything is seemingly a random jump from one interaction to the next.

   • Quarks: smaller particles inside protons and neutrons named by American physicist Murray Gellmann after a nonsensical phrase in *Finnegans Wake*(!)

- In *Finnegans Wake* (1939) Joyce made up his own vocabulary. Critic called this "dreamspeak."
- *Irish Times* on *Finnegan's Wake*: "the reader is faced with an acute bewilderment from the beginning, which is no beginning, to the end, which is no end."

5. Space is not empty. No such thing as a void as there are always elementary particles

The pain in my head has become an intensity—more ecstasy than agony: an opening. I am opening my eye again. I shouldn't though, should I? But then *shouldn't* is a *shouldn't* as well so what am I to do? Ben wants me to be more free-flowing but he also wants me to stop my quest to make everything make sense, make it right, make it perfect, and let things go, ease up, slow down. Yet when I flow freely the opposite happens. I end up here, forking across the cloud cap like lightning, surrounded by elementary particles that suddenly look so reminiscent of camassia bulbs. And I'm desperate to find a link between the two, using whatever I can gather with my frantic fingers on the keyboard—James Joyce, quarks, and hydrogen—in an attempt to discover and explain it. They have to fit. Why won't they fit? Why does none of this fit? Why don't I feel the benefits of the help I'm getting? Why do this timetable and these mandates to give up on the way I've been running/ruining my life feel like being crushed.

Because they are based on a faulty assumption. The words arrive in my head, as certain as morning and I return to Carlo Rovelli's words, and they color in something of myself I have been erasing. He writes that "new ideas do not fall from the sky" but are born by immersing yourself intensely in the subject, turning over the questions relentlessly, trying every avenue again and again and again until, when you are not expecting it you discover, "a fissure, a way through. Something that nobody had noticed before . . . something minuscule on which to exert leverage, to scratch the smooth and unreliable edge of our unfathomable ignorance, to open a breach on to new territory."

Ben is trying to help me, I am trying to help myself, and I *know* I'm not perfect (ha!). I do want help, but this isn't help. Everything that flows from the "provisional diagnosis" is making things worse because that diagnosis is at odds with the perpetual, permanent reality of being me.

The timetable and instruction to give up my rules and apps are supposedly temporary constraints. They are being imposed from the outside as a way of revealing a presumed truth to me. Ben's assumption is that my lifelong, self-imposed constraints are unnecessary to the point of being pathological. He is finding ways to show me, as kindly as he can, that I worry, fuss, overthink and tie myself in knots for no reason. He wants me to see that I would do just fine if I walked a little less carefully and stopped treating my life as a tightrope, relaxed my sharp gaze, and stopped finding it so unbearable when my instincts spot something small that doesn't match up.

But my repeated, roving search for answers, my need to spot and make patterns out of the jumble, the desire to understand fully and my inability to let things that niggle go feels exactly like Rovelli's description of how new ideas are found. My instincts always told me that something was off with this process, with this diagnosis—and I was right. The restless impulse to keep turning it over until the mismatch revealed itself to me wasn't pathological; it was scientific.

New ideas do not fall from the sky; they come to you when you open your eye. I open my eye, as I have been longing to do, and I remember. The CBT wasn't what I wanted. I knew from the beginning that it wouldn't help. Both the doctor and I thought I should see a psychiatrist. But I was tired. It was too hard to resist. After a while I gave in, stopped struggling, and agreed that I was a perfectionist, shutting myself down—stuffing a rag in my mouth and putting a blindfold over my eyes to disable my inner scientist.

I've dissociated my way through fall because it was the only way to get the help I needed, contingent as it was on ignoring the truth. Every part of me knew this wasn't the answer and I am angry and let down and unsure whether I have been betrayed or if I have betrayed myself.

I scrunch my fill-in-the-blanks timetable up and put it straight into the recycling. One by one I reinstate the rules that help me avoid disasters like the double meeting mess-up, and I turn my apps on with relief. These constraints I have made for myself are far from perfect, but they aren't built on a lie. My head has stopped hurting and I have opened my eye again. Looking with my other eye the view is brighter, busier, more confused and, with it open, the world is more full of disturbing question marks. But at least, seen this way, though the certainties are few and far between when I find them they resonate truth. And I spot one solid certainty now among the vibrating vision of old oaks, forgotten meetings, rock-lined pit ovens, meadows full of sharp scissors and parallel lines crossing in the seascape of space. I am not holding back an absolutely fine normality. It was not all in my head. The chaos is real.

December

THE MIND SCRAMBLER

The waning moon is still shining possessively over the plot at 7:30 AM today as I put on Jared's coat over my pajamas. According to the official Greenwich observatory website, the full moon that has just passed was a Cold Moon, and this morning that seems about right. I fetch the goats a couple more bales of hay, patting myself on the back when, for once, the baling-twine scissors are there on the hook that I screwed into the shed ceiling for just this purpose.

The puddle at the field gate has become a real pond once more. Rain and earth—I thought I knew all about how they mix, but the ground this December is the wettest I have seen. Victor has lived here for forty years and even he is shocked by the rising water. Last week our plot's former owners visited to find the road turned to river; the lawns, a series of lakes; and the east-facing flower beds nearly a foot deep in flood. They said that in all their thirty-three years of living here, there hadn't been a winter like it. It's frightening: the pace and suddenness of the changing climate evidenced by mold growing along our skirting board and ducks swimming happily on the carriageway. I like my winters cold and metallic—hard, blue, and fractal—not soggy and mild. There is beauty to be found in this sludge, I am sure, but it is not obvious to me.

After a short break I have my last CBT sessions coming up and there is pressure—though only from myself—to draw a line under this difficult period. I have my eye open for what it is inked in but haven't found it yet. I glance at the oak as I return to the house, sending assertive thoughts in her direction. Whatever it is that I'm supposed to draw a line with, I very much hope it is not going to turn out to be mud.

I have always loved Christmas and today I stoke my festive feelings by preparing presents. I am giving my mother plants, wanting to give something I have grown to the person who taught me about what you can find in a garden. I pot the Queen Anne's lace, larkspur, and stocks into larger containers and then move on to filling decorative pots with hyacinth and narcissus bulbs. When the last are covered with soil, following instructions from the floatiest YouTuber on the internet, I hide the ugly joins between the inner and outer planters with moss I pulled from the lawn, feeling like a bird in spring.

As I sweep up the moss squiggles, I consider where to plant the spring bulbs a friend has given me. To help, I open an album in my phone's photo library where I've stored pictures taken sporadically over the growing season. Some are prompts, annotated with instructions: "move peony—too deep," "need more white here next year," "rotate veg beds—potatoes are here 2019." Others are reminders; the photo revealing where now invisible, died-back plants lie dormant, and stopping me from plunging a fork into them.

I scroll through the images, held by the knowledge that the me of summer, even in her wobbly state, managed to leave this trail to keep the next season on track. My finger swipes the screen again and again until plants are replaced by five screenshots of text, interlopers in my garden album. Before deleting them I give the first image a cursory read.

It is an article from the online magazine The Cut, authored by ten women writers sharing what it feels like to have attention deficit hyperactivity disorder—ADHD—and not be diagnosed until their twenties or thirties.

Because of the work I sometimes do writing about women's health, and a friend who has recently found out that she has this condition, I know a little about how ADHD has been underdiagnosed in women and girls. As I skim the introduction I don't learn anything new. I am about to put the screenshots in my phone's trash, when I reach the section where the women tell their stories, the first of which starts like this:

> There's this carnival ride called the Mind Scrambler that spins the seats past each other, gradually gaining speed while slinging you out to one corner and then another, over and over again. ADHD kind of feels like that—not in the fun way, but in the way that all you can really do is hold on and hope that it slows down.

I get to the end of this sentence and go back to its start, cycling through a few more times and not really breathing. Then I pull up the original piece, this screenshot not feeling real enough, and I reread, seeing the ride spinning faster and faster while someone who looks like me holds on and tries to slow down but finds everything spins more violently instead.

Eventually I move beyond the first sentence to hear more of the story of this woman who finds the world a smorgasbord of inspiration and importance and says, "I'm aware of so much that seems interesting and it's really hard to cut anything off."

Another talks about her energy as "the best and worst thing in the world." She is, she writes, "a medium-sized hurricane," adding that it can be amazing "when that power is directed in a positive way," but damaging and difficult when the energy is destructive and restlessness makes her lash out. She describes being flooded by emotion—entirely consumed by whatever it is she is feeling—and the meltdowns that follow.

These are clever, successful, professional women, including a medic who was diagnosed as an adult. She was really bright and tried really hard, and she got excellent grades and so ADHD wasn't ever considered; meanwhile she suffered and stressed and took herself beyond any normal breaking point, thinking that was just how it would always be for her. Convoluted systems and reminders that allowed her to pretend she was like everyone else got weightier as her responsibilities grew. And when she slipped up, a tidal wave of self-hatred crashed down and she nearly drowned in her own life.

The Mind Scrambler: a carnival ride, a metaphor in an article that has just begun to unscramble something in me. I sit for a minute flicking back to particular sentences and then applying them to my own life. Underneath the story I have been telling myself for decades, I might really have been on this ride every single day. My bedside table, the desk drawer, the closet (and the other closet) appear like a series of slides behind my eyes all full of tangled crap pushed out of sight. Not because I don't care about the mess—I really care—but because I just can't seem to avoid it, however hard I try.

Constantly feeling as though I might be caught out, discovered, or revealed is normal for me, and the words of these women are, for the first time, giving me a context for this. The spinning vortex in my head; the systems, the repeated checks and always being early for everything in case I forget a meeting, someone sees a hair out of place or—horror—I am late; there are explanations for all these things here.

I travel across this new information with my usual speed, already trying to unpick and apply it, and then turning it into this single realization. Maybe everything feels so hard all the time because, for me, it is.

The past few days have been a more obsessive than usual frenzy of googling, bookmarking, and note taking. I am now familiar with the condition's diagnostic criteria, have read papers about high-functioning people with ADHD, discovered support groups, completed several questionnaires and pored over online forums.

This is my way—a laser beam of focus on a shiny new idea that puts everything else into the shadows. Even this tendency itself has become something to be discovered. It is, I now know, not just deficit of attention that's the issue for people with ADHD but also poorly regulated attention: too much of it sometimes, too little at others.

This intense concentration that I know so well could be "hyperfocus," awareness exclusively directed in one place for an abnormally long time to the exclusion of all else. The scattered thoughts, the hitting myself on the side of my head in math lessons until I could make a number connect to a synapse, the way my thoughts slow down and stutter to a stop when overwhelmed: It all fits. If I have a brain like the ones I am reading about now, it stops working when it is bored and flicks on like a floodlight at a new scheme.

I am welded to this new discovery and it is a relief to return to the subject after each time I have to divert from it and engage with the rest of my life. Today I've made my way to a piece on "emotional dysregulation" and find in it explanations for so much of how I feel. Somewhere between the amygdala region of my brain and the cerebral cortex are a series of connections that might, according to the doctor-author, be abnormally weak.

When something happens that provokes an emotional reaction, my amygdala does an overzealous job of flooding me with panic or fear. The cerebral cortex is supposed to get in the way and inhibit that emotion, giving me time to pause, think, and deescalate. But if I have ADHD then it might not do its job as well, so I stay stuck in the heightened state, flooded with my response to that negative thing. Apparently huge mood swings, meltdowns, and rages are common and they are made all the worse by how disproportionate they feel to the small thing that set them off. I wish this didn't sound like me, but it really, really does.

From here I move to other familiar issues: a sensitivity to noise and other sensory stimulation, suggestions that a lack of dopamine transmitters and/or reduced serotonin activity could play a role in the higher-than-average anxiety and depression diagnoses among the group. Others write of the mental health side effects being less of a chemical issue and more a sign of what it costs to try to fit in. Distress can turn into "symptoms" because of a chasm between the world and you, the things you are supposed to do without thought being inexplicably difficult.

The word *disorder* quickly grates on me, but perhaps it is appropriate for a condition bound up with mess, lateness, and chaos. I let myself roam the new plain of disorder for hours without stopping. Neither food nor water would satisfy me; all I need nourishment from is being in this wide place where my brain always wants to go and reading about that very trait while I am in it. The big-picture view, lateral thinking, something that many ADHD people naturally seem to have.

Other parts of my life take on new meaning. My need to know every stage of a seed's or chick's development, my love of breaking down words into their component parts, this project of peeling back each layer of the plot: ways of trying to track back the enormity of the destination I have arrived at until I have understood the series of logical steps that were skipped in between it and where I started.

This, according to self-help strategies, is what they, we—those of us with "executive dysfunction"—are told to do. Break it down, make a sequenced plan where one small thing leads to another. That is how you get to the end of a project. Or, in my case, how I get to the end without disintegrating.

It feels as if, without knowing why I needed to, I have been trying to help the circuits of my brain's neural networks work in a normal way for years. I haven't ever known about the glitches and deficits in my cerebellum, subcortical structures, or my prefrontal cortex, yet some part of me sensed them.

Buzzing with all of this and unable or unwilling to be dragged away, I duck out of as much of spelling practice, bath, and story time as I can and explore more. Clumsiness could have its root in ADHD too. There seem to be links, and though they are not well understood it feels like the beginning of an answer to why I am always falling over and breaking things.

I emerge only after the children are in bed. Over dinner I fire this new information out at Jared for the first time—as calmly as I can, which isn't very calmly at all. It is a lot, of course, for anyone. Not just the change of tack but how much I already seem to know about it—the pace at which I move. Yet he takes in what he can and agrees that, unlike anything else suggested so far, this really does sound a lot like the me he knows.

The school term has ended and Arthur helps me do my evening rounds at 3:00 PM. One of the hens hasn't been coming out of the coop much and I take a look at her. She seems OK, but I feel sure there's something that will make itself known soon, old age perhaps. We watch her for a bit and then I spot Alert, Arthur's small rooster, sitting near a builder's bag, perched in a way that makes me wonder.

As if from a distance, I observe what happens inside my mind next. Here is a tiny abnormality that many wouldn't notice. I see it and then it grows in size, taking up the space that the story it suggests deserves. I zoom in on the rooster and then out from him in every direction, looking for something that I haven't yet seen and itching with the need to find it. My eyes, ears, and nose get to work in the here and now; my brain roves backward, forward, and sideways—across things I have experienced, am planning, or heard of once five years ago. Then it clicks and the itch stops. I think I have worked it out.

At my instruction Arthur steps forward and opens the bag. We peer in and then he laughs and points: I was right. Inside, hidden under the folded cover, sits Speckles the hen, as I knew she would be. Though I've never consciously noticed, I realize I have long known that she is Alert's favorite and that the rooster never strays too far from her feathery side. He has been guarding her as she sits. I tell Arthur to carefully reach and feel underneath—she is a good hen, a good biddy, and doesn't peck him, broody as she is. He feels for and then finds them, a little nest of white eggs as warm as the fireside and it's as if I have won a prize.

This is what I am for. Spotting things before they happen and attuned to hidden moments. I naturally look for and find clues and bring them together to make a solution before anyone has mentioned that there is a puzzle. It is hard to reconcile this with a "deficit" of attention and understand how they are just two expressions on the same face.

The day's jobs are not yet done, so I step back into the wind and drizzle, spotting a flash of orange in the narrow west-facing bed near the door as I step through it. I rummage behind hollyhocks sown in August and find a nasturtium vine still in flower. There is frost damage in parts, but most of it has survived in the shelter of the house.

I break off one of the flowers and put it in my mouth, soil and all, and it is as delicious as July: sweet and spicy—a treat. I have earned this taste of summer and am going to enjoy it, alone, because I deserve this moment, and no one else here likes nasturtiums. I stand outside and eat every last flower from the vine before moving on to strip the plant of each leaf as if gorging on the final layer of a box of chocolates hidden under the bed. I make a promise to myself to try letting the New Year unfold as gently as each nasturtium dissolves. The sensation of fragmentation, of unraveling, is still here. The beginnings of an understanding of why and how does offer the hope of help, but it hasn't made the sensation go away.

Neither has my need to grasp my land's size and importance disappeared. I still want to know what the enormous force that a small patch of earth exerts is made of. I have an inkling now as to why I can't leave paradoxes like these alone; agitated by the knowledge of something hidden under the surface, more than a hen this time.

I think back to the beginning, the prehuman forest and its first settlers. They braved the darkness, discovered some of the forest's secrets, cut down trees, took the land, and built themselves a home. There is a so-called wanderlust gene, associated with ADHD, say some, that certain studies have linked to people who emigrate. I have discovered a study focused on the Ariaal people, a traditionally nomadic tribe of northern Kenyan cattle herders. The researchers tested members of the tribe for the DRD4/7R allele—a version of the gene associated with the brain's dopamine receptors, and one linked to ADHD behaviors.

This allele was particularly prevalent in the Ariaal people, and when found in those still living a nomadic lifestyle it went hand in hand with markers of success such as better health. Yet, in those who had moved to a more static life the very opposite was the case. One resultant theory is that instead of being a sign of a malfunctioning brain, ADHD is part of an evolutionary process that made some people exceptional at looking toward the next day, the next move, and deciding which direction their people should take across the land. They were the gifted leaders who noticed the bigger picture, the patterns within, and drew them together to make the best decision, though not necessarily the most predictable one. But for people who thrived on a changing landscape, the world's movement to a different kind of life could well be full of struggle and suffering.

Something is itching again—a faint memory of something I once read, and I pull out my phone, take off my gloves. Here it is: the story of who walked in the forest in that gap between no humans and settlers. Kent had nomads too. It was they who made the very first openings, *dens*, in the trees—not to live permanently in but to travel to at the end of the long summer. Their herds of swine ran under the oak trees and there were sheep and cows a little later too: grazing spots mapped as names that we still use without knowing their origin: *shiphurst, cowden, cowlees*.

I wonder how they fared, the best of those nomads, once they dug up roots to put roots down and tied themselves to this single clearing year-round. Did they struggle like the Ariaal, like me—their leaders falling back now that their brains were forced to work in an unaccustomed way? Or was it a relief? Perhaps they found a way to skate the seasons and the changes in this place as I am trying to, as if each day was a new journey and their challenge, despite remaining static, still to guide their group safely to the next camp—not in space but in time.

I don't know if the nomads of this forest were broken by the constraints of permanence. But I know that their undulating existences shaped our villages, forests, and fields. The drovers' tracks they used to travel over the land still cross it today, now acting as roads and footpaths. So while historians and archaeologists place the Wealden nomads ten thousand years ago in the early Holocene period, I find them here in the Anthropocene as well. They are still here now; their move to permanence a very early loop in a thread that takes us all the way to the current environmental crises. I find them in my genes, too, and want to know which nomads I am descended from and what land I should be walking.

This time I don't even have to close my eyes. I am there in the place my DNA knows, that has been pulling me toward it with an unstoppable force. Alive with noticing—just as I should be: the path ahead, the changes in the undergrowth, the signs of water, a bird of prey in the sky to the west, a rustle—a predator?—in the distance. I see the herd as a whole, one huge undulating animal, and if a part of it slows or speeds up, threatening to break away from the mass, then I can catch it before it does.

With a movement of my arm and body I keep the herd together, yet I see them individually when it's needed. A limp, the first telltale sign of a pregnancy, a tiny change in movement makes me zoom in on something small but newly important. I spot when the people walking with me are tired, sad, bored, hungry, or fearful, often before they do, and so they feel safe even though this last grass we are chasing will soon run out. I will find some more though—it is my way, my job, my life. I am her, and she is me. These are my people at last.

However often I fear I am a madwoman, a crappy friend, a bad mother, and rubbish wife, I know I would have made a bloody good nomad.

Ben Cherry sits opposite me for this, our final session. I describe how my attempt to get rid of my unnecessary systems had gone. I did not find a middle ground, I told him. The looming pit of chaos was real—full of forgotten meetings, unclean clothes, and missed deadlines. "In the absence of anything better I think I need those rules and systems," I explained, letting this be the introduction to the idea that what feels like a drawn-out breakdown (I stammered a bit around the word) could be related to undiagnosed ADHD.

He nods but looks skeptical, having worked, he tells me, with children with ADHD—mainly boys. So I share what I am starting to learn about how the condition has been researched, understood, diagnosed, and treated with a bias to boys and men. How many women and girls present differently; less obviously hyperactive, less disruptive, less reckless with more of the emotional dysregulation symptoms. I want to leave this building knowing that he believes me so that I am more able to cross out the "clinical perfectionism" label in my medical records and mind.

I talk about my restless, hyperfocused searches; the need to follow the flow of links to make a pattern. "I don't work in bullet-point form." I take effort not to spill everything out to Ben, but we don't have time, so I say just enough to give him the gist—the bullet points coming in handy from time to time. The more I talk the more he nods, less skeptical now, especially when I tell him that I have already been to see my doctor and he has agreed, it could well be possible. Because I do not want another one of those suicide-hotline letters, he has referred me to a specialist psychiatrist whom I am going to see privately, asking for help with a credit card this time.

Our closing session draws to an end. I hand Ben a letter of thanks into which I've sealed a packet of seeds saved from the June flowers that were blooming when I needed help and couldn't get it. He has helped me, though perhaps not exactly in the way he planned. Though I am beginning to see how the process we went through was unwittingly encouraging me to torture myself, it forced me into a corner that I had been exhausting myself trying to avoid. It was only because of Ben that I had to look at and see what the problem might be and begin to move toward something that feels truthful.

I wish I could do more for someone working in a system like this and managing to keep hold of their kindness. Then again, he has just shown me the line graph charting my symptoms since the summer—their frequency and severity plummeting from extreme to the safer end of moderate, with nothing but the land to explain this dramatic improvement. Perhaps the gift of seeds is enough—one of the most meaningful things to give or to receive, as they have always been.

I walk to the parking lot thinking of all the things I didn't have time to tell Ben. Of my childhood, of the other eye, and the rest of what I've gathered to support the idea that ADHD could be a factor for me. As I do I continue a process I've been engaged in all month, taking the line breaks out of my recent bullet-point notes and thoughts and allowing the links to live and grow into those spaces I had actively been suppressing them in.

- Camassia harvested by Kalapuyan and Clackamas people in Willamette Valley

Clac-kamas: Kamas? Camassia? When did the harvests stop? Why did they stop? Who stopped them? Stopped. Stop!

- A new exhibition at Five Oaks Museum, entitled, *This IS Kalapuyan Land*, is guest curated by Steph Littlebird Fogel (Grand Ronde, Kalapuya).

Five oaks. One oldest oak. The Grand Ronde Reservation: an excision, a heritage, a place of belonging. Layers of identity added; a refusal to be removed even as removal takes place and meaning made in spite of and because.

- Fogel has edited the museum's prior exhibit on Kalapuyan peoples, adding historical content from David G. Lewis, PhD. The Willamette Meteorite, a sacred item known as *tamanawas*, the "Heavenly Visitor," to the Clackamas people [STOLEN] by local settler, Ellis Hughes and taken to his homestead in 1902. "Stolen" replaces the original exhibits word "moved."

Iron, nickel, cobalt, phosphorous thrown down from the sky. An alien made "native" to both continent and the earth by the passage of tens of thousands of years.

- "We have always been here, we will always be here." Excerpt from *Decentering Whiteness in the Museum*, by Steph Littlebird Fogel. The sentence "acts as both a museum exhibition title and land acknowledgment. It is also a declaration of perpetual stewardship by the Kalapuyan people."

Have always been here. Will always be here.
Will. Always. Be.
Have. Always. Been.
Is. Was. Am. I. Always.

- The exhibit includes "curated contemporary Native artwork." *The Sun Bathed Everything*, Angelica Trimble Yanu (Oglala Lakota Sioux), "a monotype print of sacred landscapes referencing cultural presence across layers of time."

"Native" artwork, "native" peoples, "native" plants. "Native": a metamorphosis of a word that holds: meadow bulbs, a yellow sunlight bath, the hammering in of fences (legal or wooden) and iron shackles within its six letter span.

Natif (Old French): born in; raw, unspoiled. From the Latin nativus: innate, produced by birth. Natus, nasci, gnasci: to be born. And gignere: to beget.

The root word, the originator of native is "gene:" a code, an instruction that has shaped our lives and land, "native" or migrant. "Gene": genetic, degenerate, generation. Indigenous, gender, gentry, genocide, eugenics, genealogy. Naïve, gentle, germination. Nation. Kin.

The words fill my head and the landscape of the town center and I use them to activate my brain's newest filter, transforming the usual stressors of the street into something both more familiar and engaging. As I weave through the other pedestrians on the sidewalk, I'm a nomad moving my flock expertly through the obstacles of a challenging land. My feet walk through this ordinary town but my body and mind are plotting the best course and journeying smoothly along it, riding the rails of the world like a ride.

Not the Mind Scrambler though. On this ride I'm in charge. I choose the pace and nimbly switch direction according to what lies ahead. And all is well and beautiful as long as I keep moving. Why do I ever stop moving? Why did we stop moving, us nomads? What compelled us to settle down?

Christmas is about to leave the smallholding. A time of cinnamon smells, charades, and magic that I love to dust the house with, like powdered sugar on mince pies, as my mother did for me, with Jared calmly handling the hecticness of turkey, roasted parsnips I sowed in April, and Christmas pudding. He glides through it in a way that I can't imagine being able to do. I am grateful for him and for the festive season. Bracketed from the usual and operating along its own golden meridian—a line of curve and candlelight that we are pulled along by reindeer, minutes drifting past as snow.

Today is the last of it and I am trying to stay with the festive feeling even though I am cleaning out the hens and am fed up with them. We haven't had an egg in months. This laying strike is much longer than their normal, annual molt and break. We had to buy eggs for Christmas—at the same time as buying sacks of chicken food. I have wormed them, put apple cider vinegar in their water, changed their diet, bought them a new house and burned the old one in case blood-sucking red mites were lingering in there. All of this work and none of the reward.

I almost don't bother to check the egg boxes when I've finished but hope has been visiting of late, and so I slide one open. There in the hay are not one but four eggs, including one from the chicks I hatched in the spring. This, her first egg, is gorgeous—a deep olive green. My breeding experiment (crossing a pale-green-laying hen with a cockerel from a line that lays a dark brown) has worked. I have bred an olive-egger, I am a chicken genius, and the hens are in my good books again. Or perhaps, it occurs to me as I try not to rush and trip with these treasures, it is me who is back in the flock's good books.

I am looking for signs of progress everywhere. It has been a revelatory month and, as ever, I want to make sense of it. Four eggs when we had none—that is a sign if ever I saw one. Inside I shout to everyone to come and look: Here is a reward for our hard work and faith. The kids say "Wow!" and mean it, and then argue about whose hen laid which; Jared teases that I've unconsciously bred a hen to lay this shade of eggs so that they match the color of the kitchen walls. I hold it up to the paintwork: He might have a point. We smile at each other; I kiss him, and I remember how it all began—with love. And I remember that the door to his room is the door to mine. I like the thought of our interconnecting rooms very much.

There is still work to be done, so I slip out the back door heading to the henhouse through land that is luminous despite the grey day. My June garden is emerging from December's bog, and there's a shimmer of energy around the place. As the wind ruffles the field maples' bare branches and a carrion crow shouts above us, I ditch the chores and go to the old oak instead.

It has been too long since I found a fissure, a way through, but I have opened the egg box and with that closed the messy chapters of my life and readied for something clean, fresh, distinct, and unsullied. My eye is open and so is the oak's, and I look to the tree, asking it for something minuscule on which to lean and open a breach on to a new territory. With the help of the last Christmas magic in the air I find it in sound.

There is a cacophony of voices and sounds to tune into. Victor's old-fashioned phone already ringing, geese honking, a faraway tractor, the scratch of a hundred-year-old hoe, Harry's pigs squealing,

Mary's steps on the drovers' path, Joane's slower pace to the coops, and the hum of the battery chicken farm down the road.

Underneath all this I hear the sounds of the ancient forest and a baby crying to be fed. I exert more leverage and help these cries of many yesterdays become a roundness of skin and milk dribble tied to his mother's back. The woman is hard at work on this land, bending carefully so as not to tip the baby out, but ignoring its wails so she can finish clearing the far too heavy rocks and pull the ivy that's finally loose enough to free.

This is the moment that the forest becomes a clearing. There is pain in the trees: a keening of branches, a root-stamping of grief and protest as the wind rubs the forest against itself. Light breaks through the still-tiny hole in the canopy: a pile of logs, a makeshift shelter, a fire smoldering and pigs rooting in the distance. We are in one of the forest's dens, the nomads' summer grazing place now becoming a permanent settlement because of her. It is her I am most interested in—always her. Stubborn. Relentless. Awful. Brave.

Sweat runs down the woman's neck and its drops cool against my own skin as she finally sits on a stump next to a vast and newly felled trunk. She examines her blistered palms, eyes flicking to where an axe leans against all that is left of the ancient forest's Mother Tree. And I'm afraid she'll take it up again but instead she reaches behind, unties a knot, and loosens the shawl that has been holding the baby.

Her face changes as she brings him around to her: hard becoming . . . not soft, but flexible, as they smile at each other. He latches on, little sucks at first and then tiny pin-like fizzes of milk let down in her breast, and he gulps, then swallows. I feel it too, prickles of milk under my areolae.

The child quiets and the mother wipes her own face, leaving a smear of mud. Dirt from a place she has traveled to reach and has now claimed. In this small spot she's the primary link in a new human chain that runs up to and beyond us. The first to strip this place back and turn the earth into her survival and her child's shelter. For better and for worse she will carry on claiming it across continents and generations.

For now the smallholding's first settler just sits and sways the baby to sleep, as she always has, as she always will. She has always been here. She will always be here. She is the one to credit. She is the one to blame.

> This woman is the settler: the invader, the oppressor, the destroyer of all things.
>
> She is the nomad who stayed: the solution, the protector, the bringer-to-life.
>
> The peasant. The queen.
>
> I search for her shadow. I walk in her footsteps. I tremble in her wake.
>
> I kiss her ankles. I tread on her toes.

I finish my outdoor jobs—half here, half there—and return to the fireside's warmth. Jared is cooking, and as I pass him to boil the kettle he asks if I'm OK. My face must look strange. I keep smiling, frowning, and shaking my head, and a moment later there are tears in my eyes. I try to explain why to him but the words tumble out too fast and I am pacing and gesticulating; eggs, peasants, nomads, queens, and fresh starts.

If I could burst out of myself I would. Hyper. Active. Two words made one that drop into my head now: another gift, another curse. It has always been there. It always will be, confusing the fresh start of the New Year.

Jared scoops my miracle end-of-an-era eggs from the counter, and I have the urge to stop him using them as ordinary cake ingredients.

I've turned them from eggs into something else, and though I can see it slipping away I want to hold on.

Every ordinary step I've taken on this last day of the last month of the last year of the decade has felt full of possible meaning to find and decode. These hours have felt to me as if they should function as a final full stop on the long sentence of the past twelve months. Offer a tight conclusion to the biggest, busiest, fullest, emptiest, most beautiful and awful decade of my life so far.

I have been waiting for a last-minute Christmas miracle, a sign that everything broken is now mended, that would allow me to wrap up and put away the ten years in which I became a mother—twice—changed careers more times than even I can remember, made two big moves away from friends and homes we loved, had more joy but also more distress than ever before.

These four little eggs, found after I'd almost given up hope of them, swiftly became a good omen, giving me permission to draw a line between the bad times of the recent past and better times now surely ahead. I know it was stupid to think that way after all that's happened. A mistake, but such a lovely one to make for the little while I could pretend everything difficult was over and the future would be clear and calm.

So though part of me crumples and wants to cry and shout, a reawakened sliver of my brain tells me it is for the best when Jared stumbles, juggles, and cries out as each perfect egg hits the floor. They were an omen after all, but a more realistic one. This chapter won't close neatly at midnight to make way for a shiny new one to follow. Seeing everything in neat chapters that progress steadfastly forward to a tidy ending and an immovable conclusion is only possible for me if I shut part of myself down.

Whatever comes next is a continuation and the future will be full of messy smashes. The next chapter might be something that has happened before.

missing you,

The woman in her twenties,
is amazed she's an anomaly. She's
doing fine—if fine means living breathing, getting married, having
children—without the chunk that in us normals holds. half
of all our neurons. Her brain, the jaw-dropped doctors think,
became expert in alternatives,
workarounds, diversions. Who's to say
she's not finer than the rest,
Our signals
take no chances, walk
the roads most travelled by, while hers,
                                    double-joined,
                                              are dancing.

—Tania Hershman, from *and what if we were
                              all allowed to disappear*

PART FOUR

THE NEXT SEASON

THE TEST

TEST START

Blue square, red square, red circle, blue circle, red square, red square: CLICK.

Red square? I don't remember what a square is, but I am sure I never want to see one again. I can't think why I have to click this button but I'm certain that I must. I look for the horizon, a point of focus, and there is something: a red square—no, a red circle—no. A circle? A hole? A great absence: darkening, deepening, pulling me toward it. I click. I don't click. I click. But I'm past the point of no return. CLICK. CLICK. CLICK.

I stretch.

I bend.

I disappear.

I have become earth now. Crumbled to a fine tilth and blown into the cracks of the keyboard: lost between the *A* and the *S* and the *D*. I am sifted so fine that I could plant carrots in myself and they would grow straight and true.

But it is too dark for anything to grow here in this place where I am lost. There are only squares and circles flying past me relentlessly, seemingly at random, an endlessness of commas, never a full stop,

red, blue, red, blue, , , ,

The world as I know it has ended: the homestead demolished, the animals vanished, the crops and the flowers died back.

A felled forest, a black hole, white noise, and then silence.
Even the swirl of the wind has stopped.

"You're all done." The psychiatrist's assistant is speaking but her voice takes a while to reach the other universe where I am lost. My senses have been disconnected from my brain. My head is empty. Circles and squares play on a loop behind my eyes, and it takes me awhile to notice that they have gone from the screen. There (here?) was nothingness, here (there?) is too muchness but I can't dither. The equipment that bridged the two places is already being dismantled, my next task is to find a way to do the reverse and come back to this world, this room, before it is too late.

"How was that?" she repeats. How. Was. That? There is a pause and then the word *awful* crashes into the room, and I am surprised and then embarrassed to realize that I am the one who lobbed it in. The right side of my jaw is still wet from the tears and my hand is gripping the clicker as if it had been welded on permanently. My thighs shake as I stand and I feel faint as I force myself to unfurl my fingers and drop the clicker on the desk. "I know it's ridiculous," I say. "But, yes, it was awful." It was awful? Was? Is?

The assistant moves in her jerky way and I watch her and will myself to let her become less of a 2D character and more of a person. I can tell that she's stressed by the elderly laptop's refusal to connect to a hotspot on her phone and to do whatever else she needs it to so that this isn't a wasted effort. Finally, the computer stops circling and connects. A couple of clicks, a quick scan—her whole head moving left and right along with her eyes—and then the left-hand corner of her mouth hooks upward in the half-smile of someone who thought as much.

"I don't usually do this. If there's any doubt—you don't want to interpret this wrongly. Give the wrong result." Her words tumble out disjointedly but I catch some and stick them together to make a sentence that switches me on a little more. She can give me the results right now.

Results. The test. Little LEDs light up green inside me as I remember why I am here. A diagnosis. Something solid, a certainty after all the waiting. What if it is finally over? What if it isn't?

She doesn't make me wait, this woman who understands the now, now, nowness of life. Within seconds of me clenching my hands into tight fists and confirming that, yes, I would like to know, thank you, she turns and looks at me and says, "This is very definitive. You are in the ninety-ninth percentile for inattention and hyperactivity."

I know what this means, but I pause my reaction and check because I am still foggy and this is an important number to get right. "As in, at the very top of the spectrum? The most inattentive and hyperactive?" I ask. "Yes," she nods, turning the laptop screen to me so I can see incomprehensible graphs, scribbles, and numbers. "If there were a hundred people in this room, all ninety-nine others would be more attentive and less hyperactive than you. You would be the least attentive and the most hyperactive one of all."

It's a bucket of water over the head of information that instantly takes me from where I was a quarter second ago to a completely different place. I have my head in my hands and—even though the walls are thin and there are fifteen occupational therapists working in the room outside, fat sobs come out of me. I am crying with my elbows, my spleen, every microscopic red blood cell traveling the paths inside me and the hairs on my legs are weeping, even the ones on my big toes that I pretend don't exist are wicking tears.

This drench of feelings isn't separated out into distinct thoughts yet. All I can understand is that a minute ago an ivy vine that had been cinching tighter around me since I was little was cut at the base. When you cut ivy it's not an instant untangling. The ropes of green take a long time to peel off whatever tree they have been smothering.

You have to wait until they are brown and dry before getting your fingers underneath to pull them off, checking carefully for nests, as all manner of stuff lands in your hair and on your face.

Even after the ivy is gone and the trunk feels the air properly for the first time in years, the marks and indentations will remain—some for a lifetime. I have all this ahead of me and it will be hard, nail-splitting, backbreaking work. This is just the beginning.

She is still talking, explaining that anyone in the ninety-sixth percentile and above would be likely to have an ADHD diagnosis but that there's a big difference between the ninety-sixth percentile and ninety-ninth—the percentile where I, apparently, live. I say, the thought forming as the words leave my mouth, that I can't believe I am hyperactive, that I would never have recognized myself as a hyperactive person. She describes all the women she sees whose almost constant movements are tiny, demure, socially acceptable: tugs on skirts, twirls of hair, little twitches that you wouldn't notice unless you were looking for them. The men, she explains, are usually in contrast—moving dramatically and freely—less inhibited and so more likely to be diagnosed as little boys.

I listen to her while roving over this new information and marking up sections to return to later, these notes-to-self competing for internal space with images of climbing, jumping, and swinging from one tree branch to the next because I can't not. I can't help it. I never could. My right hand feels strange, still in a loose gripping position, the clicker phantom-pressing against my thumb. I am more here than I was, but I am still there, too. I am in a thousand different places, traveling on a thousand other plains but on this plane, it is time for me to pay and collect as much of myself up as I can. The assistant makes an appointment for me to see the psychiatrist who arranged the test—this time for a diagnostic interview—and I step out into the city daytime with every single thing I have ever known loose and clanking inside me like a recycling bin wheeled across cobblestones.

STORM DENIS

Storm Dennis has blown in today, the day after the test, and it's hot on the heels of its predecessor Ciara. Dennis's destructive tendencies are familiar to me. Denis, the son of a farmer from Kilkenny who claimed not to have been clever enough to become a vet and became a doctor instead, was my paternal grandfather. Like his namesake he often clattered around sending things flying. Granny's most withering looks were saved for her husband when the sleeve of his jacket turned one of her treasures into fragments on the floor.

I find it hard to imagine him as a six-foot city doctor with four sons, a cigarette always on the go, and presiding over an array of vegetables and fruits in an ornate Victorian glasshouse in their Birmingham suburban garden. By the time I came along he had bent himself short and downsized his growing to an eight-by-six-foot garden-center greenhouse of tomatoes, each plant named after a granddaughter. The Gramps of my memories wears his third-best gardening trousers, which look as if they need a swift demotion to fourth-best and a dewdrop that forever threatens to fall from the end of his nose.

I feel the storm's blast on my cheek as I open the animal sheds and watch the livestock peer out nervously. I coax them out, feeling a little guilty but reminding myself of the field shelters and that if I let them spend every wild, wet day penned in and hiding from the weather, half their year would pass cramped and frustrated in the gloom.

I stack six garden chairs to make a single unit, hoping that their combined weight will stop them from blowing away. A study I read last night found that 41 percent of mothers and 51 percent of fathers of children with ADHD received a diagnosis of the condition themselves. There are things I want to pass on to my children, but I suppose, however hard I try, they won't necessarily agree to take them. And there must be many things that I have been given and already passed on unknowingly whether any of us like it or not. The chain of ancestors and descendants I will never meet stretches in many directions, not a straight line but the pattern of the past; its gifts and curses waiting silently in our cells, our lives so much less ours than we like to think.

Knowing that this acronym of difference between me and many others is likely a genetic hand-me-down makes it hard not to look through the generations and wonder who to point the finger at. Gramps, perhaps? We share a clumsiness that could be explained this way. Poor balance, less motor control, reduced spatial awareness have all been observed in ADHD people, while postural sway—the amount a person moves horizontally around their center of gravity when standing still—seems to be increased. Perhaps my grandfather felt as unsteady on his feet as I do and wondered, as I have, why the world keeps bumping into him.

Or is my maternal grandfather, Bill, a more likely candidate? The stories of him shaving half his beard off on an impulse, walking the dangerously high battlements of an old castle to bring a ghost story to life, and rumors of explosive outbursts make me look in his direction too. I discount the women at first as too capable, organized, and confident to be in the running, but then remember that those are adjectives others often use to describe me. They might be the wrong labels, but I have sweated and strained to earn them, and if I can, so can they.

It has not taken long to realize that, if ADHD is part of everything falling apart for me this decade, the real tragedy might not be my lack of diagnosis but rather the way others I love have gone undiagnosed. It is tempting to look around and explain so much in the close and distant history of my family with these four letters. The most painful and difficult things—lies, recklessness, addiction, illness, disappointment, and disaster—all are associated with this disorder and, all at once, inexplicable pain and loss might have an explanation.

Moments of brilliance and talents could also be explained this way: keen minds, electrified by ideas, unable to sit still until they have completed them. Yet I can't give into the temptation to label them. The individuals I know and love, and those I will never have the chance to, are people unafraid to pack up, move continents, break rules, speak out, and think laterally. Who am I to reduce them to a collection of symptoms and traits when, despite the comforting answer it might provide, it's so far from what I want for myself.

The rain is coming down hard enough now to make a drum roll on the metal roof. Water runs inside my clothes as the wind peels back my hood, but, despite my pleading, the goats will not cooperate. They are always the hardest to evict in bad weather, not liking to step on wet ground or walk through puddles and it is too wet to argue. I give in and let them stay in the small, covered concrete yard, which I must make larger. Amber and Belle munch on hay, looking smugly out at me as the gale picks up.

A week after the test I'm waiting for my follow-up appointment with the psychiatrist. He is running late and I was early, which is funny given what he might be about to officially diagnose in me. I see him wobble past the window on his bicycle and he appears a few minutes later, still wearing his helmet and fluorescent tabard.

Building on the hour and forty-five minutes of our first appointment, we review the results of the test and go through the formal diagnostic questionnaire. From the previous ramble and the formal answers of today, the story of the past year, the past three years, and the past thirty-seven years comes out in little spirals of disconnect.

I talk about the things that were so much part of our family mythology that I never gave them a moment's thought. My inability to learn to read until late and then being able to do it overnight after a mean comment from another child. The series of lost/broken/left-behind things of my childhood that provided funny anecdotes that seem less funny now. Then there are the moments I'd forgotten: the clever excuses for homework I couldn't make myself do, the library fines; the emotional collapse when I had to fend for myself at university; the unpaid bills, the clothes bought impulsively. All managed and hidden of course and never anything too bad. Nothing that would raise a warning flag if you couldn't see the speed of my legs increasing just to stay still.

We talk the past year and the intrusive thoughts of scissors and suicide. "It's embarrassingly performative," I say out loud, realizing it as I say it. He writes that down, saying he can tell I'm a writer, and I wish I could take it back. Yet it is a performance, but not because the feelings aren't real, they are very real, but because dramatizing them and turning them into horrible images was the only way I can let the truth begin to break through the person I have constructed—the person that everybody, including me, has thought I am. I was performing for myself too, of course, though I don't tell him that.

"Do you think you would ever hurt yourself? Kill yourself?" he asks, bringing me back from the sound of fragments of myself scattering across the kitchen floor. "Is it"—he struggles a little—"that you have to show how bad it is? How you are feeling and make someone listen?"

"Yes . . ." I start but trail off as I see the metal triangles that hold the garage roof up and remember how they started to call to me quite persuasively. I remember the interview I read with a psychologist who described the particular internal chaos and restlessness for many women living with undiagnosed ADHD. The pressure and struggle to keep up the facade under society's intense and unequal scrutiny. Gender roles and expectations that are already unfair and unachievable are made all the harder to meet. How, when mixed with shame, exhaustion, and burnout, secondary mental health conditions like depression and anxiety often plough the furrows of blame and self-loathing a little deeper.

Do I think I would ever hurt myself? I don't know how to answer him but I do know that many women with ADHD do self-harm and that a new Canadian study has been haunting me with its percentages: 23.5 percent of women subjects with ADHD had attempted suicide compared with 14 percent of ADHD men and 3.3 percent of non-ADHD women. Do I think I would ever hurt myself? Haven't I been doing that for a while?

He writes all I say down and then, after forty-five minutes, my hunch, the assistant's ninety-ninth percentile pronouncement, becomes an official diagnosis that will be written up in an eleven-page letter to my doctor. Attention deficit hyperactivity disorder: ADHD. Not a borderline case but a raging inability to concentrate without stimulation or supreme effort and a constant need to be on the move. A thing with a name and a treatment plan. A problem. A solution.

The consultation is drawing to a close when out of nowhere he asks, "Why do you think your husband is with you?" I pause. I didn't expect this question, though it's one I keep asking myself. I try to brush it off and say, in a quiet, stuttering way, that I don't know. "He's stuck with me now, I guess." The flat joke comes fast because not being able to give an answer doesn't feel like something I want to leave in the air to make its way up through ceiling tiles and out into the world.

"I imagine it's because he loves you," says the psychiatrist gently but with total confidence, as if it was the most obvious thing. He sets that short sentence down for a minute before continuing. "You are very hard on yourself. Maybe you need to be less so? Perhaps you need to love yourself more, like he does?"

I was expecting the lisdexamfetamine prescription he will be asking my GP to fill, but the one for self-love comes as something of a shock.

Storm Dennis has died away, and after clearing up fallen branches I'm harvesting a few winter crops before another storm gets in the way. The postmortem on last year's vegetable garden shows an occasional triumph, a patchwork of failures, some mild disappointments, and a few good starts tempered by later neglect. It didn't help that the weather was too cold and then too hot, but I can't blame it all on that. I put the energy I had into flowers more than food because I needed to look at beautiful things. After expending any motivation that remained on dragging myself out of June, there was nothing left for potting on peppers and feeding the squash.

The leeks, however, have worked and I kneel to evict them from clay that's holding on to water as if it remembers the summer drought. From this lowered perspective I can see the plot's swampy surface, weeds, the skeletons of frostbitten calendula, and a world of discarded pots, labels, and canes. My vegetable garden feels like a town evacuated in a disaster and then abandoned, but I am undeterred, and full of energy and plans now that I have the definitive answer I've been searching for.

I excavate enough soil around the first leek to allow me to grip its top. The ground slurps and sucks at the yellow-white vegetable, but I persist. Once I have enough of a purchase I start to twist, a little left and right at first and then in a complete circle, which breaks the little roots that tie it to the earth. With relative ease I am now able to pull it up: huge, perfect(ish), and intact—a real beauty of a leek and a whole one at that.

Since my first failed attempt at a leek harvest three years ago I have become physically stronger, but today's success is down to more than muscle. I have learned how to use my strength and become familiar with these plants; held their seeds, thinned them, and watched as they grew. Understanding a little of what they are doing under the soil's surface means I know to rotate, not pull. I have the right tools (some of them, anyway), and despite the blister appearing on my winter-soft hands, I even know how to use them.

Arthur comes out as I finish and we walk to the meadow where the bulbs I planted in November have started to flower. Large crocuses are popping up at random, little purple, white, and yellow individuals, stranded in the green of the lawn and blown to an angle by the recent gales. I know they will naturalize and make more of a carpet in time, but for now they are comically sparse, less a riot of color and more of a protest that I can't help giggling at. No daffodils or camassia yet, but they will come, and for now it is enough that Arthur spots another crocus emerging and calls to me excitedly. He's careful to look where he steps so as not to squash another bud that might be pushing up through the soil's surface. "Well done, Mummy!" he says, looking at the flowers and giving my hand a squeeze in one of those rare moments when a child notices their parent as a person who might need a bit of positive feedback sometimes.

As we walk and talk I see that the garden is getting on with spring, despite me preparing to turn away from it. Snowdrops and primroses are dotted here and there again, the hens are laying in earnest once more, and the geese are nest building too. The benefits of coming outside, working the land—an active way paying attention to the natural world around me—have been underlined even more firmly for me thanks to ADHD-specific studies. The improved concentration and swift easing of stress and anxiety reported chimes with what I have known and can feel in this moment.

The first of the purple anemones are opening. As I inhale, oxygen that has touched their petals is drawn into me. This breath is a gathering of myself, countering the too-frequent opposite pull of dispersal, and holding me more firmly to the earth. Perhaps that is all it will turn out to be, the big secret force the land exerts on humans nothing more than gravity itself.

"ADHD can be a gift," the psychiatrist had said encouragingly to me after he gave his verdict. "No one wants to do boring things, and people with ADHD can't do them. Look at the choices you've made. You have made your life around whatever you find interesting and important because you have had to. It can be such a strength if you can adapt and use it." I believe him, though quite how this fits my life and with being a woman, a mother, a wife, a person who needs to earn a living in twenty-first century Britain, I haven't yet worked out.

The smallholding could be my gift to a future self. Wrapped up clumsily by someone who didn't know what she was doing or why but had her heart and instincts in the right place. But the paradox remains. The way I have set our lives up is too big, too much, and it creates as many problems as it relieves. It is a symptom of my dysfunction that I needed all this just to be interested in it enough to get started and I may have to face up to the reality of other symptoms meaning I will never be able to cope with something on this scale.

This spring I don't ask Arthur what we should grow in the coming season. I might not grow anything, sow cover crops over the veg plot and have a year off while waiting to see if the medication I am waiting to be prescribed helps before we decide whether to stay here or sell and step away from the ground I have worked myself into.

Arthur spots another clump of snowdrops, and though I try to push the future aside and be here with him I am pulled forward by the fear of having to leave and a hope of being able to stay. My diagnosis could offer the clarity I hoped for in December and mark the beginning of a more straightforward, easier time for our family of four—for Jared and me, for everything out there too. The year 2017 was a duckling-filled secret horror show, 2018 a slog of recovery that wasn't, and 2019 the absolute worst. But 2020—I try not to think it. I want to stop believing in neat chapters, permanent resolution, fresh starts, and full stops, but the thought makes a bud and then the sunshine opens the flower: 2020 is going to be the year we need it to be.

DAFFODILS AT THEIR YELLOWEST

The phone rings. From here on the sofa cushions, which I am glued to by exhaustion, I can see the annual beginning of March daffodil show out of the living room window, and I focus on its cheery yellowness while I wait for Jared to answer. The high I experienced after the diagnosis—made of relief, clarity, and the hardest part of the journey being at an end—has been swapped out for a deep low. Ice drags the bottom of my eye sockets down into the left side of my chest where it melts and flows. The word for this coldness spreading like a spring thaw through me is *grief*. The printed sheets of the test's result have killed someone—me—and, though maybe she needed to die, I can't help but mourn her: the person I have turned myself into in order to survive. Here in place of calm, capable, focused, try hard, be good, sit still, don't rush, never late, wait your turn, be-careful-Rebecca is a back-of-an-envelope sketch of someone I have spent my life hating and hiding.

I have always been proud to be a noticer: particularly observant, switched on, and tuned in. If I looked myself up in the dictionary, "pays attention" would be in my definition. It is my thing. No, it *was* my thing. Now I have a new definition. I am sufferer of a disorder. I am someone with a deficit of attention who missed 36 percent of the clicks in the test. Might I have missed 36 percent of my life, and if so, which bits did I miss? And what was I so focused on that I tuned out over a third of everything else?

This is enough of a destabilizing puzzle but it is the hyperactivity that actively revolts me. I recoil from myself, gagging as I start to notice how it manifests and see that the shoe fits. The doesn't-fidget-girl-then-woman was a very persuasive impression based on need, made possible by luck and constant vigilance. I dressed the constant motion up as busyness, "being useful," and "getting the job done." The tiny but constant movements I make when watching TV, at my desk, eating a meal, or talking on the phone were blanked out. I see them now and I hate them along with nail-biting—shameful; skin picking even more so.

My poor attention hasn't prevented me from noticing that I will avoid waiting in line at almost any cost or that I always find a job to fill a gap because waiting quietly is torturous. If I'm filling the watering can, I'll dash off to sweep the yard or fetch hay, coming back ten minutes later to find the forgotten hose still running, a lake of wasted water on the floor.

I hate all this about myself. I hate this real me who couldn't overcome herself and moved eleven thousand times in fifteen minutes when she was trying to be still. I hate that I keep being forced to see her now. My neck, jaw, shoulders, the base of my tongue, and my glutes have become so used to tensing to keep hold of the pretense that, instead of letting go, they have gone in harder—a state of constant contraction. Even my pelvic floor, which a specialist physical therapist has told me has become hypertonic, is choosing twisting, tight pain over supposed freedom. I wanted definitive clarity, the answer. I wanted the battle to end and, once again, it hasn't.

The news outside the plot has hardly been restorative. A dangerous virus has been keeping the people of Wuhan in China locked up at home and though—like so many things—it seemed like a distant disaster at first, it's coming closer. The stories from Italy are horrifying and Jared and I have had a brief falling-out because I am becoming convinced that this is something to which we should start paying attention—and he thinks it isn't anything to do with us.

I sit with the tiredness of all this as Jared comes in, hands me the phone, and I answer to hear my father's voice. He has recently returned from skiing in the European Alps and tells me he has developed a fever and cough. This morning he visited one of the newly opened Covid-19 test sites, where a junior doctor attempted to instruct him on how to take the test via vague gesticulations through a firmly closed window. He promises to ring with any news. I say "I love you" with new emphasis and then we hang up, the news story instantly becoming a new, tangible, personal threat.

PREPARING THE GROUND

On any ordinary day I am more likely to know the predicted temperature than the exact date, which is often blurred by a freelance life and a mind that only cares about such things when they insist on being cared about. But today I do care, and so I do know that it's the twenty-third of March 2020. All four of us are sitting in front of the TV waiting for the prime minister to say what we know he is going to but which shocks us nonetheless. After two weeks in which seemingly everyone in charge was either gazing dazedly out of the wrong window or running to try and catch up with the virus, the UK is now going into lockdown.

Lockdown: a term that's passed my lips more often than many other people's because it is how poultry people refer to the period in an incubator immediately before eggs are due to hatch. On day eighteen you candle and turn the eggs one final time and then close the lid firmly, leaving them alone to settle into the best position in a sealed, humid environment protected from the fluctuations of the world outside.

The eggs I set in our incubator last week will go into lockdown in thirteen days and the chicks within should be released three days later. For us it will be longer and even less certain, the most optimistic readings of the situation having us held in place by the pandemic for months. The something that was coming has now come. Or one of the somethings anyway. There is always something coming if you are focused on the horizon and it is strangely OK now that everyone sees it.

After the announcement we reassure the children who are in an excited, summer-vacation bubble of no school, cut with disbelief and flickers of genuine fear. We put them to bed with tales of all the things we are going to do with this wonderful time together and then sit in the kitchen with glasses of wine so large that they might as well be buckets.

"Do you remember when we thought last year was bad?" I laugh slightly hysterically as I say it, but I feel even and clear in a way I am beginning to understand. A crisis is my comfort zone, a coming into my own. I am primed for sudden change, and if I'm not flung from one thing to the next, I will find a way to propel myself, unconsciously creating my own chaos while consciously trying to tidy it up. My body chemistry has always been set on a higher fight-or-flight setting than many people's and the effort of keeping watch, noticing every cue from others so as to modify myself to fit in means that this genuine emergency is oddly comfortable and congruent. It is the day-to-day that makes me wobble. I flee from low-key dissonance but run toward the clarity of disaster.

We are as ready and as fortunate in this disaster as we can be, and when I suggest we abandon any idea of not growing much and instead make this the moment we really go for it on the smallholding, Jared agrees and seems to mean it. The idea that this was a mistake, a symptom, my symptom, my mistake is being challenged robustly by circumstance. The shortage of some products, the rationing in shops and the risk that now comes with going into the outside world have made the plot seem to him like the next logical step it seemed to me before I set foot on it.

We are here now, and here the law says we must remain, and we are grateful for it: for the smallholding and for the luck and the privilege that enabled us to scrape just about enough together to get here. Despite the genuine threat to many things and people in our lives, which makes my stomach lurch, Jared and I talk in a newly united way. We smile at each other—the most certain thing each of us has in this newly uncertain time—and we plan our work on the land, which finally feels like our solution instead of my problem.

There is another reason I feel grateful tonight, though I don't voice it because it feels selfish. Even when we're allowed out again, nothing will return to normal for me. Reality has changed for good and I am not ready to face it. The pandemic is providing distance and distraction that I need, a falling out of time that isn't my fault. A grace period before the moment I have to emerge into the world with a line on all this. A softening of the timescale of processing my diagnosis. I wouldn't choose it, I promise. I would take it and all the suffering away if I could. But I can't do that anymore than I can pretend that a break from the world doesn't come with a side of relief.

I have jumped back in my garden this morning like a cool lake in summer, with Jared and the children at my side. With yesterday's lockdown announcement in our ears we dismantle that fucking greenhouse with energy and joy, leaving it in a tangle of metal and a pile of panes that will have to stay in the drive until the recycling center reopens. It feels strange to look at the rectangle of empty space it left: a rectangle of absence, arguments and disappointments which we obliterate with a sweaty hour-long frenzy of digging.

Now all four of us are busy remaking the veg plot, which will take us a few days. We are putting one of my long-held plans into action and replacing the hard-to-reach-the-middle square beds with long rows that will double the space for edible crops. The kids are helping rake the woodchips back while Jared brings over barrows full of slightly underdone compost and tips them where we have cleared. There is no need to weigh up whether we can afford to buy better compost or whether I should wait until this batch is rotted down further because it's probably full of weed seeds—there is a delicious lack of choice. Another horrible constriction for many that I am privileged enough to be able to see the best of. Without options, decisions and the usual minute balancing acts of work/friendship/marriage/doing good/staying sane, I am freed from some of the daily battles with myself. I have no choice but to go with it, discovering, as I did when living in my limbo state last summer, that there is something very natural for me in flowing from task to thought to feeling.

VERNATION

Jared and I are splitting the days in half, one of us working while the other is at the homeschooling helm. This morning it is my turn to sit at my desk trying to type at double speed and make eight hours work fit into four. Before turning on the computer I take a little blue-and-white capsule from the seven-day pill box, which has proved essential to avoiding a double dose, and wash it into my system with water.

I started taking this new stimulant medication at the beginning of April and have now been taking it daily for six weeks. Stimulants can have the opposite effect on people with ADHD to those with more standard neurology, the psychiatrist explained, asking me during the diagnosis if I had ever taken cocaine because while "everyone else at a party is bouncing off the walls, often the ADHD person finally sits down and reads a book."

This daily dose of lisdexamfetamine works in this counterintuitive way: affecting the central nervous system to increase naturally occurring norepinephrine and dopamine levels and so regulating attention span, hyperactivity, and impulsiveness, and improving concentration. Some people on the forums and Facebook groups I trawled before deciding to give it a try have found stimulants have an almost-exclusively positive impact and instantly life-changing results. For me it is less black-and-white. The meds seem to be helping, allowing me to narrow my focus when needed and step away from things more easily when it's time. I have noticed a fleeting sort of calm contentment from time to time too. Nothing dramatic, not happiness, but a quiet sense of being still and fine, which is more restful than the flinging from awful to excited to which I am accustomed.

There are downsides too. Some people report a long list of side effects, occasionally as serious as psychosis, but little positive behavior change. For me the drug's official downsides have been mild: a little insomnia, the occasional jitters, and a stiff neck, which are all fading as my body adjusts. For me it is, I think, the medication's push toward a more "normal" behavior pattern that, though useful, presents its own drawbacks. My existing coping and masking mechanisms have already programmed me to use hyperfocus across much of my life and work; deadlines, a "try-hard-or-die" conditioning, and high expectations filling in for genuine interest and switching my brain on. Some people hyperfocus only on the things that really capture their interest but I have developed a capacity to do it for almost anything.

Now that I'm experiencing fewer of my natural meanders in thought and activity, fewer pauses and cycling back over the same things, fewer tangents and digressions—traits all labeled negatively as poor concentration, distractibility, or a short attention span—I can see the positive, balancing impact of them more clearly.

Though it is easier to fit into what is expected while on the medication—especially as, with the children at home, current distractions are multiple and time is in shorter-than-ever supply—there is a different kind of tiredness to living this way. At times it is as if I am a mechanical toy wound up every morning and pointed at an arbitrary goal that I judder toward in a relentlessly straight line. I miss the digressions and what they offered as balance to my tendency to lock on and go in hard. I am not sure how long it would be good for me to exist as this much-blunter instrument. I might—I whisper it to myself, not wanting to commit out loud—not take the meds forever.

For now my doctor has agreed to my suggestion that when everything is settled enough to try, I will take a break from the medication on weekends and will be prescribed a couple dosages to choose from, tailoring the strength of the stimulants to the demands of the hours ahead. I am thankful to have successfully navigated the system and been prescribed the drugs that many struggle to access because of the high cost, for the equivalent price of three coffees a month. And I am only too aware that racism, bias, myths, and misunderstandings about ADHD mean that the way I look and speak has made accessing them easier for me. My prescription is handed over as if it were candy while a friend suffers monthly interrogations and multiple identity to obtain exactly the same drugs. She and I live in the same area, are the same age, have the same job, both of us with two children, a husband, and ADHD; but I am white and she is visibly multiracial.

So much is presumed and so little understood about ADHD. I understood so little myself until recently and even now I'm only beginning to dip my toe in the complicated waters around the acronym. The more I read the less I'm sure about the model that sees who I am as a lifelong disorder, an abnormality to be managed, and a dysfunctional set of symptoms that can be minimized but will never be overcome.

I instinctively prefer the term *neurodivergent* and am persuaded by what I have been reading about "the neurodiversity paradigm," a concept that Judy Singer, an Australian sociologist, was instrumental in developing while completing an advanced undergraduate degree in the late 1990s. Singer's research was based on personal experience as someone "in the middle of three generations of women somewhere on the Autistic Spectrum" and through creating and participating in some of the first online AS support groups.

In this emergent paradigm, autism, ADHD, dyspraxia, dyslexia, and a range of other neurological and mental health conditions are reframed. People who had been sufferers of a condition with undesirable, abnormal symptoms are transformed into individuals whose brain function may diverge from the average function more than most but who are not faulty products to be returned to the factory for fixing. Neurodiversity is a political—not a clinical—idea, which insists that variation in the way human brains work should be viewed in the same way as other infinite variation within our species.

When looking at the world through this paradigm, I do not *have* ADHD, I *am* ADHD. The issues I have faced are real and are indeed connected to ADHD. The acronym can be a helpful way to understand, overcome, or accept aspects of myself and my life, but it can also be problematic, reinforcing the idea that there is a single, correct way to think and be. The neurodiversity paradigm subverts the idea that I am abnormal or deficient and that a dysfunctional brain is the root of my problems. If we accept—and I am finding I do—that the natural world thrives on variety, and each organism in every species is meant to deviate from the others, then the normal baseline against which a deficit can be defined simply disappears. Variety is what is normal, and an agreed-upon "normal" height, weight, speed of movement, and concentration span is something societies make up for their convenience and change when they want to, without warning, according to who is in charge and what benefits them most.

Drawing on the social model of disability, those who use the idea of neurodiversity in their activism insist it is society's bias and deliberate refusal to adapt and make space for the reality of variance that is the disabling factor. Those with the most privilege and power prefer to greenlight the qualities of people who fit in most easily, are least disruptive, most productive, and who mirror the beliefs, qualities, and preferences they hold themselves: the "neurotypical." According to this way of thinking, I can't and shouldn't be corrected so as to better fit their constructed "normal." The world should recognize my right to exist as I am and allow me to do so without being harmed.

The activist in me is drawn to this, and I can feel my natural resistance to being fed into the correction program that much of the medical literature, diagnosis, treatment, ADHD life hacks and organization tips, and the broader societal understanding of ADHD evokes for me deepening. But I'm wary too. There is a large part of me who can't bear the thought of being "disordered" and "abnormal" and this approach is rather convenient for her. I would love to look away from the chaotic, hyperactive, disordered reflection I've been shown and see someone else, but I *do* have tangible issues, I *do* want help, and I'm cautious of throwing away the basis on which I've been told I can get that help. It is no mystery to me why some of those more profoundly affected by the way their brains or their child's/partner's/mother's brain works are resistant to the idea of dismissing the pathology of a condition that is causing them so much distress or which they have had to fight so hard to get recognition of and treatment for. How to assert myself as someone who struggles and needs support while resisting the idea that I am the problem is a paradox I struggle to reconcile myself to.

WHERE THE EARTH MEETS THE SKY

After lunch and a vigorous scrub of my nails I take the children on a walk to the woodland of Devil's Hole. We have been visiting it daily, tuning into the minute changes that take place overnight, and as we climb the stile Sofya points to the ground's newly blue tinge: the first bluebells starting to reveal their color. I look down at them and smile but soon my nose is back in the dry air and I'm looking up to beyond where the birds' call and the leaves are unfurling.

Sometimes it is easier to look up than it is to look down at myself. The treetops, the sky, the stars, and the enormity of space—where there is so much time, distance, and so many questions—center me. This upward view is both relaxing and freeing despite, or maybe because, it offers a glimpse of something huge beyond comprehension and guaranteed to be impossible to work out.

Last night the four of us sat together to watch a documentary about the Hubble telescope. The program took us past these clouds to billions of years away: the "pillars of creation," cosmic wombs in which stars gestated. We talk about it as we walk the circular path through the hornbeams, and I tell the children that when I couldn't sleep last night I looked up Edwin Hubble, the celebrated Missouri-born astronomer who gave the telescope its name. When asked about his beliefs and what drove him to explore the universe he once said, "The whole thing is so much bigger than I am, and I can't understand it, so I just trust myself to it; and forget about it."

"Forget about it." His words in my voice weave in and out of the tree trunks. If Hubble couldn't understand the universe, then perhaps I can be happy to look up at the sky despite the knowledge that I will never understand it either.

And I do want to look up at it and into it. I've been searching for a telescope, nominally for the children, really for me, but everywhere has sold out of them along with vegetable seeds, plant pots, and potting soil. Gazing at the stars and planting in the earth are the nation's pandemic pleasures: the land and the firmament calling to humans in this latest hard time.

The children and I emerge from the woods into the brighter light of Victor's largest pasture and stand to watch the seagulls circle. These birds are new to the skies here, forced to scavenge farther afield since lockdown started. Seaside pedestrians carrying street food have been replaced by police officers telling those who sit on a bench during their permitted daily exercise to move along. The birds must be bewildered by the sudden changes at their usual haunts; no tourists with ice cream, no overflowing trash cans, no fish and chips. I don't blame them. I am bewildered too, so I am trying to trust myself to it and forget. This surrender won't last; my nature is to struggle and probe, but this afternoon I am content just to see it—the vastness—and to feel it crackling above.

Back in the house we compromise on one more half hour of math and then settle to watch a wildlife program that will do for homeschool science for today. I am only half watching, and as my thoughts drift my eyes trace the date our house was built that's carved into our mantlepiece: 1922.

I slide out my phone surreptitiously, unable to resist the impulse to know more about the year the smallholding began but not wanting the children to see that my attention is on my own addictive little screen instead of the bigger one we're supposed to be looking at together. 1922: I read and make notes slyly—less bullet point now and more stream of consciousness, a compromise that lets me keep hold of my train of thought without hampering my natural flow through links in search of patterns.

They watch BBC Channel 1, where a family of monkeys is struggling for survival and I read about 1922, when, in a London still reeling from war, the British Broadcasting Corporation was formed. South from where the broadcaster's staff worked in their new studio, a bungalow that would become my home was built in the Weald of Kent. Across the Irish sea, women gained the same voting rights as men, though it would be another six years before any woman who lived on my plot's rights were realized this same way.

1922: White American women had already held the vote for two years and, in Massachusetts, another step toward equality was taken as all state positions of office were open to them. Meanwhile, 3,000 miles west in California, the black bear was hunted to extinction and, perhaps in protest, a twenty-ton meteorite lit up the sky before smashing into a grove of Virginia oak trees and setting them all ablaze.

1922: The USSR was created and, spurred on by the Russian Revolution and rising food prices in the aftermath of war, more American settlers than ever made the great westward journey to the Great Plains. They staked their claims on land, attempting to turn barely surviving into thriving, all the while setting about killing and exiling the indigenous people and removing the prairie grasses that were holding more than the soil together. It was hard and brutal work but the winter was mild that year and the rain fell when it should. The weather was deceptively obedient for much of that decade—a meteorological lullaby soothing the settlers as they ploughed deep furrows and expanded homestead and farmland, unwittingly helping to create the devastating Dust Bowl of the 1930s that would ruin many of them.

1922: Twelve months in which Senegalese boxer Louis Phal became the first African person to win an international professional sports title and Egypt gained its independence from a British Empire that had staked its claim to rule over a quarter of the world.

1922: A year when, in Denmark, physicist Niels Bohr was awarded the Nobel Prize for his work on quantum and atomic theory, his "complementarity principle" holding that objects have certain pairs of complementary properties that can't all be observed or measured at the same time. As Western economies boomed and *new, modern,* and *novel* were the buzzwords of the era, physicists struggled to reconcile quantum theories of how this world of moving pictures and automobiles worked with Einstein's theory of general relativity. How could inventions be made to work so successfully on the basis of predictable and measurable interactions between subatomic particles in specific locations and fixed timeframes, if time, place, observation, and measurement are actually subjective and relative—if they are not fixed at all?

"Mummy!" Sofya's voice is full of concern, and I drag myself back to the screen to see a young monkey and his father separated from the rest of the clan and huddling together for warmth on a high branch as a colder-than-usual winter sets in. They look so miserable—so much like Sofya and I would look huddled together against the storm. I promise myself I'll come back to 1922 soon, put the phone down, pull the children in close, and we root for the primate family together.

A FOREST OR A CLEARING

There isn't much give in the fabric of life at the moment. It is pulled more tautly than ever by these late-May days. We exist in a blurry mix of work, parenting, school teaching, and intensive focus on the small-holding, but I am squeezing in moments of research time, focused with new intent on discovering who first created our smallholding and whether they had similar ambitions and motivations to me.

Today my desk is keyboard-deep in documents, and on my screen is a list of properties on our road with the occupants' names and professions. I had planned to turn to the online census records and physical archives to find out who lived here in 1922 and the first decades beyond. But the pandemic has closed the archives, the census of 1921 just predated our house and that of 1931 was destroyed in a fire. By 1941, the Second World War had put paid to that decade's efforts. The record on my screen is the 1939 Register. I have signed up to yet another genealogy site to get access to this census stand-in, taken at the outbreak of fighting as part of the British war effort. It is currently my only hope of finding out something concrete about why the pasture of Church Hams was divided and who walked this land in the smallholding's earliest days.

I have already read the names of properties on our street from beginning to end and now I review them again and then again. With each scan I confirm that our plot isn't listed where it should be. It just isn't there. Disappointment deepens, my acerbic inner voice pipes up, and I try to switch my focus to shut her out, looking for what I can find rather than staring at the missing piece. I see that, in 1939, this was a road of farm laborers, tractor mechanics, and dairy workers. Families came and stayed, spilled out onto other plots as once-resident children became their adult neighbors. One couple retired here from the city, leaving their only daughter behind in one of its asylums, along with the thousand other women deemed lunatics.

The sound of that asylum fills the air around me and tips me toward meltdown. Screaming. Banging heads on the floor. Nails on a blackboard. Shuffling footsteps. The hole where the name of our house should be gapes wider and starts to feel like a conspiracy that could suck me in. Knowing something about why my brain gets flooded and then stuck in desperate anger and escalating panic helps me rationalize it after the fact, but it hasn't made this feeling go away or enabled me to escape from it more easily. This pattern I am in doesn't respond to analytical, rational thought or trying hard. It is born of something deep and dark and seemingly impossible to reason with.

At our last appointment my doctor suggested a type of therapy called EMDR: eye movement desensitization and reprocessing. I already knew a little about this odd-sounding but apparently effective treatment because of how helpful it can be for those who've suffered traumatic childbirths. Patients are helped out of the prison of being stuck in a harmful response to trauma triggers using external stimulation of both hemispheres of the brain. Therapists move a finger left to right for the patient's eyes to follow as they talk or play a beeping sound alternately in their left and right ears. This combination of identifying the negative feelings behind the trauma response ("I am going to die"), discovering the more positive alternative to replace them with ("I am safe"), and the external stimulus can bypass the stuck area of the brain and allow someone to peacefully process the traumatic event and embed a new response to the trigger.

Though I knew EMDR had been shown to be effective, lifesaving even, for sufferers of post-traumatic stress disorder I didn't know why my doctor was suggesting it for me. "Isn't it a trauma therapy?" I'd asked, confused, and he confirmed that yes, it was, sounding surprised at my confusion. "Hasn't your life been a series of smaller, hidden traumas? It isn't always the big things that traumatize us."

His words shocked me and made me recoil, but they landed as inevitable truth. I have been so lucky, haven't I? I haven't been in any serious car crashes, had any near-death experiences, or been victim to a violent attack. And yet . . .

This is another reframing of my life and some of what I have just started thinking of as symptoms of ADHD may be something else. Signs of how I've masked myself and/or trauma symptoms from living as a neurodivergent person in a world that takes what my divergent approach can offer with one hand while slapping me hard with the other for doing and being the wrong thing when it's inconvenient.

It makes me feel like a spoiled brat to consider myself traumatized by nothing more than having been this person living in this world. But here I am being triggered by a list of house names and a line in the historical records about a long-dead woman and wondering what parts of me are ADHD, what are masks, what is trauma, and whether there's anything left that's actually a person in her own right.

I'm beginning to see that common to many of my meltdowns is a sudden visibility of the gap between me and the world. It's this gap where dangers lie—this disconnect—which means it isn't enough for me to decide that this research is worthwhile. In order for it to be defensible I have to be successful and find the piece of information I set out to look for. It is essential to be able to prove I was right when the world eventually challenges or rejects me as I am always certain it will.

My instincts insist that my research is valid, reasonable, right, but that internal compass often points me in a different direction from the one set by the official rules I've learned and internalized. Thanks to the lifelong study I've made of how to stop myself and those around me from noticing there's a difference between the two, I'm good at contorting myself to straddle and bridge the distance. The *normal* is fifty miles west of me and I'm the Other, over there in the east, doing something very different and exhausting myself in the pursuit of new ways to lengthen my shadow and exist simultaneously both at sunrise and sunset.

This is why the tiny things in life have such an existential level of import for me. It is not that I am overanxious or clinically obsessed with perfection. The details are of vital import to me and the need to be vigilant to them is reinforced regularly by the outside world. In this small situation in front of my computer screen, and almost every other I can think of, it feels like survival to think carefully, make the right decision and be prepared for the emergency should it turn out to be the wrong choice. These are the conditions I have come to believe are a prerequisite for my existence in the world. I am hardwired for fight or flight. I fight with knowledge, plans, and meticulously crafted arguments; I flee by dissociation: leaving myself, not caring, becoming so angry that I might as well be someone else.

When the gap is too great and I can no longer bridge it, the trauma rises up and gets me. Which is it? A waste of time messing around looking up old records or something essential I am compelled to do, the reasons for which will become apparent. How can I choose? Which way is safety and whose problem is this anyway? Mine or the world's? Which term should I use: *ADHD* or *neurodivergent*? The panic flooding me now is real but it is not real. The anger is justified but it is not justified. I don't know why everything is always so either/ or, yet it is. All I know is that I need to move my body and calm my nervous system. I go out into the plot: legally the only place I can go and thankfully the only place I want to be.

At first I walk in unseeing loops until what I am learning to recognize as an urge to run leaves me. My heart rate slows and my eyes focus on the goats balancing on their hind legs to reach the leaves of their favorite meal: the hollow tree. I walk toward it, saying the Latin of its species name aloud. I have recently discovered that this tree that my goats perform acrobatics of desire to eat is *Salix caprea*: goat willow. I knew I had identified its species when I found an illustration of a goat stretched up on two legs to get at the branches in *Herbal*, the five-hundred-year-old book by botanist Hieronymus Bock.

Half a millennium after Bock wrote his treatise, Amber and Belle are doing their best impression of the old book's woodcut, stripping off the delicious bark from a downed branch. As I look on, the half-millennium gap in time fills itself in with trees, the sky is slowly obscured by leaves, and the air cools in the new shade they cast. There is a thud, followed by a moment of absolute silence. The goats are motionless, their eyes wide, and even the nearby hens stop their scratch-peck for a second. A faraway groan, a crash breaks the pause and in its wake we are all stilled again—both by the fall of what can only be another great oak and the loss that each of us knows through its absence.

Then, within an exhale, every living thing moves on and turns to the light, celebrating the new warmth. The trunks thin out again, the sun reappears, and I remember how much I love this clearing in which I have made my life. I need this space, light, and heat to exist—to grow. Progress is necessary, change comes anyway, and I am grateful for it. Yet however deeply I know the present is true, the outline of the past persists—its leaves always in bud—reminding me of something else I love and long for, insisting that this is a place where the ancient forest should be. I have such a confused response to both. A forest or a clearing: which is it that I want?

The next day over dinner I tell Jared of my latest livestock plan. Shortly after lockdown was announced we agreed this would be the year we'd breed the goats for the first time. It's already twelve months later than is ideal, and if we miss this season they will be older and the increased risk of our inexperience, combined with a potentially more difficult first pregnancy in an older goat, is something I am keen to avoid. Instead of dealing with the logistics, expense, and stress of taking Amber and Belle to a stud billy, I make the case for why we should get our own and show him photos of Saxon, a billy goat kid born to a registered breeder this spring who will be old enough to do his job by the autumn but still small enough to train and easy to handle.

We're both aware that this could be another of my subtly impulsive ideas camouflaged by a well-reasoned argument, and agree to wait as long as possible before making the decision. Though it is the right call it's hard for me to let go of the plan to call the breeder in the morning that a part of myself was already living in. I can see my kind of impulsiveness so clearly in this disappointment and it sickens me a little.

I didn't score highly on the impulsivity portion of the test but the more I read around other ADHD people's experiences, the clearer it is that the symptoms, the diagnostic and the therapeutic processes have all been based on straight, white, male, cis-gender subjects. My subtle impulsivity was erased by that context, and if I struggle to be visible, then many others must find it harder still.

After we've eaten I cheer myself up by activating my new subscription to an agricultural history library that I've joined to read more about the post–World War I fashion for smallholding. Tens of thousands of demobilized soldiers were offered a new start on a small acreage through this official local government scheme, and a number settled in Kent. Families who had been pulled apart and battered by war found themselves on their way to a low-rent smallholding as if it was the next logical place to go after the trenches. A remedy for trauma—peace connected to war by the mud.

As I read I feel with a certainty that doesn't have its basis in a stack of documents, that our smallholding was created for this purpose and that, in the aftermath of conflict a family arrived here hoping to escape the volatility of the world inside and outside their heads.

For what I promise myself is the last time, I pull up the 1939 Register, in which I tried and failed to find our plot, scanning it as if it might have grown a new shoot of information during the intervening days. And after a while I see it, a tiny tendril now visible to me: a house name that is similar enough to ours to attract the gaze of my other eye. There are no street numbers on these rural roads, no easy way to tell which name corresponds to which contemporary property, so I flick through my folder of maps and records somewhat randomly and try to make sense of this possible clue. I pay attention to my instincts rather than what I should do and am led to a document I'd previously skimmed and dismissed.

This time, I slow down and read carefully. There, at the top of the second page, is exactly what I have been looking for: confirmation that our plot originally went by another name—one that is an exact match for the one I've just spotted on the register. I have found it: a single word that leads me in a flurry of clicks to a widower called James Sanders, who occupied this place at the outbreak of the Second World War. He was a small-time poultry farmer, living off this land, as I had hoped he would be and I can be certain that this place was a smallholding seventeen years after it was originally built, most likely from its very first moments. A little more research leads me to the other occupant: Lucy Kempson, a widow of seventy-seven who used to run a grocer's shop in another part of Kent, but who by 1939 was living here, on the plot, as "unpaid domestic help." I raise an eyebrow at "unpaid" and share a wry smile with her inky imprint.

The skin of my cheeks is unaccustomed to the tightness of smiling. I am delighted by all I have found: the glimpse of these two individuals, the birth of our smallholding, the confirmation that my instincts are sound. But I have gained something extra, a surprise gift, and it is this that has pushed me from happy to joyful. This plot's real name is *Oakleigh*. I love how it sounds when I say the word aloud and as I do it breaks down into its component parts in my mouth: Oak Leigh. Leigh. I know about "oak" but what is "leigh?" For once unfettered by *shoulds*, I follow the instructions of my instincts without conflict and look up this new word.

Leigh: from the Middle English *legh*—an open ground. The thread runs back to the Old English *leage*: a clearing in the forest. I find it in the languages before: *lauhaz*: meadow; *lówkos*: field; and then, hidden in the Old Saxon and the Middle Dutch, is the older word and meaning from which the clearing, the "leigh," was made: *lh*—a forest. Oakleigh: a clearing surrounded by oaks. Oakleigh: open ground newly cut into the forest of Andredesleage. Oakleigh: the great oak forest itself.

Oakleigh: The forest has been here all along just as I sensed it was. There isn't a paradox. There isn't a gap to hide or bridge. A forest and a clearing: It can be both and so can I. I can be a forest and a clearing too.

THE VASTNESS ABOVE

I leave my desk, and glad of the long, light evenings, I walk out into my clearing and see the trunks of the forest that still grow here. Trying to learn to flow instead of battle and accepting that both and all can be visible and true scares me. The belief that I must conceal the divide or make a choice between opposites will likely take a lifetime to undo. Every time I think I've broken free I seem to find another contradiction or shackle and am pulled back. This sensation of freedom may not last long, and the prospect of being imprisoned by my own thoughts again is overwhelming. I look up, hoping to find it all a little easier in the context of the comforting vastness above.

The gulls are up there again and a wood pigeon is throwing her bulky body through the air below. I breathe out and try to sink into being both: a multiplicity, not a dichotomy. Up there, down here; a gull, a wood pigeon; the air under their wings. From this bird's-eye view I see the smallholding. I am both *now* and *then*, both *here* and *there*, both *up* and *down*, and I see newly created boundaries that have existed for a century. New/old fences, new/old sheds, a little home and a vegetable patch, three human figures at work.

Oakleigh, 1922: the scant letters and digits develop heartbeats. A man, a little boy, and then her: the first woman of my smallholding. I don't need to read her details on a land record or birth certificate to know she was real then and is real now. Her husband calls out her name, "Aggie!," and that is enough for me to travel through time and matter and settle easily into her apron-wearing flesh. I am her and she is me and we both lean our tired forearms against the fence and turn our eyes to the sky for comfort.

He's got a nerve, John. Shouting my name out like that and asking why I'm standing here all gormless, doing nothing and staring up into the heavens when we have so much to do.

"I'm looking up, like you did." He forgets it was his idea, written in his hand in a letter to me. He's the one who said it was easier to look up sometimes. Easier to look up and see a barn owl, hunting for mice and rats, than it was to stare at his boots or across at the line and the wire and . . . but he would never say what it was he was looking away from.

He wrote about the birds instead. He said he'd been watching the owls hunting at the wrong time of day—in broad daylight. My husband never wrote more than a word about himself. He didn't ask for anything either, just sent me a long list of birds seen at odd times and said it showed that even they knew none of the normal rules applied in wartime.

He wrote me a bit about the cathedral and the shelling once—though I had to guess at half of it because the censor had hidden so much with his black pen marks. "Wallows," apparently, their "s" lost under the ink, were building nests in the cathedral. The swallows didn't seem to mind the shells, he said. Swallows. Wallows. *Wallow*: Oh, I wanted to but I couldn't, you had to keep going—everyone said it. Don't wallow in it. Do your bit and wait for them to come back—maybe in the spring.

He did come back eventually. "Wounded in action." Action—
funny really given that he couldn't move. The doctors said there
wasn't a thing wrong with his legs or his back. It was shell shock
and they sent him off to a hospital where officers who'd gone
dumb and ordinary men like him who were crippled, learned that
their heads had told their bodies to stop making an effort.

Before this war he'd have been shot as a coward, wouldn't he?
Or sent to the asylum maybe. But it turns out any rule can be
changed if and when it suits. So they helped him and by the time
the war ended, and they discharged him, my John walked back to
me and we sat and stared at each other wondering who the hell
the other one had become.

It wasn't long before he came home with drink in him and told
me they offered him a smallholding and he'd slammed his hand
down on the table and said, "Yes, bloody please and thank you
very fucking much." He signed for this land I am looking up from
today without asking me. I didn't argue, I didn't ask why, just got
up and started to pack.

Mud. We have a lot in this new life and I'm supposed to grow
things in it. I didn't want to but I didn't want the war either. I
didn't want to spend the first three years with our boy on my
own, biting my nails, getting thin, and taking comfort where I
shouldn't—making the soft parts of myself hard. Not wanting
these things made no difference to them happening.

And today we're planting young cabbages and our little boy
is helping, liking the feeling of making a hole in the soil with
his finger and then dropping the roots in. John is moving the
hoe over the weeds and I love to look at him for a while until
it gets too much and my eyes burn. I see his hands shake and
remember that they shake even more when I drop a pan or slam
a door. I remember his screams in the night and the feeling of my
heart thwacking against my ribs every time I hear a knock at the
door. He is here but he is also there—and so am I and it hurts.
Sometimes I have to find another way to see him, to get to him.
Sometimes it's too much to stare down at our boots on the earth.
Sometimes I make the only choice I can: I choose to look up, like
he did, and find that he was right, it is easier that way: beautiful
and full of birds.

Aggie looks up and so do I. We look up in 1922 and we look up in 2020. In both years there is a field, a vegetable patch, a clearing, and a forest. In both, a family stuck together with mud. In both, a woman turns to the land and the sky to cope. And in both there is a single moment, made of the soft brown wren who appears above them in fast flight.

THE LONG DAYS OF FOGBOWS AND CORONAE

It is July, the tipping point of a summer that began in late March, as the human world folded itself inward and the sun shone on regardless. I am on my way outside to water the mildew-prone zucchini with a well-water-pump system I've fashioned.

It hasn't really rained on the plot since winter when it was flooded. The Met Office, which has been tracking UK weather since 1855, says this is going to be the way of it now: a boom and bust of wet and dry, and every year's heat pushing up a little further. An inconvenience for most of us for now, but already a matter of life and death for some. I'm working on a plan to store large quantities of rainwater in the winter so that I can give it back to the ground in the following summer's shortage. A drop in the ocean, a Band-Aid on a compound fracture, but I tell myself that a drop is still wet and a bandage stops a little blood. I keep hold of these small things. With my boots on and long sleeves between me and the dawn air, I step out. There has never been a brighter sky over the land than this morning, but as every day for the past few weeks, mist winds around my ankles like a cat, hovering just above the bird's-foot trefoil and clover in the field, obscuring the narrow path that the animals have worn to the gate, and confusing the edges of the boundary trees.

It swirls elsewhere too—across the country and the world, covering what we usually see and exposing other things instead. Even the vision of the linear, forward thrust of time is altered by it. Friends, family, and online articles talk of months flattening out endlessly before accelerating and then, without the punctuations of the usual, how they vanish and are lost. The pandemic mist has made time behave for many others as it often does for me.

Despite the months of dry weather, the sky is a paradox of water droplets: unexpected obstacles getting in the way of the light waves as they try to reach my eyes from the sun or the moon. As the wave meets the water it is forced to bend, scatter, and split, and then white becomes red, yellow, green, and blue. To the layers of time and place I have already learned to see on this land, this year has added another: fogbows and coronae—eerie, shimmering patterns with extraordinary rings of soft, distorting color that may or may not be more beautiful than rainbows.

I see them as I work, finishing the animals and garden jobs before moving on to begin fencing in a small paddock for our new billy goat, Saxon, who will soon arrive.

I have been working outside since five as I now do most mornings, up early to enjoy the lack of interruptions that have become constant with all of us at home. It is 9PM now and I'm in my favorite safe place, the bath, but living dangerously by reading on my phone with slippery hands.

WE ARE ENTERING AN ERA OF PANDEMICS—IT WILL END ONLY WHEN WE PROTECT THE RAINFOREST, reads the headline of an article I probably shouldn't be absorbing at the close of this long day. An era of pandemics. Great. I read on, some facts I know, some I don't, and new connections form between them. Powerful people, people who look a bit like me, have been snatching from the rainforests and elsewhere for a long time, often taking from those with a deeper understanding of the ways all human lives are woven with it. These thefts are catching up with us now and the consequences would serve us right were it not for the predictable horror that indigenous peoples are hit hardest.

The scientists quoted in the article say that this pandemic—and those to come—reached us humans because of our ecological smash and grab. We have been crashing around in the wildest places and taking from them—taking more than we bargained for. It is all connected, as I always feel it to be. The maps and the lines, the thoughts joining this to that and leaving me in a spin are not madness. They are sanity. Everything is interlinked, everything is important. The rainforests are burning farther and faster than they did in last year's record-breaking fires. They have been alight since the colonists showed up and they—we—started extracting everything.

It is not an easy time for anyone. During the pandemic, waiting lists for diagnosis and treatment for autistic and ADHD people have lengthened. And though some accommodations, such as remote working—things that neurodivergent and disabled people have long been asking for and often denied—have now been put in place, there's a fear that a system that grades us against a convenient normal will take these things away as soon as they suit the "normal" cohort less.

I have been reading about how Judy Singer has updated her ideas around neurodivergence in light of the pandemic and related environmental disasters. She sees the links too and wonders if the idea of respecting biodiversity, and its subset neurodiversity, and seeing them "as the very foundation of the stability of our floating global home" is more important than ever. In times of loss of diversity, threat of economic collapse, and increased competition for scarce resources, she says we need a strong argument against a simplistic "survival of the fittest" fortress mentality against "outsiders," however they are defined. Equality is made of diversity, not uniformity.

"Hands, face, space," reads the government's snappy new pandemic slogan. These emergency orders presume a safe home, an adequate space, a hot tap, and an outdoors where you are welcome. My family has enormous privilege and it has never been more obvious that it's not a happy accident that we have this and others do not. The Black Lives Matter protests following George Floyd's murder have come at a time when people of color in the UK and across the world are at greater risk of dying from this new disease and more likely to work in jobs where they will be exposed to it. It is not lockdown for everyone. And lockdown for most is not the same as it is for us here.

I put my phone out of splash range and wash my hair with as little shampoo as possible because we'll bail the bath out with the mop bucket later and give this water to the plants. My ears fill as I submerge my head, full of thoughts of lands vandalized. I can't absolve myself from this rampage—I've felt its benefits too and ignored the reality of damage and destruction of places and people. I probably shouldn't use shampoo at all.

My right hand struggles to close the bottle's lid, still half fixed in a grip around the fence post basher's handle, and I hear the sound of its metal striking the wood now. I have been outside putting up my new fence. I have been elsewhere putting up other fences too. I am the white woman putting up the fence. I am the settler. I am John Wanstall, rioting, protesting, and then leaving the English village I have known my whole life because of oppression, but, once in Australia, becoming the oppressor myself.

No matter how much I want to be a guardian of this land, I am a newcomer. No matter how much I connect with the words of peoples more connected to each other and the ecosystem in which they live, I am made, at least in part, of a people who seem intent on destruction, denial, othering, and homogenization. I don't want to be a settler, but I am and now I have to learn—and learn fast—how to become a guardian. It is urgent work in a world this screwed up, and I'm in danger of screwing it up further.

I sit up, water running down my face into the bath and later back to the ground. If we are all connected—people, places, animals, trees—if I and my actions are as linked to charred stumps and mutating viruses, then is it OK to pace myself, to have a car, to turn the lights on, to laugh?

I am not sure about the car (though we still have one) or the lights (until they aren't at the expense of something else), but it has to be OK to laugh even when this vast network of connections becomes visible. There must be a way to crack a smile without stuffing my fingers in my ears or shouting "LA-LA-LA-LA!" to drown out reality—I just haven't quite worked it out yet. The Gᐧaandlee Guu Jaalang—the Daughters of the Rivers of the Haida First Nation people—are who I would ask for advice if I had any right to.

The Haida people are the opposite of newcomers but even they must have arrived as settlers long ago, making their home on an archipelago dotted off the North Pacific coast of Canada. Since then they have grown through the land like a vein of mineral.

I want to ask the Daughters of the Rivers how they learned to be these guardians of a community made up of more than people, but they don't exist to help me fill a void. I catch myself doing it over and over again, turning individuals with strengths and weaknesses, wisdom and foolishness, like we all have, into a caricature made of my entitlement and a history of setting indigenous people apart.

In any case, the Daughters of the Rivers are busy with more important things right now. A fishing lodge's wealthy American clientele have long been trespassing on Haida land and spoiling the earth by using it as their playground. All but wiped out by the smallpox, the Gaandlee Guu Jaalang know and fear the impact this new pandemic could have and want the lodge to be closed.

As the bathwater cools further, I click the link again to watch their video message to the media that first caught my attention. The Gaandlee Guu Jaalang look straight into the camera lens and stand behind their spokesperson, Kuun Jaadas, as she explains how it is going to work now. How it should always have worked: "As people of Haida Gwaii we uphold our responsibility as stewards of the air, land, and sea, and assert our inherent right to safety and food security in our unceded lands and waters."

The Haida women pitch blue tents under evergreen trees. "We are here. We never left." They take to their fishing boats and sail the waters that lap the edges of their ancestral shores. Grey sky meets grey water and they glide across its surface of rights and responsibilities. This is what I need to learn for myself: rights and responsibilities.

I have the right to exist as I am but I am responsible for my behavior. I have to work on the things that are unhelpful for me and my family. "I am here," though I am in the bath, I am outside too, putting my palm on the land as I say the words, trying the idea on for size. It is like trying on my mother's shoes as a toddler—I have so much more growing to do until they fit. However much I want to live in a world where the Daughters of the Rivers are in charge of everything, where the rules match some of my instinct, they are not and they do not. Something is still coming and it could be worse than what has already arrived. That's why I will keep on trying and why more of us are going to have to learn—and quickly—what it means to be a steward of the air, land, and water.

None of this is easy and these kinds of thoughts still make my words come too quickly, open me up into the wide place that I have spent a lifetime torn between using and trying to suppress—a fight that has me pinching my side again now. Fingers leaving another bruise before I can remind myself to see the forest and the clearing and learn to be both.

THE DAY OF THE FOUR-YEAR HARVEST

We are sitting outside for lunch. I know neither the day or the date but I know what is ripe and ready to pick and eat and so am fairly sure it is August. The last forkful of cauliflower I eat tastes as nutty and good as the first. It has taken me four years of sowing cauliflower seeds to get to this point of actually eating one. Some things do take more than one season and one pair of hands.

Sofya sits opposite me, eleven at her next birthday, covered in bruises from falling over and banging into things and busy spooning food onto her plate and the table. Her body is sitting down but her mind is at work in the fully equipped equestrian center world she has made a game of, complete with rodeo lessons, a horse called Nightmare, and a dressage arena where her brother, who has little idea what dressage is, trots around on an invisible pony.

Arthur is next to me holding a book about space, which he can now read by himself—though quite how that's happened with our haphazard homeschooling we aren't sure. He will be seven soon: bangs flopping over his eyes, yesterday's mud on his cheek and knees, hay stuck to the back of a baked-bean-stained sweater. Our new ducklings and gosling are standing as close as they can to him despite the fence that separates them. He is their favorite person and the only one who can coax them into their house at night and I stay close to him too, this boy who looks like love and smells like a farmyard.

Everything we have just eaten was grown here. It turns out that it is possible for me to have a really productive year on the smallholding: I just need to put in thirty-five hours a week and have three dedicated helpers. I remembered to do second and third sowings, staked almost everything before the wind could snap it, and have finally cracked how to net everything to successfully defeat the cabbage whites. Every patch of the smallholding has been worked for the first time. It is still not neat enough for the part of me that needs to prove to the world how organized I am, but I am trying to let the truce continue.

Jared and I have talked of a need to redefine success for ourselves—tell a different story about what a good life means. I've read that you can change your brain structure by changing and retelling a story enough times. Today I tell myself a story of how some seasons last four years and how mess is beautiful. I try to feel my brain shift but I guess it will take a few more repeats.

This evening we are watching a PBS documentary, *Âs Nutayuneân: We Still Live Here*, directed by Anne Makepeace. It tells of how Jessie Little Doe Baird, a Mashpee woman from Massachusetts, has brought the Wôpanâak language (the language of the Wampanoag people) back from extinction over the past twenty years. Despite having no background in linguistics or academia she has led a project to successfully reconstruct the language and begin to teach children and adults in the community to speak the once-forgotten tongue.

Jessie speaks straight to camera telling us that her journey to a master's degree, a MacArthur Fellowship, and an honorary doctorate began in the early 1990s, when the voices and faces of ancestors she had never met appeared in her dreams, speaking in a language she didn't yet understand.

When the film has finished I read about the first Bible ever printed in America, printed not in English but in Wôpanâak. The Bible and the settler colonialism it represented played a leading role in the language's demise but has now been repurposed as a central source for its resurrection too. I laugh when I learn that with no need for a word for "clock," the puritan's timepieces were called "that thing that makes a lot of noise and is no good to anyone." I've never come across a name for anything that hit the spot for me so exactly.

What lingers as we turn off the light and go to bed is the emotion felt and expressed by those interviewed as they described regaining their language. Something in the way Wôpanâak captures and conveys the world has allowed those who speak it to express themselves more fully, more truthfully, and with less compromise. It was pain, I think, that made their voices crack at times, a painful realization that until now they had been unable to understand and share the stories of their lives fully because the words available wouldn't bend to that purpose.

I sleep only briefly and wake in the early hours still thinking of the documentary, of the stories it told, and of my own story. Dialing the brightness as far down on my screen as possible I try and bore myself back to sleep with a search for a secondhand tap we need. Soon I wander off my deliberately boring course though and am reaching for my headphones so I can watch a recent video of a famed expert talking about ADHD and time.

"ADHD," he asserts, "is, to summarize it, time-blindness. People with ADHD cannot deal with time and that includes looking back, to look ahead, to get ready for what's coming at you."

He talks about the chaos we cause ourselves and others because of our inability to see time and therefore function properly. His speech is confident. There's no wiggle room, no space for interpretation. Time for him is a universally understood, accepted, objective, fixed, tangible, and visible thing that ADHD renders invisible. It is something you either do wrong or right, that you see or you don't, and I'm glad Jared's asleep and I need to be quiet, as I might not otherwise be able to stop myself throwing my phone at the wall in fury.

Time-blindness. The offensive use of *blind* as synonym for *incompetent* is only one of the layers of ablism in this phrase that makes me want scream. I've expended a lifetime's energy on reacting to an internalized version of the narrative this man is peddling without knowing which side of it I'm on. Believing there's one true version of events and working desperately to learn it and act it out; making sure no one, even me, sees that underneath the act I do time all wrong. When ADHD became a factor in my life I updated my location in the story but not the story itself. I stopped being someone on the right side of time and tried to accept that my malfunctioning brain couldn't cope with it.

Now I'm ready to tell a different story because, here in exactly the kind of darkness that first allowed Joane Newman to stretch her hand out of the past to me, it is very clear that the expert's version is bullshit, nonsense, a whole bucket of perniciousness crap. There are many ways to see. Our perception, vision; the pictures we create with our minds, senses, cultures and histories—personal or collective—are relative rather than fixed. "His" time is just a thing that makes a lot of noise and is no good to me and millions of others.

Look at me! I want to stick my head into the internet and shout at him. *Look at who I am and what I see!* I want to force him to stare into my eyes and really see me and then ask him how honest it feels to tell me that I "can't deal" with looking back, to look ahead, to get ready for what's coming at me.

I am not time-blind.

I am time-luminous.

My experience of time is different from this "expert's," and I use it like a candle in the dark, lighting up the supposedly straight line of history and showing the truth of its tangle. I glow with the need to make some minutes denser and others less so. Many other people do too: the neurodivergent, women, those from other cultures, queer and trans and nonbinary people, figures from the past, indigenous people. In fact, I'd bet almost everyone experiences time a little differently. There are moments when none of us can deal with what time is supposed to be.

My whole body and brain are as awake as they have ever been. There's a glow in the eastern sky and the sun is rising, so I get up, make coffee, and take it outside to think and learn more. I sit on the south-facing patio with the out-of-control grapevine at my back and read the words of Marta Rose, an activist who defines herself as "neuroemergent." She wants to be defined by what she is, not by what she diverges from and in her booklet on "neuroemergent time"

Marta Rose sets out a story of time that I like a lot more than the one I know.

Here there are layers of time, looping, spiraling, and coexisting like mist, and the undeniable issues that we neuroemergent time travelers face is not rooted in our faulty logic or misfiring minds but rather in how at odds we are with the way the industrial and postindustrial world has constructed its logic. I don't instinctively move in an exclusively forward direction, taking equal-sized steps toward a set goal. Progress for me, as for Rose, means movement in all directions and goals that appear, disappear, and evolve. Progress means needing to stop sometimes and look out of the window. It means giving up and going back to the same things over and over again.

The small-scaled measures by which many societies currently measure success and failure don't work when applied to this kind of progress. We have to radically expand the timeframe in which we judge success to see ours. An idea sparked one month and abandoned the next is a failure and evidence of faulty concentration, distractibility, poor prioritization, and time management if success is measured from one month to the next. But what if that idea is put down for five or ten years, growing quietly in the background all the while and waiting for the right moment before it is picked back up? What if something abandoned as a teenager is what sparks the real breakthrough when you are sixty? Do those things not count?

Everything I read about time in the physics books I've added to my reading list this year undermines the idea of time as a fixed, static, objective, truth that anyone could get wrong or right. I've learned that time changes speed depending on altitude. Time bends, slows, and alters in relationship to gravity. Time shifts depending on where we are on the globe. The sun sets half an hour later even if I only go a few hundred miles from here. Even the idea of a year being three hundred and sixty-five days is revealed to be a fudge every four years or so.

The strawflowers growing here in the hottest part of the plot took varying amounts of time to germinate, though I scattered them together. If I sent their seeds to my cousin in their native Australia she would sow them in her spring, which is my autumn, my autumn being her spring. I can't be time-blind if time is not a thing anyone can defend as being solid and visible—and I refuse the idea that *blind* is a stand-in for *less*. If I struggle to fit myself into weekdays, holidays, weekends, start time, stop time, leisure time, me time, and family time, then maybe it's not me that's bad but the constructs.

The story of time this expert believes in was constructed very recently. It was written to the ticking of puritan watches, by factory bosses locked in struggle with workers' rights activists, and its main protagonists are profit and power. It is not the only story though; there are and have been many others. In the Australian languages still spoken near my cousin's home, there are other concepts, contained by other languages' words: ideas of deep time, place, and being, that I wish I could understand. We know them in English as "Dreamtime" and "The Dreaming," but those are poor translations, huge concepts squashed into sleepy words in which they don't fit.

I hear the children wake. Getting-up time. I go inside to make toast. Breakfast time. And along with the peanut butter and jelly I spread the "everywhen" on each slice.

Everywhen: the word a more tuned-in scholar used to convey some of indigenous Australian peoples' beliefs. *Daramoolen* in the Ngunnawal and Ngarigo languages, *Nura* in the Dharug language, *Tjukurpa* in Pitjantjatjara.

I can't pronounce these words and may never understand their full meaning. Yet they are still meaningful to me and it is enough to sense that what they hold is important. These terms and all they contain were not made by people in the dark about time. Their words glow with vision beyond simple sight, time-luminous.

THE APOCALYPSE

This year's Weed Moon has come and gone, and on this late-August morning my mind is on more mundane things like catching up on emails. I have decided to stop mentioning these "strange," "difficult," or "worrying" times in every communication because it feels fake. As of yet there's no word that captures what the past six months have been. We don't know what kind of times these really are yet.

After pressing Send I read the new messages in my inbox. One from a mailing list begins, "during this apocalyptic time . . ." and goes on to try and sell me loungewear. I snort, imagining cashmere jogging bottoms as the only logical response to the end of the world. Maybe they are?

Apocalyptic. It was the word used by the news reports I read in February 2019 when temperatures rose abnormally and the moors burned. An apocalyptic time. Maybe it is? It seems like less of an exaggeration today than ever. This strange, difficult, frightening time could turn out to be the beginning of an apocalypse and part of a collapse that ends everything.

An apocalypse: the end of the world that we keep saying we don't want though the thud of our boots suggests otherwise. It's an odd word, *apocalypse.* Apo-calypse, apo-calypso? I linger on the sounds and, of course, I have to look it up.

> "Apocalypse": old English, via old French; from the Latin—from the pulpit—from John of Patmos, the supposed author of the bible's Book of Revelation.

> "Apocalypse": the meaning I have always thought it held a very modern one, only dropped into the Oxford English Dictionary in 1989, when I was seven.

> "Apocalypse": defined as an awful end-of-days disaster by anyone I'd care to ask. How quickly we've forgotten that it was never meant to mean that.

"Apocalypse": from *apocalypsis*—a four-beat hidey-hole of a word. *Apo-*, Greek—un, off. And *kalyptein*: to hide, to cover, to conceal. Apo-kalyptein, *apokalupsis*: it is an uncovering, an unearthing, a revelation: a little round something that has just been dug up.

"Apocalypse": its Proto-Indo-European root word *kel* meaning "to hide," "to save," "to keep."

Kel, a root word from which so many branches split. *Kel* to *kalyptein* to apocalypse. *Kel* to *kalyptos* to eucalyptus: an evergreen tree whose leaves were crushed by the Kulin people for aching joints and open wounds. Eucalyptus: hardwood made into *tarnuks*—water bowls—carved by those who steered their boats' narrow hulls through the falling Birrarung River waters.

"Hull": a word that spirals back to: *hulu, hulla, huls,* and then—yes—it boomerangs to *kel* again.

"Hull": it is the concealing case of a tree, like a eucalyptus, named for its hull, its operculum, its elf-hat cover slipping slowly from the bud.

"Operculum": a word to describe both the little lid that protects a flower and the one that covers the brain's cortex— the soft insides of my skull where consciousness rests— though it never rests. Grey matter, dark matter, chattering and chattering while I wait for the end that might already be here. That might never come. That I dream of at night.

"Night": *neht* (Old English). Light: *leht* (Old English). Light: from the dawn on the path; light from the candle on the wood, on the hull, on the walls of the hold of my small ship that is still empty—stuffed full—an apocalypse of stems.

This light falling on my face through the open window feels like the first rays of a new day. My eyes are closed as if I've been sleeping, but I wake now, warm from the sun and luminous with time. An "apocalypse" is a beginning, not an end. It is a time of revelations, wild, wide apparitions and stream-clear insights; new ways to look at old things.

"It's not the language that is lost; it's you." The words Jessie Little Doe Baird's ancestors spoke to her are running around in my skull as my brain reboots. I can almost hear the zaps as synapses meet at each revelation, new connections form, and out-of-date thoughts are archived.

ZAP! I thought it was the land that pulled me here and that forging a connection to the earth would help me feel grounded and whole.

ZAP! The land isn't there to heal me or complete me. It, we, everything are already parts of a wholeness that just is. Fences have been put up to obscure that truth; I put some up myself. My job now is to take them down so as to see, feel, share in, and protect it.

ZAP! The force I have been trying to discern, the one that draws me and many others back to the land is truth. We sense the truth of the whole, we know we need it and some have held on tightly even when it seemed like a small thing, a small holding.

ZAP! I know what I have been roving the world and searching for. I have found it but the quest will never end. It isn't a journey with a destination or a question with an answer. It's not a diagnosis, a label, a treatment, a place, a time, a piece of information, or even a feeling.

ZAP! What I have been searching for is a language of my own. And languages are never finished.

DJEDJENKUMAKA

The porch floor is warm on my bare feet and so is the grass that I walk across on my way to the oldest oak. A language of my own, that's what all this has been about. The words I learned as a baby aren't enough. The concepts don't fit, the grammar is wrong and some of the best bits were shaken out along the way.

The language I am making now is for the whole spreading wide

world out there and for in here, inside my mind. It is made of time
that bends, stretches, loops, and spirals. It is made of multiplicity and
designed for a world where molecules can spin clockwise and counterclockwise at the same time. It is a tongue in its infancy; a raggedy
bag of sounds, actions, observations, and words I have magpied from
other places and times in the hope they will grow and cross-pollinate.

I need to learn the language of plants, of birds, of stars, of worms,
of water, wind, and storm. From all this I hope to make a language
that can catch the specific feeling in my elbow after a day of fence
building. And I want to speak it not only with words but with movement, with my actions and my body. I want to utter it as the roots of
a seedling do and as the chick bashing its egg tooth on the shell does.
I have been building my own language here and one day it might
allow me to be in dialogue with this queen of the woodland: the oak
tree.

I look up at her and another little word lands on my tongue like
an acorn on the ground: *dóru*, the six-thousand-year-old, Proto-Indo-European root word for tree. *Dóru* from *deru*, meaning hardy,
strong, and true. Though its four letters contain a lot, for now only
one thing matters: a lost language, growing more branches until the
word *tree* was first used to refer to anything that had a trunk.

I put my fingers into where the Proto-Indo-European language
hides in the oak bark's cracks. They are perfect handholds for climbing, and so I do. I probe each one until I find the gap, the fissure, the
breach, and I climb up. *Tree* was not meant to mean any old woody
perennial. *Deru*, the adjective, was chosen specifically for "the sturdy
ones," the truest and most important tree to those restless nomads
who moved across Europe and Asia for many thousands of years.
Tree was intended to be the word for an oak.

In Russian *dóru* became дéрево (*derevo*); in Sanskrit दरु (drú), and
in Persian, it morphed into 'ﺩﺍﺭ (dâr). Swathes of the world's forests are described with syllables from a single forgotten word. The

Celtic languages show the link too: Welsh: *derwen*, Cornish: *derow-en*, Irish: *dair*, Scottish Gaelic: *darach*, Breton: *dervenn*, and Manx: *daragh*. I say the words aloud as I scratch and scrape my way up the old oak's trunk using the ivy's coil as rope, exerting leverage on the gaps in its surface, and pulling myself up.

It was only 1,300 years ago that the Vikings came to England as invaders, the latest wave of settlers interpreting a new land, a new language, and trying to conquer it. For those who were invaded, the most important being that grew in the forest was an oak. For the invading force it was an *eik*, and somewhere in the linguistic muddle of all this the word that the ancient Britons had used for their sacred tree became the word for every tree and the Old Norse *eik*, the name for an oak.

I am up high enough in this old *eik* now. I stop climbing, find its strongest branch, and start to swing from it knowing that this story—the story of how a single word shows that all trees are oak trees at heart—is true. I swing harder in the knowledge that it was all made up and that neither piece of information contradicts the other. When searching for the origins of our modern tongues, linguists went back as far as they could and then simply ran out of written records.

Dóru: from the Proto-Indo-European language, a language of starts, of myths. A dark place at the center of it all, rendered invisible by the absence of light and lost—until we found it—down the back of the sofa? No. We guessed it back, found the void, and made an estimation to fill it. The linguists made the Proto-Indo-European language from pieces of themselves. They made it up. *(It's all made up.)*

I swing back and forth on the oak's branch, my wrists aching, my grip loosening against the buildup of lactic acid, the swing threatening to become another fall. But I remember how humans came to be, and the primate hiding in my cells shows me what should happen next. I let go of the oak's branch, flinging myself across, toward, away, and over—choosing to jump from tree to tree rather than fall, and knowing that this "everytree" can take me anywhere I need to go.

I swing and jump, swing and jump, and then it is time to drop down. It is not an easy landing. Branches smack against my skull, my back, my stomach, as I crash through the forest's upper boundary and down through its layers onto its floor. I lie muddled for a moment, taking in the softness of my battered tissue, and then I look up at this new *dóru* and forget my bruises in a breath.

I have come to rest under a globe of a tree. The canopy stretches up beyond comprehension and there are frogs living in its nooks and grooves and colorful bracts of bromeliads decorate the nine-foot circle of its trunk. A sloth moves on her own timeline above my head. She was born, has lived, and will die in this single djendjenkumaka tree—a tree big enough for whole lives to play out in its branches at whatever speed they choose.

It is really loud here, but then there is a bat colony in the branches above and nearly half the known bird species in the world are busy asking me what the hell I am doing in their forest. Here at the tree's base where I have landed, the light barely breaks, and I have to sense rather than see the thousands of insect species creeping here in this great rainforest of Suriname.

Djendjenkumaka, the Kapok tree. Latin name: *Ceiba pentandra*. Djendjenkumaka: the Saamakan name for a tree that tells the story of one of the six Maroon peoples of Suriname: the Ndyuka, the Matawai, the Aluku, the Paramaka, the Kwinti, and the Saamaka. Tonight the djendjenkumaka's leaves shake in the light wind, and the sound evokes the Baule people of Africa who gave the tree this name.

Ripped from Sakassou, in what would be stamped, mapped, and redrawn as the Côte d'Ivoire, the Baule people were forced here to South America for a new reality of enslavement. Those who survived the voyage worked long, blood-soaked days growing sugarcane on this, another land that had been stolen.

Djendjenkumaka: I prise open the spaces between its consonants and vowels and am shown a people who risked the fragments they had left to reclaim their freedom by running, escaping, and sheltering in this rainforest: a green mystery, full of danger. Their only option. An apocalypse.

The Baule people made a new life here and by thriving they defied those who had tried to diminish them—resisting their former captors and forcing them to recognize their identity and acknowledge their power in a peace treaty. The Baule people turned themselves into the Saamaka, and as they transformed, they had to find a new language for a new life. How do you find a new language? You make it up.

Djendjenkumaka: the Baule people forged this tree's name from what they knew, *egnien*, and what they were learning, *kumaka*. Egnien, the Baule name for this species of tree. Because, once their eyes had adjusted to the dark of the forest, they recognized it as a tree that also grew in their home, Sakassou.

Kumaka, the Lokono people's Arawakan name for this tree, spoken by a people who already understood what the forest could offer and how to live in and with it and heard by the newcomers across the humid air. Djendjenkumaka: made up from two pasts and two presents for the future. A tree, a *dóru*, an oak with a complexity of stories to tell.

I put my hands into the unfamiliar earth and see that if I dig down a little farther I will reach the familiarity of the tree's roots, a route back to my plot if I want to return or a path to elsewhere. There are so many directions in which I could go from here. Ireland, Rwanda, Gran Canaria, Peru—where the Ancón-Supe people dug and planted seed potatoes and then freeze-dried the harvest, the bitter night air keeping the roots fresh through the long winter and across thousands of years.

Which way to go? Instead of being caught by indecision I open my eye, pay attention to the sounds of the rainforest, and wait for the next apocalypse, the revelation of where to go next. Backward in time, diagonally across to another place or . . . ?

Yes, that's it, the direction I have been putting it off. The one I struggle with most. The future. It is the glow around the black hole where the light has been bent, the time that encircles any apocalypse. It is anathema to me because I already feel I am in it most of the time, embodying the next season just by thinking of it. Something that no one seems to understand, something that has made me feel unwanted and cast out. Though the future always pulls me towards it, I have become afraid of it. I have to face it now.

I run through the rainforest-wet air toward a darkness that opens wider and wider. My arms open, my legs move at speed, and I shout as if I'm psyching myself up to jump in a freezing mountain lake.

SPIRAL TIME

Evening light: my favorite. It hurts to move my face toward the open window to see the sun glow orange on the top of the old oaks' canopy, but I do it anyway. A square of two-tone trees, skyward leaves lit up as if from their insides. I know that this ordinary, magical thing will happen again tomorrow and the next day, but I won't be here to see it—not from this vantage point anyway.

The vegetable garden is now a blur that I can decipher only by taste, but the little oaks are still clear to me. They've come a long way from the sticks with roots that we planted one rainy March afternoon: healthy, green, and over thirty feet tall now. I suppose I should stop calling them the "little" oaks—but it's an old habit and old habits die hard.

I hope old habits and old women can die gently too: it sounds less painful that way. Though, if I'm honest, it sounds a little boring as well, and I'm not good at boring. I've never done gently well, either.

I hold my eyelids apart until the sky dims and all the trees revert to green, and then I let my eyes fall closed and enjoy the blackness. It seems I am dimming too: going back to the land—a place I used to think I'd already returned to. It was so beautiful to try to do it, and fail, and then to try again and again. I'm smiling at my mistakes and it hurts my jaw to do it; mandible and maxilla alliterations of pain that turn an easy smile into something more: better, deeper.

The air has the taint of bonfire and I close my eyes and breathe it in. It is the smell of a chick in the pocket of my overalls, kissing Jared against the wall of the goat house on a hot August afternoon, crying alone in the shed, and working it out with the turn of a sharp-edged spade and a barrowful of woodchips. Freckles and fires with the little ones, who became the so-much-bigger ones in such a long/short time. Rough hands and red-rimmed eyes more alive with every rough day to how beautiful the pattern of holes was in the orange dahlia's petals, even though it was made by small slugs on their way to ruin my strawberries. Those slimy, sluggy bastards.

Bettering, worsening, perfecting, destroying: it all depends on the way you squint at it, doesn't it? A consequence of little holes, small spaces that opened up to be filled with love and sweat and all the other things that brushed against my skin here on this land.

I sleep a little and wake to the day's last light and a moss carder bee passing the window. It lands on the rose that I propagated a few years back, a quick rest on its way to the clover it loves so much. I gave this rose its name: "Sunrise." *The Name of the Rose*—that rings a bell somewhere, an echo of standing at the window by my father's bookcase; hands on a creased spine, heart away in the valley, and eyes looking out over the garden of my childhood.

Every story tells a story that has already been told. Does it?

No. The 'Sunrise' rose is here only because of me. Because I did and I could and I will and I would, in the way that only I can.

Yes. Every story is a repeat that repeats itself over and over again. I cut the stem that made 'Sunrise' from a bush that came, in its turn, from another—one I propagated decades before from snips my mother gifted me from her own rose garden.

My mother's garden is now stones and thigh-high grasses. The broken walls and weeds with meadow flowers poking untidily above the rubble would drive her absolutely mad.

But, on the plus side, she'd be thrilled that next door's trees—the ones she hated in a way that no one, before or since, has ever hated a tree—blew down one stormy day. Their trunks still lie somewhere under the brambles, rotting gently and sheltering another world of tiny lives.

Her garden is now a buzzing, teeming, wild communal place of hidden passageways for the voles and mice who dedicate themselves to eating the nearby gardens' pea seeds before they can germinate.

On balance, I think she would have loved to see this expanse of mice, flowers, and birds, and know that we played our part in making an equal space for everyone—even in the center of the big city where she gave birth to me. A city remade from the best of the past with the best of the present: the only possible future and a world we had to rebuild even though it was already far too late.

Or maybe this is nothing but a fairy tale I like to tell myself: a hopeful fiction laid over a ruin. Because surely, when the dial was turned up another degree and everything they had said would happen—and worse—really did happen it was chaos. Everyone panicking and pretending to be shocked—as though this was something being done to them, instead of done by them.

And if that's the case, then my mother's garden is long gone still, but under concrete and cement and the mechanized quiet of slow-choking air. A place that isn't a home to anything because there's no need to make homes for things that no longer exist.

I don't know which of these stories is true. I used to and I know I played my part, but I can't catch it now: what happened out there, what's happening today: it's all so long ago and none of it has happened yet.

Truth isn't a solid thing anyway. It's not like one of the muddy

rocks that Arthur liked to dig up and clean, turning the dishpan water brown as he exposed sharply defined edges: the clarity of quartz.

There are always truths in the lies and lies in the truths. We always
make it up. I'll let it go and look up at the darkening sky of now instead. Never a truer thing existed than this sky and never was there a
sight more made of lies and tricks of the light.

Drawing the outside air into my warm body, in the pointless pretense that they are two separate things, has become an irritant, and
there are only a few more times that I'm prepared to do it.

I'm going to be a difficult person to the end: always walking the
opposite way with my ears, eyes, and heart open, making everything
harder than it needs to be. This is who I am and what I do and, finally, I don't pretend to be anything else.

I am seconds away from it and I still don't believe in it. Of course
not. This end is another fiction: a deluxe death, tied up neatly with
a ribbon and a bow, not the real one I should expect given what we
have all seen. Surely, by now, the plot, the oaks, the moss carder bee,
the rose, the love: none of them exist. Stubborn-headed to my last
breath, I take a run at the death I want, and I grab it and bite into it as
though it's the last apple in the orchard, letting the last air out of my
chest in a relief of long rattle: the juddering *click-clack* of the crack
willow's branches on a squally day.

No in breath comes. I wait.

Nothing.

And then . . .

Can there be a "then" after I've emptied my lungs? The final exhale is a full stop rather than a comma, isn't it?

I wait

and wait

and wait,

ah!

I am going, going, gone . . . but also more here than I have ever been.

I don't need the air anymore because I am of the air. I don't need the earth because I am of the earth and the wind, and the trees, and the rain. We all come and soon go from this place, leaving prints behind to be brushed away or followed.

Stillness gives way to movement: I am time traveling, like always. Flying off the horse's back through the valley's air and landing face-down in the Runnel; the girl with two left feet, on her knees in the playground, on the woodland floor, on the cobbles outside the pub; a body turning itself inside out ("This is awful . . . tell me I can do it; I need you to tell me I can do it"), and a baby is born on the bathroom floor ("It was you all along!"); making plans in the sheepy idyll of a Welsh summer; sowing seeds in shortening autumn evenings; milking goats and wild goose chases; watching the gulls circle; crying, throwing, smashing, apologizing, kissing; pumping water up from the well and discovering that the can is becoming too heavy to hold.

I stretch myself further: making a clearing in the great forest; holding a candle up to eggs I take from my apron—still warm from the broody hen—and seeing the spiders of red veins in them; closing the gate behind me after letting the cows into Church Hams pastures, and then, moving over the centuries in milliseconds, bashing fence posts in to divide the land and writing OAKLEIGH on a makeshift sign.

I am everywhere all at once: whooshing, zipping, and somersaulting along the thread that I felt sure existed but had never been able to see in full until this moment.

And yes, just as I thought, this thread isn't on its own. It weaves over and under so many others, an infinity of stories reaching in every direction and touching in more ways than I could ever count, that together make a vast, eternal, universal rope with the currents of life and death, finales and beginnings.

I meet something hard with deep grooves in its surface. This huge

and solid object is not rock, not polished or static; it is something per-
meable, alive, damp even. Suddenly I know what it is. I wrap myself
around the trunk of the huge oak tree and, for a half second, I think
I have reached a final destination, a goal. I hold on and know her and
am her: the rings, the sap, the roots, the other eye, the mother.

Then a jolt and an awful lurching hook as I am ripped away. Nothing under my palms now; nothing anywhere but color and wind that
I swirl through as I fall and fall, wondering how the hell I am still that
child, braids undone, Band-Aids on my knees? Why did I get falling
as "my thing?"

Then, as abruptly as it started, the freefall ends with a surprisingly gentle landing—like sitting down on grass.

I don't see anything yet but I can hear birds, a constant electric
hum in the distance, an occasional engine, the screaming of pigs, a
faraway voice or two, and even an old phone ringing.

When my pupils have expanded enough I find I'm sitting under
the oldest oak tree. Though the sun is shining, the air is refusing to
warm in response to it and the ground is hard with a frost that hasn't
melted yet. The pond is frozen solid for sure; I don't need to see it to
know.

I hear an engine in the distance getting closer and closer. There's a
blue flash behind the hedge, then the car, stuffed full of lives and objects, crunches onto the driveway and I wait for what I know is about
to happen but cannot be happening. A lifetime of seconds later and,
as I knew he would, the man opens the passenger door and steps out
into the January day.

He has his back to me, as he often does, and I stare at it for a few
seconds, overwhelmed, before walking quickly toward him. I stand
very close, pressing my own back against his—each hill of my vertebra
fits into each valley of his and makes us two halves of a whole. I feel
his muscles loosen a little, and he leans back into me, unknowingly
of course.

The rear car door opens and I move back. The little girl jumps out and runs around the car in a blur of six-year-old, a single curl helter-skeltering in her otherwise straight hair. She opens the other rear door, reaches in, and helps the littler boy out: a sleepy, grumpy wobble in his step and a plump fist in his big sister's hand. His feet are hidden by brown boots but I know the upward curve of their tops by heart: fleshy, puddingy little toddler feet that demand kisses, no matter they've been dancing shoeless in the mud.

The woman opens her door last, and I know how she is feeling as she straightens up and looks out across the plot for the first time, imagining their new life stretching out over it: rushing excitement, the beginnings of an out-of-control web of ideas, plans, and connections spreading in her head.

"I can't believe that we live here, that this is all ours!" she says to the man, and I bristle. I find myself shouting as loud as I can, my voice ricocheting silently off the old garage, *It isn't yours and it never will be!*

Nothing happens because (damn it!) she can't hear me; of course she can't. But before I get too frustrated I see them: the sound waves suspended in the air, waiting for their vibrations to be provoked into action.

And as she breathes in, yes, she sets them off. The woman catches something—a half whisper—and it's enough for a first flicker of recognition to appear in her eyes. I realize that I will find a thousand other ways to show her that this land isn't hers.

It's not a gift; she didn't earn it, and it's not a prize that she won. She is only its custodian and I am going to prepare a lifetime's worth of sharp lessons until she learns that this land is on loan: a right still to be earned, a responsibility that must be taken.

I hear a baby's cry and the babble of voices in the distance. This task isn't mine to face alone. A compass, a psalter, a basket of eggs, and a candle on the ground nearby. Other women are emerging to be with me, and with her. This is spiral time. Luminous. Infinite. And we will always be here. We never left.

We turn to face her, the plot's new custodian, the thirty-four-year-old me, who will take more than a lifetime to discover that she's the answer to her own question. She's still a bag of bones and notions, a collection of disguises stuffed into a body that she hasn't learned to find the edges of yet. And I love her for it. She is my life's work, my goal, my love story, my spiral, my end result made into a beginning. I see my younger self clearly in this cold light, every cell of her: so fragile and unaware. She turns to her husband; reaching out, pointing, speaking in excited twirls and explaining how everything will be wonderful from now on.

And it will be.

And it won't.

I reach out to her, keen, as ever, to get started, and then my eyes focus on the object in my hand. A button-clicker.

Red, blue, circle, square.

It has been a very long day, a very full life, and it takes me a moment to work it out.

The test. That supposedly finished decades ago. The shapes slide in front of my eyes as if the screen was never turned off.

Red/blue, circle/square, CLICK/NO CLICK. I am supposed to see the distinction and make a choice, but it is hard to keep up. The shapes want to merge as they did years ago, when I couldn't choose and so was given a diagnosis.

It helped.

It didn't help.

Diagnosis? From the Latin, from the Greek. *Dia*: across, out, other. *Gnosis*: knowledge.

A "dia-gnosis": illness, abnormality defined at last thanks to the test and the expert who knows best which is right/wrong, red/blue.

Diabolical. Diabolos. Devil. Cast out. Thrown away. Other.

But also: *Diagonal. Diaphanous. Dialogue.*

Light shining, words traveling, time spiraling—across, through, in different directions.

A "dia-gnosis": an other-knowledge. A way of being, of seeing, of speaking diagonally.

Red square, blue circle, red circle, red, blue, bled, rue, circed, squircle, squed, ircle, irqucle, uare, eu.

Blue circle, red square, blue square, red, red, blue, blue, rose, delphinium, dahlia, anemone, bluebell, tulip, forget-me-not.

But this time I remember.

And what I remember best is that red mixed with blue makes purple. There are a thousand ways to pay attention. I open my eye and the shapes and colors blur, becoming the parts of the whole they always wanted to be.

Red, blue, red, blue, red, rose, delphinium, foxglove, aster, iris, lavender, camassia.

Red, blue, and then the purple I have been waiting my whole life for.

It was always both.

CLICK.

Map Art to come

AUTHOR'S NOTE

All the historical figures, dates, happenings, words, and references included in *A Thousand Ways to Pay Attention* are based on research and corresponds to recorded evidence I found of individuals, places, times, events, traditions, and movements. All the historical characters mentioned by name are documented living by the name, at the time, and in the place that I have written them, save some small alterations for the reader's clarity. You can read more about them on page 000. The additional life I have breathed into this history is based on a mixture of research into what was likely or plausible and an instinct about what felt right.

Some names, places, place names, and identifying details within my own story have been changed to protect my family and other individuals. All the events I describe from my life have indeed happened to me but these pages are not intended to be definitive or give the last word on anything. Everyone involved has their own equally valid versions and I know even my own version will shift as time passes.

I have tried to tell my story with the kind of deep honesty which my neurodivergent mind insists on but which the masking I have learned sometimes makes challenging. As part of my ongoing process of understanding my own experience of time and place, and in a conscious attempt to reject some of the time-rules that have been unhelpful to me, I have placed events in the narrative according to where they felt they belonged as I was writing.

In this memoir I am choosing to be honest by acknowledging that we tell, retell, revise, and reexperience our stories. I have written with awareness that events, feelings, and conclusions shift—and will continue to shift—in time, place, and importance during our lives. I am equally aware that this doesn't make today's reality any less real or any less true.

The significant differences between the original version of this book (published in the UK as *Earthed*) and *A Thousand Ways to Pay Attention* are evidence of my shifting awareness at work. A lot has happened in the year between the two publications and I'm grateful to many writers and scholars as well as to my editor, Elisabeth Plumlee-Watson, whose work and guidance has helped me realize that allowing my story to evolve was the most honest approach.

I wanted to write in a way that shows how my brain works and so this book covers a lot of ground. I am not a historian, a horticulturalist, a social anthropologist, or a physicist and this is not a reference book. I might not have it all exactly right. And I am trying to be OK with that and remember that honesty and accuracy can be two very different things.

ACKNOWLEDGMENTS

When I sent Elisabeth Plumlee-Watson a proof copy of *Earthed* I had no idea that she could (and would) send it to The Experiment and become my editor. Working with Elisabeth has been a very beautiful experience and I am deeply grateful to her for having such enthusiasm for the book and for bringing so much of herself and her family life to the work.

I would like to thank Matthew Lore and all of The Experiment team, especially Jennifer Hergenroeder, Zach Pace, and Beth Bugler for taking on this unusual project, putting their weight behind it, and for their faith in and creative support for this book.

Sarah Moore's painting of my house and plot of land is the most perfect continuity of the magic that has surrounded me as I have worked on this book and its predecessor. I am thankful to Sarah not just for her talent and vision but for sharing her own experience of ADHD and being such a champion for the book.

I'm grateful, as ever, to my agent Julia Silk who continues to go above and beyond to support me. And I'd like to thank Sarah Rigby and Lorne Forsyth of Elliot & Thompson for supporting me as I wrote *Earthed* and for making *A Thousand Ways* possible through their kindness and flexibility.

My thanks are also due to Gary Sampson and everyone at the Woodchurch Ancestry Society for their painstaking work cataloguing parish records and researching the history of our village and its inhabitants. In particular, I would like to thank Josie Mackie for taking the time to share her knowledge, experience, and memories with me and for leading me to Joane Newman.

Thank you to William Bisbee and the Bisbee Family Genealogical Society, the Wôpanâak Language Reclamation Project, Professor Lisa Brooks, Dr Sharon Blackie, Jessie Little Doe Baird, Anne Makepeace, Cheryl Bryce, Steph Littlebird Fogel, David G. Lewis, Robin Wall Kimmerer; to the Gaandlee Guu Jaalang and Kuun Jaadas, Marta Rose, Carlo Rovelli, Landworkers Alliance, La Via Campesina, Land In Our Names, Leah Penniman, Sara Limback, Justin Robinson, Remi Sade, Cel Robertson, Sui Searle, Claire Ratinon, and the many others whose work or direct assistance has been of great help and inspiration during the writing of this book.

I have only been able to get through these years because of the help of many medical professionals along with the support of my friends and other writers. I am indebted to you all.

I am especially grateful to my parents for giving me the time and space I have needed for writing and processing this year. We are all very lucky to have you both in our lives.

Sofya and Arthur. Thank you for continuing to bear with me. I'm home now.

Jared. Here's to finding our own new language.

ABOUT THE AUTHOR

REBECCA SCHILLER is cofounder and trustee of the human rights organization Birthrights and a regular contributor to *The Guardian*. Rebecca and her family raise a motley crew of goats and fowl and work their small homestead in the English countryside to grow vegetables, fruit, and flowers and to restore wildlife to the land. She lives in Kent, UK.

rebeccaschiller.co.uk